Richard Barthelmess
A Life in Pictures

by David W. Menefee

Richard Barthelmess
A Life in Pictures
©2009 David W. Menefee

All rights reserved.

No part of this book may be reproduced in any form or by any means, electronic, mechanical, digital, photocopying, or recording, except for in the inclusion of a review, without permission in writing from the publisher.

Published in the USA by:
BearManor Media
P.O. Box 71426
Albany, Georgia 31708
www.BearManorMedia.com

ISBN-10: 1-59393-328-2 (alk. paper)

Book design and layout by Valerie Thompson

Table of Contents

ACKNOWLEDGMENTS . . . **1**

FOREWORD . . . **2**

PREFACE . . . **5**

PART 1 BIOGRAPHY . . . **7**

CHAPTER 1 FROM STUDENT TO STAR . . . **7**

CHAPTER 2 ENTER GRIFFITH AND GISH . . . **23**

CHAPTER 3 DISCOVERED BY GRIFFITH . . . **29**

CHAPTER 4 WAY DOWN EAST . . . **40**

CHAPTER 5 MARY HAY . . . **46**

CHAPTER 6 INSPIRATION PICTURES . . . **55**

CHAPTER 7 THE SILENT STARS GO BY . . . **88**

CHAPTER 8 GOODBYE TO YOUTH . . . **125**

PART 2 FILMOGRAPHY . . . **153**

PART 3 PORTRAIT GALLERY . . . **387**

APPENDIX: THE PLAYS AND MOTION PICTURES OF MARY HAY . . . **425**

BIBLIOGRAPHY . . . **429**

INDEX . . . **452**

Dedication

As a young child growing up in Long Island, I became aware of my relation to Richard Barthelmess from talks with my grandmother, the late Helen Barthelmess. Grandma spoke of his career with pride and enthusiasm regarding the many films he participated in as an actor. I was particularly intrigued with the fact that a vast majority of his work was done in the silent film era, which I had never been exposed to as a child.

Richard was my grandfather's cousin, which makes him my third cousin. I vividly remember my grandmother telling me how famous he was back in the golden movie era, as John Wayne debuted in one of his early films as a supporting actor. She often spoke of Dorothy Gish's statement that his face was "the most beautiful of any man who ever went before a camera." She commented that all of the Barthelmess men shared Richard's solemn and piercing eyes. I beamed with pride as she suggested that I also born resemblance to him.

As time went by, I was rarely questioned by others as to my relation to him until I moved to California in 1981. It was then that I began to be questioned by folks who were familiar with his work and career in the Hollywood and Los Angeles area. Many of these individuals were Hollywood "film aficionados" and were keenly aware of the mark he left in the industry.

It was at that time that I began to explore and hear more about his career and films, as technology facilitated the re-release of many Richard Barthelmess films on VHS and DVD. Of all his films that I have seen, my favorite is The Dawn Patrol. *I began to pay more attention to his life-work and started to collect posters, movie cards, photos, and other memorabilia as I traveled to various places in California. It was then that I began to feel excitement as well as a personal pride regarding his work and our blood lines.*

I particularly remember a tour guide at Hearst Castle commenting on the fact that Richard was often a guest at the famed property in the early 1900's. I remember the pride I felt when I told her of my relation. I was excited to find a book in the gift shop that featured several photos of Richard and the many other early Hollywood stars who were frequent guests of Hearst.

Richard Barthelmess: A Life In Pictures *is a seminal piece of work that is richly researched by author David Menefee. The forthcoming chapters not only accurately capture the filmography of Barthelmess' career, but provide a unique insight into the personal life and integrity of the man and relative that I had never known. This book will certainly be a welcome addition to the libraries of those who admire classic films. I hope that you enjoy reading it as much as I have.*

— DON BARTHELMESS

Acknowledgments

This enormous research project requires assistance from many contributors. It began with encouragement from my mother and father, Eunice and Doyle Menefee, who reminded me that all things are possible with faith in Jesus Christ. I am grateful for Lois Welborn Peyton, who shared her personal love for Richard Barthelmess and many rare items of memorabilia that had been gathered over many years. Others to whom I am indebted include Don Barthelmess, Ronald Raburn, Randy Jones, Michael Derfler, Richard Maturi, Randy Miller, Candice Danaher, the Academy of Motion Picture Arts and Sciences, and the entire staff of the Dallas Public Library Fine Arts Department.

Foreword

"Who is Richard Barthelmess? This is the common response often heard when his name is brought up to the average person today. When the movies were young, Richard Barthelmess was one of the most popular and loved of the first film stars that appeared on theater screens shortly after World War One, and he was one of the few actors trained exclusively in motion picture acting. A pleasant leading man and producer, Richard won a special Academy Award for *The Patent Leather Kid* (1927), and was individually nominated as Best Actor for his work in *The Noose* (1928).

Richard was equally admired by both men and women for his handsome dark looks and all-American personality. Women loved his open and innocent face and his smoldering, soulful, expressive eyes, and men admired him for his innate masculinity and frequent depictions of heroism. Richard had an unusual facial characteristic: a slightly crooked mouth that slanted at the lower corner when he smiled. It was an endearing quality that set him apart from the physical perfection of other leading film stars.

His long, stellar career is one of the clearest examples of the transitory nature of stage or film "stardom," proving just how fleeting is the fame that is bestowed on those who achieve a film career. Although some of his films have been lost, many examples of his work are still seen today, including the outstanding D. W. Griffith films, *The Love Flower, The Idol Dancer, Broken Blossoms* and *Way Down East*, as well as Howard Hawks' *The Dawn Patrol* and *Only Angels Have Wings*. A perennial favorite on "the late show" is *Cabin in the Cotton* with Bette Davis. With that strong connection to popular culture, it is odd that he has passed into the shadows of obscurity.

How is it that a movie star of the highest stature, having played in seventy-nine films over more than thirty years, can be virtually forgotten? One reason is that fifty-seven of his films were silent, even though he was one of the few silent film stars to enjoy equal success in talking pictures. Despite these facts, he is unknown to many people.

Richard was one of the anomalies of the film industry: an aloof, withdrawn lad, a young man of inherent reticence, who was thrust by a fluke of circumstance and financial necessity into the limelight that beamed on those with a high-profile motion picture career. He was frightened by fame, a status that was usually considered by others to be a reward for accomplishment. To Richard, fame was one of his life's greatest penalties, and his attitude about it is illustrated by this telling comment he made at the midway point in his career. "It isn't as if we were really important," he later said. "Nothing will ever convince me that I am actually important to anyone in the world outside of my dependents and the few people besides who are fond of me. We aren't celebrities. We are curiosities."

His well-grounded grasp of celebrity's status mirrored his sure-footed sense about his role in life. No cloud of scandal ever shadowed him. All who knew him said that he was as thoughtful and sensible in his work as he was in his private life. This book brings to life the both the public image that was so thoroughly exploited and the private man so carefully reserved for the privileged few. The title of this book refers to his "life in pictures," meaning the many lives he impersonated within film scenarios as well as his private life.

For the first time, the story is told about how his handsome looks inspired Russian star, Alla Nazimova, to pluck him from youthful obscurity to play opposite her in her first film, *War Brides*; how he risked his own life to rescue Lillian Gish from certain death on an ice floe as it was about to plummet over a waterfall in a scene from D. W. Griffith's *Way Down East*, a stunt that went terribly wrong and nearly cost both actors their lives; how he produced *The Patent Leather Kid* and won an Academy Award; how he nearly fell victim to the topsy turvy mayhem of Hollywood's transition from silent to talking pictures when he used a voice double to sing for him in *Weary River*; how his work in *The Dawn Patrol* was nearly eclipsed when he followed America's call to arms, walked away from his movie career, and joined the US Navy in World War Two. By the time the weary veteran returned, Richard found that his career had taken an unfortunate turn. An entire generation had grown up never seeing him on the screen. His determination to regain his position as one of Warner Bros. top stars established him once again as a star and a valiant survivor of the fickle frailty of public attention. The book contains an extensive biographical treatment, a Filmography, and a gallery of rare portraits, posters, and lobby cards that illustrate how vast was his impact and how prolific was his work.

In this biography, the author makes no judgment of Richard's work, but represents the opinions that were shown by contemporary critics, who reveal how he was viewed in his time and the effect he had on motion pictures as the medium grew from short films to feature-length films, and then evolved from silence to sound.

For those who remember him with pleasure, this book will rekindle the reasons why they loved him, and for those who are discovering him for the first time, it will reveal a personality and artist with many fascinating dimensions.

Preface

Richard Barthelmess: A Life in Pictures is more than a biography. It is also the story of the evolution of the film art as it progressed from silent to talking pictures. A pioneer in films, Richard worked in early, silent shorts and silent feature-length films, and then he survived the chaotic transition from silent films to talking pictures.

This biography traces information from a variety of sources, including interviews given by Richard Barthelmess to writers while he was in his youth and in his autumn years. In addition, many people who were close to him in his motion picture work shared their memories of film-making experiences when they wrote their own autobiographical articles and books. These manuscripts were extremely important in revealing how Richard was accepted in his time and how he affected their lives and work. Their personal stories are juxtaposed with his, and they include the pioneering efforts of D. W. Griffith, Lillian Gish, Henry King, and many others.

Story synopses were compiled by viewing surviving prints, and for those films that are considered lost or unavailable for review, synopses were reconstructed by merging production notes, advertising reviews, and comments made by critics that were published in many newspapers and magazines.

Contemporary reviews were gleaned from a wide selection of sources, including the prominent magazines, *Photoplay, Screenland, Motion Picture,* and *Motion Picture Classic.* The *New York Times* offered insights from the perspective of major metropolitan critics, and *Variety* revealed opinions from a film industry point of view that often differed from those held by observers from outside the industry. In addition, the appeal of his many films has been gauged by the reviews found in small town newspapers across America, which often countered the sometimes-jaded reflections that were expressed by more prominent sources from the major newspapers.

The book is constructed in three parts: biography, filmography, and portrait gallery. There are scores of rare candid photographs from his personal life. Analyses of his films are illustrated with advertisements, lobby cards, poster art, scene stills, story synopses, and production notes. The concluding section presents portraits of Richard Barthelmess that reveal his personality and image as it evolved over the span of his long career.

Part 1: Biography

Chapter 1
From Student to Star

On Thursday, May 9, 1895, at 7:07 in the morning, Richard Semler Bartelemys, was born in the Central Park West area of New York City, the son of actress Caroline Harris and Alfred Bartelemys, who was an importer by trade. Richard was the tenth generation of males born to the French house of Bartelemy, all of whom were christened Richard. They were men enriched with a fine combination of French and Dutch bloods.

Alfred died soon after Richard was born, and that same year, his young widow turned to the stage as a means of livelihood. She adopted the stage name "Caroline," and joined stock and road shows. She played with Sidney Drew in *Billy*, Mme. Petrova in *Panthea*, Shakespeare with Viola Allen, Robert B. Mantell and others, and appeared with Thomas Ross in *The Only Son*.

Caroline and Richard lived in a three-room apartment on West 50th Street. There were no servants, and Caroline cooked their dinners in the kitchenette. Meals were served in the living room in front of windows providing a mesmeric view of New York. From this view, Caroline often thought about her son's future, wondering how she could provide the opportunities he would need to succeed among the millions thronging New York.

Caroline was responsible for Richard's first experience in a professional role. She was engaged with a Boston stock company in *Little Princess*, a popular success of the day that boasted an illustrious cast that included Edward Ellis, George Le Guere, Juliette Day, and Clara Mersereau. There was a scene at a party in a girl's school. For one week, Richard filled out one of the roles as "Donald," the only boy in the play. When the play was brought to

(LEFT) **Five-year old Richard, and** (RIGHT) **ten-year old Richard. The Spanish War influence was still strong in military costuming when this photo was taken while he played in "Fatty" Brown's back yard. He had a sword, so the kids elected him General.**

New York, he again played the role. Richard performed well, but he was uncomfortable being in front of the footlights.

There was nothing about Richard in manner or temperament to suggest he would have been associated with the theater. Solemn, meditative, always conservatively dressed in dark suits, white shirts, and black ties, he was the pattern for a judge, an archbishop, or a partner in a financial institution. Having seen the dark side of the tinsel and glamour of the theater behind the scenes with his mother, he had no desire for a theatrical career. From his father, he inherited Dutch frugality and a desire for financial security.

As he grew to school age, his education became a problem for Caroline because she frequently had to go out on the road on tours. At the age of ten, Richard began studies for two years at the Hudson River Military Academy in Nyack, New York, which was not far from where Caroline worked. He spent most evenings after school watching his mother on the stage. Before he was twelve, he had seen from the stage wings Shakespeare's *King Lear* so many

Richard with his mother, actress Caroline Harris.

times that he knew the entire script. Later, he attended Manor School, a private military school in Stamford, Connecticut. He never thought of an acting career, and only took part in theater work when he and his mother needed extra money. At that, the two of them had much in common with other struggling actors. Shortly after the turn of the century, the new and sudden popularity of motion pictures opened up a strange, innovative source for financially fraught actors to earn much-needed cash.

"Dickie, there's a new thing called moving pictures," his mother told him when he was about eleven years old. "Some really nice actors are going into them. I have had an offer, but I don't know . . . I feel funny about it. What shall I do? There's a company called the Biograph, way down on Fourteenth Street. Do you think I ought to do it?"

In a 1925 *Movie Weekly* interview, Richard remembered being flattered that Caroline consulted him about this decision, but he did not know how to advise her.

"There are some people named Pickford there — children. And a man named Sennett, another one named Arthur Johnson . . . all very nice. There's a Mr. Kirkwood, too, and a young man named Owen Moore," his mother pointed out optimistically.

Together, they went down to the Biograph to investigate the strange goings on before drawing any conclusions about the odd new business. Neither of them knew at the time that they were taking the first steps toward the people and events that would change their lives forever.

"When we got there, I was all eyes," Richard thought back. "I remember how a little boy kept getting under everyone's feet . . . Jack Pickford. I remember two innocent-looking, wide-eyed children . . . the Gishes, and a strange, dark little individual who later emerged into the personality of Lottie Pickford. I don't remember what they were working on at the time, but I got a job and $5 a day. The first day they let me work, I had the trying bit of *walking down a street*. Just walking down, expressionless, that was all. *That was my first job in pictures.*"

While he was still a boy, the great Russian actress, Alla Nazimova, was preparing for her American theater debut in the Schubert Brothers' production of *Hedda Gabler.* Alla was struggling studiously to enhance her speech and bring the Ibsen classic to New York audiences, so the Shuberts enlisted Richard's mother to teach the English language to her. She brought Richard to Alla's home during the lessons. While practicing English, Alla had many hours to study Richard's handsome, angular face, and in his sensitive expression, she saw what she thought was a typical, clean-cut, all-American youth. Alla kept the memory of his face in the back of her mind.

In 1913, Richard needed money, and he first ventured onto the professional stage playing with the Hamilton Stock Company in Montreal, Canada. He appeared in parts ranging from the peg-legged boy in *Mrs. Wiggs of the Cabbage Patch* to Tom Brown and Uncle Tom. When his mother paid a visit to the theater for the purpose of seeing her son perform, she discovered him shuffling about in the guise of an old farmer with spectacles on his nose and a bandana covering his head.

The manager, who sat in the seat next to her, turned and remarked, "You have an actor on your hands, Miss Harris."

"I'm afraid so," she reluctantly replied.

As a teenager, Richard went to Trinity College in Hartford, Connecticut. "My mother was on the stage," he later recalled in an interview in *Motion Picture Magazine*. "My father died before I was a year old, and while both my mother and I felt college was the thing, I often used to do something in the way of dramatics during my vacations." His mother encouraged him to appear in the university stage productions. He was also a member of the Psi Upsilon fraternity, President of "The Jesters," a dramatic club, sang in the glee club, and was a cheerleader. While there, he legally revised his birth name to "Barthelmess."

Holidays and vacations were spent watching from the wings while his mother performed on the stage. When Richard was between school years, he enjoyed taking part in local plays in summer stock with his mother, often playing small roles in her stage productions when there was need for a young man. He grew up with this knowledge of the theater as part of his background, but in spite of his experience, he harbored no serious aspirations of his own. He was young, all-American, and full of the same spit and fire as any other boy. He had no desire to wear make-up or become a professional actor.

At Trinity College, Richard was in a fight with another boy. He took the hard blows, and severely aroused the anger of his professors by diving in with his fists. He was suspended for six months. Dumped out on the streets, he had to fend for himself for the very first time. Finding work as a teenager was not easy, but he had to survive.

Desperate for money, he haunted the Philadelphia theater circuit looking for work in the winter of February 1914. Like other out of work actors, he trudged through man-high drifts of snow and wind blizzards, a stranger in town, knowing no one and having almost no money to his name. He found lodging at a seedy hotel near the train station, a room that was stained, narrow, insect ridden, and gloomy. He took a trolley out to Columbia Avenue where the Emily Smiley Players put on two shows a week at a little theater in Wildwood, New Jersey, and Philadelphia. There, he found work as a callboy, stage manager, curtain ringer, sceneshifter, and property boy. He played a part in *The Girl of the Golden West*. It was marvelous training for an eighteen-year-old, but the $20 a week he earned barely paid for a minimum existence. Richard took the experience on the chin, thinking it was the punishment he deserved for being kicked out of school. He resolved to make the best of the grim situation.

"You couldn't call it a life," he remembered in a 1925 *Movie Weekly* interview. "I couldn't buy clothes with this sum, not suits or coats, or anything of that sort. Now and then, I bought a new pair of shoes or replaced a storm-battered and dust-crusted hat with a new one — that was all. When I could, after I had eaten and paid for my room, I would tuck away a dollar or two against the time when my six months of penance should be done and I could turn my face toward Trinity College again."

Richard finished his experience with the Emily Smiley Players, and then returned to New York without a clue what to do next. He reconnected with an old friend, who got him a job in Ottawa, Canada for $25 a week. The gig ended, and he then went back to college, made his peace with the professors, and bore down for more serious study. He was forced to take the freshman course all over again.

In the summer of 1914, the conflict began that escalated into what was later called World War One. While on vacation from Trinity College, Richard worked as a stage manager in summer stock. The following year in the summer of 1915, Richard decided to parlay his experience in dramatics with the Hartford Film Corporation, a newly formed organization that had high hopes of turning the wilds of Connecticut into another Hollywood. The film company came to a nearby village on location to film a two-reel, slapstick comedy. Richard was impressed with their work, and participated as an extra. As often happened with independent companies, the corporation went bankrupt within a few weeks, and Richard spent the rest of the summer working for the Travelers Insurance Company. His original purpose remained focused on entering business when he left college. The summer of 1915 had not been a very profitable one, but it was an exciting experience, and it planted the idea of film work firmly in his mind.

"Dick wasn't very enthusiastic about this sort of thing," said Caroline later, "but he was able to earn some little money. It all helped, and Dick was determined to do everything in his power to aid. He is a good boy. He always was," she added.

"My mother enabled me to enjoy the advantages of a college education," Richard told an interviewer for *Picturegoer Weekly*. "She battled against reverses to keep me at Trinity College, Connecticut. And during holidays, I took 'extra' roles in movies to keep my end up. The glamour of the screen got me completely."

Motion pictures had overtaken the live theater as the entertainment medium for the masses. When Metro announced grand plans for a large-scale production of William Shakespeare's *Romeo and Juliet*, teaming Francis X. Bushman with Beverly Bayne in a silent movie adaptation of the tale of the star-crossed lovers of Verona, it was cause for great excitement. Richard went forward to be involved in this magnificent production.

Frances Marion, who was an avowed screenwriter for Adolph Zukor, marveled at the audacity of Metro's competitor, William Fox, when he announced that their version of the same story would be filmed starring none other than Theda Bara, the most celebrated vamp of them all. In Frances' book, *Off With Their Heads*, she illustrated the competitive situation looming within the film industry with the pending release of two versions of *Romeo and Juliet*: "We had no sooner recovered from this shock when it was announced that Francis X. Bushman and Beverly Bayne were to appear in another screen version of Shakespeare's immortal play," she remembered. "We wondered if sophisticated viewers might laugh, and nothing was more dreaded than laughter when drama was being enacted (not acted) on a broad scale."

In the short history of motion picture, and even through the centuries of theater since Shakespeare's day, no stars were ever gilded in costumes more elaborate than those worn by Bayne and Bushman in their filmed version of *Romeo and Juliet*. No sets for a Shakespearean drama boasted such baronial halls or buried actors under more profuse arrangements of flowers than in this impressive production.

Beverly Bayne had never played Shakespeare prior to this first attempt, but she triumphed in competition against the powerful presence of Francis X. Bushman. Metro's sumptuous presentation was a gallant attempt to translate the spoken word into silent, moving images.

In the summer of 1915, principal photography on the film was completed. This early, feature-length film was mounted on eight reels, running about ninety minutes. Their artistic challenge was to present the all-dialogue play in silence with subtitles. Metro advertised the spectacle as having a cast of 600 and a cost of $250,000, the first full-length version of the timeless romance of the two star-crossed lovers. They succeeded in translating the classic words into floating images, and earned tremendous plaudits for their effort.

Romeo and Juliet joined this imposing array of outstanding titles demanding its audience share around the world. Metro released the film with great fanfare, and the film was lauded by George Blaisdell in the November, 1916 *Moving Picture World* as "a great production, one that easily will rank with the best cinematographic efforts that have gone before." Blaisdell went on to write:

"Francis X. Bushman and Beverly Bayne head the cast. It is an ideal combination. Mr. Bushman, above all else, possesses the physique of a 'well-governed youth,' of a 'man to encounter Tybalt', he appears to unusual advantage in the scanty garb of the period — in the language of Juliet's Nurse, 'his leg excels all men's.' He fits the part, and he plays it.

Miss Bayne is a rare Juliet. Kindly endowed by nature in figure and feature, she has entered into the interpretation of the role of the heroine with marked sympathy and feeling."

Supporting these two stars was a splendid cast — also the longest cast in the history of motion pictures up to that time, excepting the multiple-storied *Intolerance*. There were exactly one hundred names in the cast list furnished by Metro, including a Booth, a Sothern, a Mantell, a Kemble, and a Davenport, all famous names in the annals of American theater. In several scenes, Richard Barthelmess played an unaccredited role as a townsperson in Verona.

At the Broadway Theater on the initial presentation the night of October 19, nearly two and one-quarter hours were devoted to the running of the eight thousand feet of film. The dramatization was taut, and approximately a full reel was devoted to the balcony scene during which Romeo climbs the Capulet wall following the feast of the Capulets. The conversation from Romeo on the ground to Juliet on the balcony was a romantic highlight of the production. Great care was given to insure the portrayal of this great epic of this famous play would reach the same dramatic heights on the screen as viewers experienced in the stage play would expect. The balcony scene was considered remarkable on its own merit, and when taken with the film's entirety, a crowd-pleasing standout. The balcony scene was framed in an exquisite bower of foliage, and some of the love scenes took place in a beautiful garden. The few glimpses of the Capulet castle added to the atmosphere. The background never intruded; it was subtly appropriate framing for the story's events. The natural settings seemed to be those with the best effect. Studio art in 1915 had not reached a rivalry with reality, but the artificial settings were painstaking and sufficient.

Both the Fox and Metro versions were successfully released simultaneously, and industry observers realized how impossible it was to prophesy whether a film would succeed or fail. For Richard, it was his first taste of the excitement of being in a major motion picture. He started looking for other opportunities within the fledgling industry.

After another year at Trinity, he went back to New York for a vacation during the summer of 1916. Rather than remaining idle, he secured work at $10 a day as an extra in a motion picture starring Billie Burke, one of the brightest stars of the American stage.

Billie Burke was born Mary William Ethelbert Appleton Burke on August 7, 1885, in Washington, D.C. As a child, she toured the US and Europe with her father, a circus clown. After many years of sawdust and one-night stands, her family settled in London. Billie was fortunate to see many plays in London's historic west side, and she fostered a desire to be a stage actress.

At the age of eighteen, she made her debut as an actress. Four years later, she came to New York and appeared in many plays. The movie industry soon beckoned, and she made *Peggy*, her first film, in 1916. Its success was immediate, and later that year, she starred in a serial, *Gloria's Romance*. Richard played one of his earliest roles in several episodes of the popular series.

According to the *Frederick Maryland News*, the producers paid $25,000 for the picture rights to the novel of the same name by Mr. and Mrs. Rupert Hughes. The weekly chapters were serialized in the *Chicago Sunday Tribune*, as well as many other newspapers around the country, allowing audiences to follow the story developments as the series unfolded throughout the twenty chapters.

During Richard's 1916 vacation, Alla Nazimova was preparing her own film debut in a motion picture version of her sensational vaudeville play, *War Brides*. She thought back to the handsome face of the boy who had sat at her feet while his mother tutored her in English. She wanted him for the small role of her son, Arno.

"While plans for *War Brides* were going on, I was getting terribly discouraged. I had spent weeks making the usual rounds of the Fort Lee and New York studios," Richard recalled, "and had about made up my mind that there was no room for me in motion picture work. I suddenly decided to sign up for a naval training cruise to tide me over the summer. I had always loved the sea, and this seemed like an opportunity to do something before going back to Trinity College for my senior year. On the evening when I was to depart on the cruise, fate smiled ironically and decided to alter my life. A telephone call came from Nazimova asking me to see her at the hotel."

Richard left college to eagerly take part in the film for $7.50 a day.

"I was not yet twenty-one when this turning point in my life occurred, but had the call come the next day, I would have been away on the cruise and probably become a second-rate business man at the end of my college days," Richard later remembered. "A small part was going begging in the film, and after screwing up

Richard Barthelmess taking a break during production of an early silent film.

my courage to a sticking point, I diffidently ventured to ask for it." Richard later confessed he had always harbored an inferiority complex, and applying for the job required stepping outside of his inherent shyness. It was to prove a fateful step.

War Brides, the play by Marion Craig Wentworth, had a theme of tremendous proportions, and required intense emotional acting. When *War Brides*, in screen form, had its initial showing at the Broadway Theater in New York, it was presented to a packed house. The audience was brimming with enthusiasm, and the gala occasion accorded much applause. Notables of all sorts were present, including many screen and stage stars. The lobby was banked with blowers, and the director, Herbert Brenon, was called upon for a speech. He delivered one gracefully, including specific thanks to everyone concerned. A charming musical accompaniment enhanced the effect of the film presentation, and the resulting film gripped and held the spectators. It was thought to be a masterful production,

Two scenes from *War Brides* (1916).

(LEFT) **Richard Barthelmess as Arno, and Alla Nazimova as Joan.**

(BOTTOM) **Gertrude Berkeley, Charles Hutchinson, William Bailey, Richard Barthelmess, Nila Mac, and Charles Bryant.**

and according to one reviewer who attended, "clutches the heartstrings and holds them taut until the moment when they shall be released with a snap that is almost excruciating."

Alla Nazimova gave herself over to superb abandon in the role, which was one that required high emotional powers. It was a challenge to masterfully express the story in the simple form of silent movie pantomime. The film was constructed with swift flashes of rapid action, contained very little of actual war, and featured many intimate scenes of home life. It was supported by well-chosen subtitles, superb action, and excellent photography. The film was calculated to stir the emotions to a pitch, which would have a pronounced psychological effect upon the individual viewer, and in turn, affect the outcome of World War One with its pacifist message. Richard rode the film's success to overnight recognition. Both audiences and film producers took notice.

On completion of his role in *War Brides*, director Herbert Brenon was greatly impressed with Richard's work. When Brenon left Selznick to produce films on his own, he brought Richard to his new company with a one-year contract at $50 a week. While still in his junior year, Richard dismissed all further thoughts of a business career, and left Trinity College to seek a career as an actor in motion pictures. It was financial security that motivated him, not a desire for further fame.

He later said, "When I saw my friends earning $7 to $8 a week in banks, I decided I better go after it." At this time, Richard was just another good-looking, masculine personality with little about him to suggest his soon-to-arrive popularity.

The motion picture version of *War Brides* proved to be a sensation, and brought much renown to all who participated in it. Richard was concerned about leaving college, but felt he could not deny himself the golden opportunity for work in the film industry.

"Later on, I got a chance to go to California," he later recalled. "On the journey out I thought things over and decided to stick to pictures. I knew they meant more or less travel — travel for which I hankered, and which I would probably never get in any other way. They meant a great deal of time outdoors. I have a soft spot for the sunshine. I don't think I'd like an office job. And motion pictures meant good money."

Women immediately noticed him in *War Brides*. He was immediately asked to play opposite Marguerite Clark in *Snow White* (1916), and then appeared in *The Eternal Sin*, his first film for Brenon's independent company, cast as a young man who did not know his mother was the infamous Lucretia Borgia.

Richard's initial success came by being paired with the outstanding feminine stars of the silent cinema. After small roles in several films in 1917 and in 1918, including *Just a Song at Twilight* starring Evelyn Greely, and *The Soul of a Magdalen* with Olga Petrova, Richard played a part in *Camille* with the incomparable vamp, Theda Bara. While promoting the film on her first trip across the United States, Miss Bara paused to meet with prominent newspaper interviewers, including Kitty Kelly of the *Chicago Examiner*. Miss Kelly described her startling encounter with the mysterious artiste:

"We've had almost every kind of motion picture personage in our midst, but never yet a vampire, so it was necessary to arrange hospitable vampire states of mind, and the reviewers assembled in debate of what was vampire etiquette. The velvet-voiced one bade us enter. We did. At the far corner of the long room, in a rose-incrusted cretonne chair, Theda Bara, swathed in a mysterious, high-necked, black silk garment, inlaid with brocaded roses in pink and gold, floated in an indefinable aroma. And then she spoke. Illusion shattered before her voice like mist before the sun. Peacefully, she took command of the situation, graciously, intelligently, cleverly, she talked; ideas flowing from her like perfume from roses, her laughter broke like tinkling glass. Theda Bara, audible, was a revelation. She is a real person. Her eyes, big and bright, but ranging within limits, laugh with you. Her cheeks are flushed pink from nature's cosmetic box; her lips are just the ordinary red ones ordinary folks wear." It must have been a touching scene.

Marguerite Clark, with whom Richard had played in *Snow White*, again paired with him in a series of pictures, including the highly popular *Bab's Diary*, and *Bab's Burglar*. These were adapted from a famous series of "Sub-Deb" stories, which appeared in the *Saturday Evening Post*, and were written by Mary Robert Rhinehart. Titles for the film were taken from the original book, and their charm lay in the droll spelling and naivety of Bab's own script. The

J. Searle Dawley production was the first time that filming an actual diary, page by page, had been attempted.

By 1917, World War One was raging across Europe, and Marguerite Clark did her wartime duty selling bonds for the Liberty Loan program. She went from town to town, appearing where theaters were opening her *Bab* films, and sold bonds at public appearances. The demand for her time exceeded the limits. It was impossible for her to physically be at every city where she was invited.

A Newark theater manager, Mr. George M. Fenberg, received the following telegram on October 18, 1917:

> So sorry it will be impossible to stop in Newark. I have had to refuse a dozen invitations on way out. Cincinnati, my hometown, and Washington are all I can possibly manage. Please explain to Newark how sorry I am and ask if they won't send their subscriptions to me to Cincinnati Chamber of Commerce all good wishes, Marguerite Clark.

In these pictures, playing the diminutive Miss Clark's handsome boyfriend, Richard found his first strong personal connection with audiences. Reviewers began to take serious notice of him, and other film producers vied for his services. Many prominent female stars in Hollywood began to grab him for their male lead. Between 1917 and 1919, he appeared in an astounding twenty-eight motion pictures.

In 1918, Ann Pennington, a famous dancer, was a featured performer of the *Ziegfeld Follies*, *Miss 1917*, and other attractions. Richard appeared with her in the Paramount film, *Sunshine Nan*. It was a tale of a girl of the slums, described as a "dainty alley rat." As McPherson Clark, the son of a rich factory owner, Richard had his life saved by the diminutive girl. Feminine hearts fluttered around American at every close-up of Richard and his soulful eyes. It seemed like everyone loved him.

Years later, Adolph Zukor said in a *New York Times* interview, ". . . as I look back over these twenty-five years, I think the most significant development is the change in the people in the industry.

When we started out, remember, we took whomever we could get. There were few standards. We were experimenting. Richard Barthelmess and Wallace Reid were the first two actors trained altogether in the movies, and they were good. But before we developed our own actors and actresses we picked them off the sidewalk, so to speak. If a woman was good-looking, with an attractive figure and screen personality — which was a very different thing on the silent screen — that was sufficient. They made a great deal of money, more than they had ever dreamed of, and it went to their heads. That was not true of all of them, of course, but it was the rule. Hollywood blossomed out into a bizarre place like nothing on earth."

There was great excitement within the mushrooming industry. For Richard, a tremendous turn of events was about to occur: D. W. Griffith, the preeminent director of *The Birth of a Nation*, had taken notice of him . . . and so had Lillian and Dorothy Gish, two of Griffith's most popular stars.

Chapter 2
Enter Griffith and Gish

While Richard was growing up on the fringes of the New York theater, another young man had been struggling to gain a foothold as a writer and actor.

David Wark Griffith was a dreamy Southerner with roots that were deeply embedded in American history. His father, Colonel Jacob Wark Griffith, was a soldier in the Confederacy during the Civil War. He was known as "Thundering Jake," because when he went into a charge, his voice was heard above the din of guns and combat, urging his men to victory. Before him, his grandfather was David Griffith, a stormy, fierce man, who fought in the War of 1812, and refused to have anything to do with the English.

The Negro slaves on their family plantation were so endeared to the kind treatment afforded by their home with the Griffiths that they preferred to stay with them after their emancipation. A highly educated man, Jacob regaled his son with reminisces of his first-hand adventures in the conflict. This son of American pioneers grew up with these powerful accounts of heroism in battle and suffering in war fresh on his mind, and perhaps, romanticized by the old soldier, who enjoyed retelling his adventures.

"My first, and my last ambition, until Fate turned me into a picture man, was to be a writer," Griffith told an interviewer in 1916. "I determined on that when I was six years old. My father's sword and its early effect on my mind, his noble career, his wounds, for he was shot all to pieces, did impart a martial trend to my character, but there was no war, and the scholarly atmosphere of my home, I suppose, was responsible for my inclination to become a great literary man."

Richard Barthelmess with D. W. Griffith, who directed him in *The Girl Who Stayed at Home, Broken Blossoms, Way Down East, Scarlet Days, The Idol Dancer,* and *The Love Flower.*

His first job was at the *Louisville Courier-Journal.* The first play he saw was *Romola* with Julia Marlowe and Robert Taber. The combined effect of literature and theater entranced the young man, and he determined to become a writer of dramas. He called on the stage manager of a Louisville theater and told him of his ambition. The wise manager advised him to first become an actor and learn the craft. Griffith accepted his advice, and took small roles in stock plays in his hometown. At about the age of twenty, he joined Walker Whiteside on tour, and enjoyed a wide experience playing characters, heavies, and leads on the road. He earned some good notices, played a season of Shakespeare and Ibsen with Nance O'Neill, and continued to write in his off-stage hours. As an actor, he called himself Lawrence Griffith, and reserved his true name for his literary efforts.

In the early 1900s, Griffith headed for the West coast in a show called *Miss Petticoats*, starring Katherine Osterman. The company stranded in San Francisco. A fledgling actress, Linda Arvidson, was to appear there at the Grand Opera House as a servant in *Fedora* the week the stranded actor known as Lawrence Griffith played a role with her in a courtroom scene. The two young people had polite conversation behind the stage, and Linda invited him home for lunch.

"He had a trunk full of manuscripts — one-act plays, long plays, and short stories and poems," Linda recalled in her autobiography. "To my unsophisticated soul it was all very wonderful . . . on pleasant days when the winds were quiet and the fogs hung no nearer than Tamalpais across the Gate, we would spirit ourselves to the Ocean Beach, where, fortified with note-book and pencil, the actor-poet would dictate new poems and stories."

When their funds hit rock bottom, Griffith picked hops in the fields for quick cash, and worked in the theater at night. Linda and "Lawrence" were soon married, and for a time, appeared together in various plays. Their friend, Max Davidson, exchanged confidences one day about a place where the couple could earn quick cash.

"Mr. Davidson had been going down to a place on 11 East Fourteenth Street and doing some kind of weird acting before a camera — little plays, he explained, of which a camera took pictures," Linda remembered.

Always in need of money, they each earned $5 a day posing for motion pictures in New York at the Biograph Company in 1907. These early films promised anonymity for a day spent in a studio or outdoors riding horses. The fledgling industry intrigued them, and they asked many questions of the other actors who were between stage assignments. They learned quickly.

". . . those tawdry and cheap moving pictures, the existence of which we had hitherto been aware of only through lurid posters in front of the motion picture places — those terrible moving picture places where we wouldn't be caught dead. But we could find use for as many of those little 'fives' as might come our way," Linda confessed.

Their $5 bills began to stack up, and when 'Lawrence' was asked to direct films and offered a one year contract calling for $45 per week with a royalty of a mill a foot on all film sold, Griffith gambled on the new adventure and took a chance on the lucrative new industry. They were not finding great success in the theater, and the new job helped fund their little flat that was filled with rented furniture. It also gave Griffith time to work on his writing. For the first time in her life, Linda opened a bank account to deposit their weekly earnings.

In August of their first year with Biograph, Griffith turned out two releases a week. The Biograph Company readily acknowledged its young director's achievements. His films with beautiful girls like Florence Lawrence and Mary Pickford were hugely successful. "Once in the race, we were there to win," Linda stated. "Biograph pictures came to mean something just a little different from what had been. There was a sure artistic touch to them; the fine shadings were there that mark the line between talent and genius. David Griffith had found his place; found it long before he knew it . . . ."

Exhibitors found crowds filling theaters when they stuck a poster out front advertising "Biograph Night." The public loved their little films. To their complete surprise, on October 4, 1909, the *New York Times* actually reviewed his one-reel film, *Pippa Passes*. By the time he signed his third contract, Griffith finally dared to drop the pseudonym "Lawrence" and use his real name. Linda's trips to the bank to make deposits came more frequently after that review.

"When the royalty checks before the end of the second year amounted to $900 and $1,000 a month, we still maintained a $35 dollar a month apartment," Linda thought back. "Never dreamed of getting stylish. No time for it. So each month there was a nice little roll to bank, and it was put right into the Bowery Savings Bank. The trouble with a savings bank was they wouldn't accept more than $3,000, so we secured a list of them, and I went the rounds depositing honest movie money with rapidity quite unbelievable."

In 1912, Lillian and Dorothy Gish, two little girls, who had been thrust onto the stage in traveling melodramas since their childhood, were attending a local movie theater that had a bill made up entirely of Biograph films, which were their favorites. The two sisters went into the nickelodeon to enjoy the show, and they were startled to see their friend, Gladys Smith, in a film called *Lena and the Geese*. When the show ended, they raced to tell their mother. In *The Movies, Mr. Griffith, and Me*, Lillian remembered her mother saying, "The Smiths must have fallen on hard times if Gladys has to pose for pictures. We must look them up when we get to New York."

They investigated the Biograph Company, and discovered that their friend, Gladys Smith, was now known as "Mary Pickford." She introduced the two girls to Griffith. Within days, they appeared in a one-reel melodrama, *An Unseen Enemy*. Griffith loved the ethereal beauty of the thin and softly feminine Lillian, and found a place for the jovial and comic sister, Dorothy. The two became regularly featured in his Biograph films.

Griffith left Biograph in 1913, and within a few years, his masterpiece, *The Birth of a Nation*, a full-length film synthesizing all the popular elements of the Biograph one-reel films, erupted onto the world's film theaters like a firestorm. The movies had arrived, and Griffith headed the list of esteemed directors. Within a few years, he was independently making full-length features, and he had entirely abandoned the production of one and two-reel short films.

In 1918, D. W. Griffith was busy releasing *Hearts of the World*. A dancer was needed for a small, unaccredited role. Griffith had noticed Mary Hay, a cute teenager then making waves in New York on the nightclub circuit. He hired her to be herself in *Hearts of the World*, appearing as a dancer in once scene, swirling a full-bodied skirt as she moved toward the camera. She performed as required and thoroughly charmed Griffith.

In the back of his mind, Griffith was also thinking ahead for actors to cast in a full-blown motion picture version of the timeworn theatrical melodrama, *Way Down East*. The role of Kate Bartlett, the Squire's niece, seemed to call for the same bubbling personality radiating from the teenage dancer. Griffith kept in touch with Mary. Though she had not acted in films or on the stage, he felt he could mold her adequately for the small role in his upcoming film.

While Griffith prepared his next feature, Dorothy Gish was starring in an extremely popular series of comedy films for Artcraft. When she saw Richard Barthelmess in *War Brides*, she said, "I want him for my pictures." Lillian Gish remembered in her autobiography, "Dorothy had an instinct for picking potential stars. Her costar in many of her films was Richard Barthelmess, who had the most beautiful face of any man who ever went before a camera." His appearance suggested both gentleness and masculine strength, attributes that made him an appealing and virile hero immediately popular with audiences everywhere. Griffith sent Dorothy to investigate the young actor. She liked what she saw on the screen, but after meeting him in person, she was terribly disappointed to find that he was much shorter than she imagined. At first, she was against the idea of working with him, and told Griffith it was because he was too short. When Richard proved to be so highly popular with other stars, she changed her opinion.

Dorothy had to wait a while before she could get him. He was already busy playing opposite Marguerite Clark, Olga Petrova, Gladys Hulette, Theda Bara, Madge Kennedy, Winifred Allen and Ann Pennington. Even George M. Cohen, the celebrated Broadway star and singer of "Yankee Doodle Dandy," nabbed Richard for one of his few films, *Hit The Trail Holiday* (1919).

By the time Griffith was ready to begin work on *Way Down East*, Mary Hay, the cute dancer featured by Griffith in *Hearts of the World*, had appeared in her first acting role in a motion picture. *Eastward Ho!* (1919), which was directed by Emmett J. Flynn. It featured her in the third lead as "Kitty Mason." Griffith felt that she was ready to advance in film work. He also had his thoughts set on bringing Richard into his troupe of stock players. Richard obtained an appointment with Griffith, but the wheels of fate turned fatefully against the two men meeting.

Chapter 3
Discovered by Griffith

On the day of the appointment, Richard hurried to Griffith's office.

"Too late," said the official he met. "Mr. Griffith *did* want someone of your type, but he is leaving for California."

"I heard Griffith was leaving for California," Richard said. "Is he still here?"

"Leaving?" repeated the surprised office boy. "He's left!"

"When?" demanded Richard.

"Just now," replied the boy.

"When does his train leave?" asked Richard anxiously.

"3:45 at Grand Central."

Richard looked at his watch and saw that he had just fifteen minutes to rush downstairs, hail a taxi, and reach Grand Central station. He arrived just three minutes before the train's departure. Luckily, Griffith was standing at the gate.

"I heard you wanted to see me," began the panting young actor.

"Who are you?" inquired the director, who knew full well who he was.

"Richard Barthelmess."

"Well," answered the director, "telegraph me at the Alexandria in Los Angeles." With that, he climbed aboard the train, and then was gone.

"I was broken hearted," Richard later said in telling the story of his encounter with Griffith. "Of course, I wired. And I wrote too. But I never heard a word; indeed, it wasn't until a year later, when I wrote once more, that I received a reply. Then, Mr. Griffith summoned me. He had remembered all about me from that brief glimpse at the train gates, just as he always remembers every incident with uncanny exactness."

In late 1918, Dorothy Gish finally got Richard for two motion pictures, *The Hope Chest*, and *Boots*. Richard's life was never the same. Shortly after watching these films over which he officially served as producer, D. W. Griffith saw in Richard the ideal, all-American hero that he needed for several of his own upcoming pictures. He signed Richard to a contract to work under his personal direction.

In early 1919, Griffith filmed *The Girl Who Stayed at Home*, in which Richard was featured as Ralph Grey, one of two brothers enlisting in the war. The United States Government cooperated in allowing Griffith to use footage shot in the House of Representatives in exchange for the publicity generated by the film's theme of enlistment and acceptance of the selective draft amendment. The real star of the picture was Bobby Harron, playing Richard's brother, an unpleasant "oily" cad resisting the draft, but ultimately cooperating and finding maturity in the war.

The Girl Who Stayed at Home premiered on March 23, 1919, at the Strand Theater in New York. The *New York Times* reviewer noted Griffith's special use of a new soft focus lens: ". . . in some way, which has not yet become general, he dramatically emphasizes the central figures of a scene by throwing all the other objects so out of focus that they remain to provide suitable background and environment for the action without competing with it for the interest of the spectators. This is an artistic development of the close-up and something else. It makes the action more eloquent by keeping it in its environment, it preserves the continuity of the story, and it adds smoothness and beauty to the picture as a whole. And when Griffith does make a close-up, it is a soft, delicately shaded portrait."

Griffith was soon preparing *Scarlet Days*, and he turned to Dorothy Gish for her opinion of another young man he was considering along with Richard. Dorothy had plucked a slender and dark-haired Italian from obscurity, and then cast him as a gigolo in her picture, *Out of Luck* (1919). In one scene, the gigolo was supposed to be making love in a café to a rich woman. Griffith watched rehearsals and was pleased with the young man's performance. He suggested a bit of 'business' for the scene between the gigolo and a woman wearing a glittering string of pearls. As she turns her head to watch some dancers, he fondles her strand of pearls, singles one out, and tests it with his teeth to see if it is real. It was a perfect touch for the character and has since been copied many times with equal success."

When Griffith saw the finished film, he was impressed with the young man, who was then known as Rodolpho, and he hired him to dance in an on-stage prologue preceding the premier screening of his new film, *The Greatest Question* (1919). The dance paired him with Carol Dempster, and it was such a hit that Griffith extended it for three weeks. The young dancer called himself Rudolpho Di Valantina, a slight variation of his real name and one he thought had a more romantic and pleasing sound. Rudolpho had succeeded in obtaining other roles in two Universal pictures and two at Paramount, but real success had eluded him. Griffith tested him for the lead in *Scarlet Days*, but held off making a final decision until he could talk to Richard.

Griffith's assistant cameraman, Karl Brown, recalled in his autobiography preparing for active duty in World War One and finding Hollywood overrun with strangers, Bolsheviks, and deposed counts operating the film industry then under severe shortages and rationing. "Only Griffith remained unchanged," he pointed out. "He was still the same White Knight of *Alice*, forever noble, forever gallant, forever dreaming, and forever falling off his horse. Needing money, he was practical-minded enough to make the little pictures that make money — obvious pictures that anyone could understand. No art. Melodrama in the Al Woods manner. There was one, appropriately mistitled *Scarlet Days*, in which an Eastern girl goes all the way to early San Francisco during the gold rush to be with her rich mother, who has been sending her lots and lots of money, only to discover that Mamma is making all this money through owning and operating the fanciest fancy house in all the West. I don't know how he ever got a happy ending out of that situation, because before it was finished, I was ordered to report to the Arcade station to board a troop train to take me to Camp Kearny . . . ."

Ultimately, Griffith chose Richard over Rudolpho Di Valantina for the lead in *Scarlet Days*, the first Western story he had personally filmed since his work at Biograph. The story told the tale of "Alvarez," a Western Robin Hood. Although Dorothy Gish thought her Latin discovery would have made a better Alvarez than Richard, Griffith told her, "I agree with you, Dorothy. But women are apt to find him too foreign-looking." Clearly, Griffith miscalculated, but his attention was fixated on molding Richard to fit the character of Alvarez. With an added moustache and a Latin costume complete with a sombrero, Richard was made over to resemble Rudolpho and, to everyone's surprise, fit the role well. Both he and Griffith hoped the added moustache would make him look older.

Griffith missed the opportunity to work with the actor soon to be known as Rudolph Valentino. Lillian Gish remembered that Bobby Harron, her friend and co-star in many films, brought Rudolpho into their group of intimate friends because he was a newcomer to films and shy. She, her sister Dorothy, and Bobby rode horses with Rudolpho. They found his two great loves were horses and dancing. In addition, he designed riding clothes for both Lillian and Dorothy, and was a good cook.

A few years later, Griffith studied the rapid progress that Rudolpho had made within the industry and before the public. "I declare I don't know," replied Griffith. "All the time I was looking at him in *The Four Horsemen*, I kept asking myself, 'Is this fellow really acting or is he so perfectly the type that he doesn't need to act?'"

As filming progressed on *Scarlet Days*, Richard told an interviewer, "In Griffith's new picture — the one we're making now — I'll do an outlaw; a young Spaniard, picturesque chap, with a sash and all that. That's where this blamed moustache comes in. Nobody paid much attention to me before I went with Dorothy's company, although I've been playing on and off in pictures for a long time. I was with Nazimova in *War Brides* and with Marguerite Clark in several pictures. I was working all the time, but they didn't see me. The best thing for a man to do in pictures is to make a series with a well-known star. Then, he begins to get the letters and appreciation. Trouble is, though, somebody usually comes along and wants to star him. Then, the fans that made him a star turn around and begin to look for someone else to write letters about. It's a great life."

The company traveled to a location at Tuolumne County, California, to replicate the 1849 California locale of the story. The seven-reel finished film was well received, and earned impressive contemporary reviews for the director and star.

Griffith followed *Scarlet Days* with four films in a row featuring Richard as his leading man: *Broken Blossoms, The Idol Dancer, The Love Flower* and finally, *Way Down East* (1920). These films made Richard an enormous star.

Around this time, Mary Pickford and Douglas Fairbanks had read *Limehouse Nights*, a collection of short stories by author, Thomas Burke. They were enthusiastic about one story of a waif beaten to death by her pugilist father, and immediately brought the story to Griffith's attention as a possible vehicle for Lillian Gish. Griffith was enthusiastic, but Lillian was dismayed. A grown woman, she felt it would be impossible for her to portray a twelve-year-old girl. She offered to coach any little girl that Griffith might choose for the role, but Griffith was adamant that she was the only actress with the emotional maturity to convey the poignant range of thought required. Lillian's desire to please Griffith prevailed against her personal theories, and she dutifully took on the seemingly impossible task.

The soft focus lens with which Griffith first experimented in *The Girl Who Stayed at Home* was brought into play to help make Lillian appear to be twelve years old. Coupled with subtle lighting, her impersonation was astounding. Mindful of his success transforming Richard from an American to a Latin in *Scarlet Days*, he next tackled the challenge of making the all-American Caucasian look realistically Oriental for the lead role in *Broken Blossoms*. When asked by a reporter for *Pictures and Picturegoer* how he obtained the convincing, Oriental look for his role, Richard replied, "Why, I used hardly any make-up. I did so . . . ," and he demonstrated by pulling his forehead up until it seemed half its usual size, and with the change came a difference in facial expression. His eyes became slanted, his other features were different, and he looked remarkably Oriental. The look was accomplished by applying a tight band about his face under the hat worn by his character.

Richard was relieved to finally play someone other than a wealthy manufacturer's son. "Isn't that a fine part?" he asked Delight Evans of *Photoplay*. "I'd rather have a line of parts like Cheng Huan — characters — than my own company. Playing wealthy manufacturers' sons! I'll tell you, I'll murder the next director who gives me another wealthy manufacturer's son to play. I'm sick of them. I've played them so long that it seems to me I've never done anything else in my life."

With Richard, Griffith had found a youth that was sensitive enough to play the Chinese man of London's Limehouse section, who hoped to bring Americans the peace of Eastern religious beliefs. His only joy in the crushing poverty of his life was found in the silent adoration he felt for a winsome street waif, superlatively played by Lillian Gish.

As preparation, Griffith exposed Richard to Chinese culture by escorting him several times on forays through Los Angeles' Chinatown. They visited quaint shops, tasted authentic cuisine in restaurants, and reverently attended temple ceremonies. Richard absorbed the Chinese atmosphere, and grew to love it with an obsession that would last the rest of his life.

During the production of *Broken Blossoms*, Lillian was stricken with the Spanish Influenza, which was killing tens of thousands of people around the country. The epidemic affected more people than were killed in World War One. Five people had died at the Griffith studio, including Tessie Harron, Bobby's sister. As Lillian slowly recovered, her face was encased in a surgical mask, but she dutifully reported for work despite the fever. Rehearsals began with Griffith also wearing a surgical mask.

"As usual, we worked long hours," Lillian Gish told Ann Pinchot in her autobiography. "It was the worst time to be working so hard, for the epidemic still had not subsided. Mr. Griffith's almost neurotic fear of germs was particularly acute at that time. Nothing could keep him from his work, but throughout the shooting, he forced me to wear my facemask whenever I was off camera. And he was careful not to come within ten feet of me."

Griffith rehearsed Richard in an unusual way. He hired veteran actor, George Fawcett, to play the Chinese lad in initial rehearsals opposite Lillian Gish as Lucy, the waif. Fawcett was far too old for the role, but he had worked under Griffith for years, and he knew exactly what the director was looking for in the character. Richard

Richard Barthelmess as the Yellow Man in D. W. Griffith's *Broken Blossoms* (1919).

watched Fawcett rehearse, studied the older actor's interpretation closely, and then assumed the role in front of the cameras, cleverly duplicating Fawcett's performance as he had played it in rehearsals. That method of tutelage was very effective. Richard was able to give the most sensitive performance of his career up to that time.

Griffith's assistant cameraman, Karl Brown, returned home on a pass from his military duty and was quickly recruited by Griffith to stage a misty, opening shot of a Chinese junk drifting through fog. He was astonished to find everyone in the studio giving their attention to the oddest sight: "All attention was upon something you won't believe — a young and handsome Chinese, pigtail and all, in a black silk coat, apparently recruited from Hung Far Low's famous emporium in San Francisco. He was holding court, so to speak, smiling and chatting with his admirers in what I thought was remarkably good English for an Oriental . . . A few questions here and there revealed that the picture this was for was called *Broken Blossoms*, a title so sickly sweet that the working crew, a godless bunch by definition, never called it anything but *Busted Posies*. That young Chinese turned out to be a new actor named Richard Barthelmess . . . ."

D. W. Griffith made *Broken Blossoms* for producer Adolph Zukor. When Griffith delivered and screened the finished film, Zukor was outraged. "You bring me a picture like this and want money for it? You may as well put your hand in my pocket and steal it. Everybody in it dies. It isn't commercial!"

Zukor failed to grasp the fact that the greatness of *Broken Blossoms* was almost as fragile as its sensitive title. It was a film very easily shattered by insensitive audiences, an exquisite romance with a tragic ending, and Griffith's film eloquently asked for understanding between different races and different religious beliefs. It provided a marked contrast with the gigantic spectacles and melodramatic romances for which Griffith had previously been renowned.

Zukor's failure to realize the potential of the film spurred Griffith to send his brother, Albert, to raise $250,000 to buy the film back from Zukor. He then released it through the United Artist Corporation, a company which he had formed with Mary Pickford, Douglas Fairbanks, and Charlie Chaplin. It was an enormous hit. Despite the huge sum he had to pay to Zukor, the film eventually made more than $700,000.

Richard's performance in *Broken Blossoms* won plaudits around the world. *Broken Blossoms* premiered at the George M. Cohan Theater in New York on May 13, 1919. Audiences were spellbound by the beauty of the picture, which was uniquely enhanced by the use of colored lights projected onto the same screen as the film. The combination of these lights and further color tinting of the film by soft dyes in various colors produces a mesmerizing effect. The film was a resounding success, immediately called a "masterpiece," and with the triumph, Richard's star crested.

In 1920, Mary Hay, the pert, beautiful, young actress and Ziegfeld girl, was in the cast of a popular show in New York. She was born Mary Caldwell on August 22, 1901, and came from Fort Bliss, Texas. Mary studied dance under Ruth St. Denis at Denishawn. By the age of twenty, she was performing in *The Ziegfeld Girls of 1920*, Ziegfeld's *Nine O'Clock Frolic*, and soon after, starred in the original musical comedy, *Sally*. Mary delighted all who heard her sing a popular song, "The Orchard of Girls."

Mary visited Griffith while he made films at his studio. She and Richard fell in love while he was working on *Broken Blossoms*. He

Actress Mary Hay, a gay, blithe spirit in the *Ziegfeld Nine O'Clock Frolic*, delighted all who heard her sing "The Orchard of Girls."

later remembered when they first met. "It was the night of the opening, and at the end of the performance, I joined a party to go over to the Ziegfeld Midnight Frolic on the New Amsterdam roof. Bessie McCoy was playing up there, and Mary Hay was her understudy. It just happened that the night I was there Mary played the part, although she never had done so before."

Mary was only seventeen, and Richard was delighted with her. He asked friends, "Who is that cute little thing pinch hitting for Bessie McCoy?" They told him that she was Mary Hay, the daughter of US Army Colonel and Frank Merrill Caldwell, who was also a graduate of West Point. For Richard, it was love at first sight. He tried to secure an introduction that night, but he was unsuccessful.

Richard had been a target for all sorts of matrimonial gossip, and because of speculation, had become particular and wary. He hated theatrical gossip and scandal.

"Stage people are as moral as the public will allow them to be," he said in a later interview. "Most of them like to be let alone so they can enjoy their home life in peace. You see, I know how nice theatrical people can be. My mother is Caroline Harris, an actress, and she is also a mighty fine mother. Even if you do happen to work in a studio instead of an office, you can have a quiet, domestic life. If you do your best when you are working, you are entitled to freedom in your personal affairs. Miss Hay and I have the same ideas on the subject. I know we will be happy because, well, because this is the right sort of marriage."

Several months passed before he could return to New York again. After taking a room at the Algonquin Hotel, the first person he saw when he crossed the lobby was Mary Hay. He recognized her instantly, and as chance would have it, along came D. W. Griffith at the same moment. He boldly approached the director for an introduction, and then was invited to a luncheon with Mary. Later, he and Mary spent the entire afternoon together and had tea from 4:00 o'clock until 6:00 o'clock that day. Then, they had dinner together, and later went to the theater. For twelve straight hours, Richard enjoyed her company. He was enraptured with the young dancer. He later told Harriette Underhill, a writer for *Picture-Play Magazine*, "She is petite, sprightly, and piquant. She has a cunning little turned-up nose, and she wrinkles it across the bridge when she laughs. She is very bright and funny, and talking to her keeps one's mind up and doing. You can't sit down and mope if you want to talk to her."

In rapid succession, Griffith starred Richard in the last two films to be made under his First National contract. Two stories of the South Pacific, *The Idol Dancer*, and *The Love Flower*, were filmed with exteriors taken in Fort Lauderdale, Florida, and some interiors in a New Rochelle studio. In 1919, Fort Lauderdale consisted largely of swamps and coconut groves closely resembling the South Sea Islands, a far cry from the resort city it would become in later years. The principal acting company, featuring Carol Dempster, Clarine Seymour, Kate Bruce, Creighton Hale, and Richard, assembled for the jaunt to Florida. Work began in the fall, and then was completed by the first week of December.

The cast took a side trip to Nassau in the Bahamas. Without warning, a sudden storm blew over their boat, *The Grey Duck*, and the troupe was feared to be lost at sea. For three days, the US Navy launched a search of the charted course while the nation's newspapers speculated about what happened to the passengers on what was rapidly called "a tragic journey." After an intensive investigation of the twelve-hour route, the navy finally found the troupe at Whale Key. Rumors then flew that the entire incident was staged for publicity purposes.

In a 1944 interview, Richard defended Griffith and this incident, recalling, "In passing, I want to make sure than no injustice is done to him and, for this reason, I make particular mention of the fact that the *Grey Duck* episode was not a publicity stunt. I was in Miami at the time, and was personally aboard one of the rescue vessels, which was sent out to find him — a 110-foot ex-submarine chaser from the last war, named *The Berry Islands*. The storm was so severe that once having started the Captain could not stay out in the storm, and he then made straight for Nassau. The storm was of near hurricane intensity."

The Idol Dancer premiered on March 21, and was followed within weeks with the release of *The Love Flower* on April 2. Griffith struggled with a suitable name for the latter, first working with *The Black Beach*, the title used with the original story. At one point, *The Gamest Girl* was favored, with the ultimate name being the more romantic sounding, *The Love Flower*. Both films did much to cement Richard's popularity with audiences, but accomplished little for Griffith. The public had come to expect grand epics from the director, and films of smaller scope, though fine achievements in themselves, were disappointing to audiences expecting something exceptional.

Griffith needed to score a mammoth hit to wipe out those financial failures. In the summer of 1920, he cast his eyes on a proven-effective vehicle that had toured American towns for decades: Lottie Blaire Parker's sensational melodrama, *Way Down East*. He had Richard in mind for a key role. Unknown to Richard, making the film would nearly cost him his life.

Chapter 4
Way Down East

D. W. Griffith paid $165,000 for the film rights to *Way Down East*, which was more than twice the entire cost of *The Birth of a Nation*. Privately, his staunchest supports thought he had lost his mind.

The horse-and-buggy melodrama had been hauled around the country for more than twenty years, and nearly everyone was familiar with the tale of a country girl, Anna Moore, who is tricked into a mock marriage by a playboy cad, and then abandoned when she becomes pregnant. The poor girl wanders onto a farm owned by the kindly Bartlett family, and there she finds work and a farmer's son who falls in love with her. When the truth of her past becomes known, Squire Bartlett throws her out of the house into a raging storm. She stumbles out into the snow, falls onto ice flows that are breaking on the frozen river, and drifts unconscious toward the looming falls. The Squire's son, David Bartlett, rescues her at the last second.

This melodramatic action was merely *described* in the original play by actors watching from the stage, and in some productions, it was barely shown against prop waterfalls. On stages in nearly every town and hamlet across America, some actress playing Anna had been thrown out into the paper snow. An entire generation had grown up knowing about the girl and her trials, but D. W. Griffith had other ideas. He planned to *show* the river rescue actually taking place.

For eight weeks, the company rehearsed and expanded the action from a script by Anthony Paul Kelly, but Griffith kept only a few bits of the business created by Kelly. The rest of the action was improvised in rehearsal and followed the elements of the original play.

For the exterior scenes of the climax, Griffith gambled on Mother Nature to provide a real storm for his cameras. Insurance policies were taken out against the vagaries of the weather, and the cast settled in to wait for a real blizzard to hit. Lillian prepared for the expected exposure she would be called upon to endure by taking long walks in winter gales, and further conditioned herself to the cold by taking icy baths. For weeks, they waited for a blizzard to strike so that they could film those important scenes.

In March, the long-awaited storm suddenly descended on Long Island Sound, enshrouding the land under eight feet of deep snow drifts and lashing the trees with a roaring gale. The cast and crew bundled up in full winter coats, ready to dash out into the fury and stage the scenes. It was so cold that a fire had to be lit under Billy Bitzer's camera tripods to keep the film from freezing. Lillian was sent out into the icy winds wearing only a flimsy wool dress. The cameras turned, and Griffith filmed her as Anna wandering aimlessly through the drifts. The fury of the wind required three men to lie on the ground gripping the legs of the camera to keep it from blowing over. Her face became caked with crusts of ice and snow, and icicles formed little spikes on her eyelashes.

Griffith saw that she could barely keep her eyes open, and shouted over the howling storm, "Billy, move in! Get that face! That face — *get that face!*"

Billy moved the camera closer and recorded Lillian's frozen face, which was by then covered with inch-thick icicles hanging from her eyelashes. All that day and night, they filmed under the torture of the excruciating cold. At one point, Lillian fainted and was hauled back on a sled that passed the crew who were enveloped safely in coats, mufflers, hats, and gloves. They thawed her with hot tea, and then she was again thrust back out into the stinging winter storm. Richard stood by watching in horror, as the storm grew more intense. His moment to plunge out onto the icy floes was about to take place. The company worked for three weeks at White River Junction for the filming of these scenes, and spent those weeks entirely in temperatures hovering around zero.

For the climax of the film, Griffith had Lillian lay on a slab of ice while it floated down the river. Richard, as the Squire's son, was to

Filming the dangerous climax to *Way Down East* (1920). The camera was mounted on a suspended platform dangling perilously out over the waterfall to capture the moment Richard catches the heroine up in his arms, saving her from certain death, as the ice floe on which he stands begins to tumble over the waterfall.

see her in danger, run from the shore onto the bobbing floes, scoop her up in his arms, and then make a dash to the shore to complete the rescue while cameras cranked. It all seemed so perfectly planned, but then something went terribly wrong.

"Though he worked with his back to the wind whenever possible, Mr. Griffith's face froze," Lillian recounted. "The scene of Anna's rescue from the falls was all too realistically re-created. Mr. Griffith was directing Dick from a bridge over the river, but the noise of the falls drowned out his directions. Dick, a slight young man, was hampered by the heavy raccoon coat and spiked boots he had to wear. As I headed toward the falls on my slab of ice, Mr. Griffith shouted to Dick that he was moving too slowly, but Dick couldn't hear him. The people on the banks were also yelling frantically. As Dick ran toward me he became excited, leaped, and landed on a piece of ice that was too small. He sank into the water . . . ."

The director and crew could not believe what they were seeing. Staring in shock and horror while the cameras continued to grind,

Richard Barthelmess as David at the moment of his attempt to rescue Anna in *Way Down East* (1920).

the ice floe on which Lillian lay with her arm dangling in the below-freezing water floated beyond the point where Richard was to have rescued her. To make matters worse, the struggling actor had slipped from one ice floe into the icy waves, and the floe was only a few yards from the cascading water at the falls. Lillian raised her head for a fleeting moment, saw that the planned stunt had failed, and realized that she was doomed to face a reality worse than any peril Anna Moore ever suffered. Resigned to her fate, she sank back onto the ice floe powerless to save herself. The flow was only a few feet from the falls and was dipping in the water as it angled to go over the plunge.

At the moment that the floe was teetering on the brink of the falls, Richard desperately pulled himself from the water onto the slippery ice, struggled uncertainly to his feet, and then lifted Lillian into his arms. The slab of frozen river on which he stood began to angle and lean into the waterfall. There was not even one second to spare, but with one step, he shifted his uncertain balance while cradling Lillian in a firm grip, and then took another step onto the ice rock behind them. He heard the first floe plunge over the precipice, but did not turn to watch. In rapid succession, he leapt from one bobbing ice floe to the next. Cameras cranked during every breathtaking moment, and the crew that was watching on the shore stood gasping and astonished that he had somehow defied death and made his way safely to the shore.

The near tragedy that they photographed that day was cut into the finished film. The chase at the climax of *Way Down East* shows Richard and Lillian risking their lives, as crumbling ice floes pitch one upon another over the waterfall. The footage of their death race was horrifyingly real, and promised to be a thrilling standout in the completed picture. The shocking realism of this part of the story was unprecedented. The two stars used no stuntmen or doubles for the life-threatening scene. The exciting climax was one of the most suspenseful moments ever depicted in a dramatic motion picture.

Another tragedy struck the production of this film. Clarine Seymour died suddenly, and Griffith needed another actress — a small, dark girl — one who looked very much like Clarine — to quickly step in and play her part in the film. Richard was delighted when Griffith chose Mary Hay along with him in *Way Down East*. Because of Mary's similarity in appearance to Clarine, some of the long shots featuring Clarine did not have to be remade.

Years later, at a screening of *Way Down East* at Richard's home, he and Lillian reminisced about the ice floe scene.

"I wonder why we went through with it. We could have been killed. There isn't enough money in the world to pay me to do it today," he told Lillian.

"But we weren't doing it for money," Lillian reminded him.

Richard's virile masculinity was in sharp contrast to that of Griffith's other leading man, Bobby Harron, a fine actor, but one whose physical appearance restricted him to playing certain sensitive types. He soon found himself replaced by Richard as Griffith's first choice for leading man.

Griffith had every intention of featuring Harron, the one-time Biograph office boy, in a series of comedy films. The first of these, *Coincidence*, directed by Chester Withey, had been completed by the end of the summer of 1920. Then, tragedy struck just before the New York premier of *Way Down East*. The twenty-six-year-old actor had come east for the event. The night before, a telephone operator in the hotel saw the small light from his room telephone flash suddenly.

"I've shot myself . . . send for a doctor," she heard him gasp.

Bellevue Hospital received him by ambulance, but the actor was already in a coma. He briefly came back to consciousness long enough to tell a priest the gunshot was accidental, but then he died a few days later.

Griffith lost several members of his crew from pneumonia as the result of the exposure they endured while making *Way Down East*.

When *Way Down East* finally reached movie screens, breathless audiences sat on the edges of their seats while Richard raced on the ice floes that were about to plunge over the waterfall. The moment when his foot touched the adjacent floe brought audiences to their feet cheering.

The filmed proved to be an enormous success at the box office, but it was also the last time Richard worked with Griffith. He had decided to form his own production company, but there was another interest deep in his heart: he was in love with Mary Hay.

Way Down East had ended with a scene of Richard and Mary Hay getting married, not to each other, but to other characters in the film. Although they had a marriage license for nearly a week, they played the wedding scene for D. W. Griffith just the day before getting married in real life.

Chapter 5
Mary Hay

Richard and Mary were married by Dr. Herbert Shipman at the Church of the Heavenly Rest in New York at 45th and 5th Avenue on June 18, 1920. In attendance were Mary's sisters, Dorothy and Jane Caldwell, and Richard's mother. Richard's best man was H. Montgomery Smith, a classmate from Trinity College. D. W. Griffith was also among the party, having taken part in keeping the impending marriage quiet for some months, and sincerely happy for their newly found romance. Immediately after the ceremony, the newlywed couple went on the road promoting *Way Down East*, and attended the premier at the 44th Street Theater in New York on September 3, 1920.

About her new husband, Mary said, "I loved my husband first for his dominant trait — the clean, fine thought shown in his clean, fine manner of living. He seemed to me to be an example of the day when men will be as clean and fine as they expect the women they marry to be. My husband is fifty-fifty all the time. What is fair for him, is fair for me. I admire my husband's reserve, his natural dignity, and his seriousness. He is *so* serious — and so funny — when he tries to handle our daughter. He is as earnest and conscientious in this as when doing a picture. I must admit that he has moods, but they constitute a very small fly in a very large pot of ointment."

By 1920, Richard was getting huge stacks of mail, much of it from middle-aged women, and he found that he had become an unwilling focal point for their romantic fantasies. Millions of women adored him with blinding devotion, and they vented their feelings in letters to the film magazines of the day.

Her real name was Mary Hay Caldwell, and she hailed from Fort Bliss, Texas, the daughter of Colonel and Mrs. Frank Merrill Caldwell. As a dancer, she studied under Ruth St. Denis, and appeared in D. W. Griffith's film, *Hearts of the World.*

This letter from Agnes J. Warde of Ellisville, Mississippi, appeared in a 1924 issue of a film magazine, and it was typical:

> Everybody please be quiet about Richard Barthelmess, and let me do all the praising by myself, for I love him so much that I would be content to see a picture with nothing else in it but close-ups of him, and I would love to see that picture three hundred and sixty-five times a year! I can beat Charles

Mank, Jr., for I traveled in a storm over a road ready to wash away just to see Dick in *The Bond Boy*, and he was so delicious in the scene where he told the lady that she was pretty, and then deliberately read on in his little book, that I sat through the next show just to see him again in that one scene. I have seen every one of his pictures except *The Fighting Blade*, but he can never do better than he did in that one scene, and no other actor can do as well, so let's not call him a perfect lover, but the 'perfect actor.' Besides that, he is the handsomest male actor on the screen; he has the most adorable eyes in all the world; he is cool and deliberate, not self-conscious, and always at perfect ease, and I am no flapper."

"But I think it's just wonderful to have them feel that way," Richard told an interviewer for *Pantomime*. "It's not me they see, but a character I've portrayed. Please don't think I'm conceited," he laughed. "Perhaps I'd better just whisper it — but the Richard Barthelmess you see on the screen is just acting." He was accurately gauging his appeal to fans, not as an actor or a hero, but as a friend and a good fellow.

Some time after Mary and Richard's wedding, the couple took up residence at Mamaroneck, New York, in a house on one of the prettiest corners of Long Island. The home was within easy motoring distance of the Griffith studio. It was a pretty, six-room cottage with an acre of ground filled with both a flower and a vegetable garden. Long Island Sound was close by and within sight of the house. The unassuming taste of the two popular players, who might easily have afforded opulence, was reflected in their simple and charming home. Richard never liked working in the summer, and was never happier than when he could idle away those months on their vine-clad porch of their little stone cottage.

Their marriage was highly publicized in newspapers and magazines. Dozens of articles presented the two young stars posing at their home on Long Island, on the beach, in studio portraits, and with family and friends. Richard had good reason to go boldly into the press with his marriage. Over recent years, he had received tens of

Official marriage portrait of Mary Hay and Richard Barthelmess after their June 18, 1920 marriage.

Two photographs of Mary and Richard after their honeymoon at their summer home on East 92nd Street, not far from the Griffith Studios.

thousands of letters from women who adored him. They made up the bulk of his fan base. He did not want to alienate them as other actors had suffered when their marriages were revealed.

Less than ten years earlier, Francis X. Bushman, popular star of Essanay and Metro pictures, found that his career was ruined when the public learned that he was married. Bushman had unwisely kept hidden the fact that he had a wife and five children. Then, when he blatantly divorced his wife of many years to marry his on-screen partner, Beverly Bayne, public outrage reached unheard-of proportions. Around the country, theaters refused to show films starring the newly married couple. Films planned to feature the two stars were cancelled, their contracts with Metro were not renewed, and they were professionally destroyed. For years afterward, Bushman worked only sporadically.

Richard's marriage was a different matter than the debacle of the Bushman divorce and remarriage to the youthful Beverly Bayne, but to be cautious, he came out publicly with the full details of his matrimony, and hoped that his fans would share his happiness. Though he may have broken some hearts, the public continued to go to his films. His popularity grew greater as a married man than when he was single.

Richard, wife Mary, and newborn daughter, Mary Hay Barthelmess, in February 1923.

On June 31, 1923, Mary Hay gave birth to a baby girl named Mary Hay Barthelmess. Their honeymoon cottage was no longer suitable, so in 1925, Mary and Richard moved, taking a three-year lease on a brownstone in the east 90s in New York. On moving day, Mary was enveloped in a huge apron that was adorned with smudges. She was buried under a profusion of rolled carpets and boxes. Mary

Richard with one-year old daughter, Mary Hay Barthelmess, at the family piano in 1924.

complained that all Richard did was hang pictures and spend hours searching for just the right place for "The Fish," a trophy of a mounted fish he helped catch in Florida. "It weights about thirty pounds," Mary said, "and he has dragged it around from room to room, trying the effect on every bit of wall space. It has ended, eventually, in his own room, on the wall opposite to his bed."

Movie stars had shaken the public out of the foolish idea that all married actors and actresses must be cloistered, so far as the public knew. By 1925, there was Mary Pickford and Douglas Fairbanks, Norma Talmadge and Joseph Schenk, Mildred Davis and Harold Lloyd, Frances Ring and Thomas Meighan, Alice Terry and Rex Ingram, and many others. Marriage seemed to help business and social position, and it helped change the reputation many actors had that they were nothing but aimless bands of wandering vagabonds.

Marital life for the couple split evenly between Richard's film work and Mary's musical comedy career. They managed to grab moments together during a twenty-minute race across town to the Imperial Theater where Mary had to arrive at her dressing room by 7:45 each evening. They ate meals that were sent in from nearby restaurants, and all too often, they merely crossed paths in her dressing room for brief minutes. As she hurriedly dressed for her performance in the musical comedy *Mary Jane McKane*, which was produced by Arthur Hammerstein from a book by Oscar Hammerstein II, Richard had fleeting moments with his new wife. From the very beginning, this arrangement put a strain on their relationship.

To observers, Mary looked like a sixteen-year-old escaping from the Child Labor Law enforcers while lugging a husky, nineteen-month-old infant through the dank alleys in the back of Broadway theaters. She was untouched by the usual wear and tear of being the wife of a famous movie star, accustomed as she was to her own madcap existence singing and dancing every evening and at matinees in a musical comedy on Broadway. On stage, the cute little girl radiated personality and wore flashy garments, but off stage, her intimate girlfriends called her "Nell." She wore simple suits, which might easily come from a department store, and adorned her self with a notable absence of jewelry and makeup, a strange image for the better half of a popular idol whose salary and earnings made the compensation of the President of the United States look like thirty cents. Four years before, Mary made critic Heywood Broun coin a new adjective of delight as he watched her eccentric dancing atop the New Amsterdam Roof: "The Delectable Mary Hay," he saluted. She was a "flapper" in an age when it was stylish to raise your skirts and bob your hair.

Despite the apparent joys of their lifestyle, the couple soon began to find their home life crumbling. In spite of their efforts to find even ground on which to establish a firm relationship, Richard could not ask Mary to give up her career, and in all fairness, he did not want her to do so. As a housewife, she would have lost the spicy vivacity he found so attractive. On the other hand, with Mary appearing in yet another musical comedy on the New York stage, their life together had been reduced to nothing more than a few hasty minutes spent together on the run.

The future loomed frighteningly in front of them, an ominous specter of endless road tours for Mary and stagnant hotel life for Richard. Mary objected to the separations they were forced to endure. For a time, Richard toyed with the idea of playing with her on the stage, but he had no singing or dancing ability. The obvious solution seemed for Mary to join him in motion picture work. They began to look for a property that could feature the two of them together on screen for the first time since *Way Down East*. The idea of taking control of his professional destiny gave inspiration to the formation of a new company to boast Richard at its helm. He also hoped that working with Mary would bring some kind of stability to their rocky marriage. It was a bold gamble, even more so for a man like Richard, who was never one to lay bets.

Chapter 6
Inspiration Pictures

Richard left D. W. Griffith to form his own film production company, and he enthusiastically left with the Griffith's good graces. "However," he explained, "he has promised to give me advice if I should come a cropper."

Griffith had purchased several of the works of author Joseph Hergesheimer as possible material for films, and among the lot was a short story, *The Happy End*. As time passed, Griffith lost interest in using the story, but it strongly appealed to Richard. He approached Griffith with an offer to buy the story. The director, who was always pressed for cash, put a price tag of $125,000 on it, and Richard went in search of a loan. Financier Averell Harriman offered to put up the money for the screen rights, and Richard formed Inspiration Pictures to manage the new opportunity.

Henry King, a former actor who had turned out competent but unspectacular works up to that time, adapted the story with Richard, expanding on a treatment put together by Edmund Goulding. Together, they turned the story into a workable scenario for the first film from Richard's fledgling company. The title was changed to *Tol'able David*.

Tol'able David is a dramatic story of a backwoods feud and a boy's revenge. Richard gave one of his best performances as a boy who saves the US Mail from outlaws. It afforded many opportunities to appear as he had in *Way Down East*, a simple country boy with a straw hat and bare feet. It also offered many close-ups of him with misty eyes and far-away expressions that showed his character yearning to grow into a man.

Director Henry King and writer Joseph Hergesheimer with Richard while filming *Tol'able David* (1921).

"David was a role which I tried not only to characterize, but also to idealize," he explained to Adele Fletcher in *Motion Picture Magazine*. "A mountain boy would not have been as I played David. His hands would have been gritty. His hair would have been uncombed. His teeth would have been yellow. I studied David and thought about David for weeks. And when I finally came to play David, I gave him a dash of poetry. I think they liked him better that way." Writer Adele Fletcher wrote what so many others have thought about Richard: "And since then when we have remembered Dick, we have, at the same time, remembered the nicest boy in our hometown. That is the atmosphere he gives you some way or another. And it is easy to like him. He is young and sane and normal. He is good to look at, too, with his firmly set mouth, his deep brown eyes and his warm brown skin — with his feet standing firmly on the ground — and his eyes finding the stars."

The film went much deeper than a typical morality play. Story lines were woven to bring the audience along several plot sequences to a simultaneous conclusion. The breathtaking result lovingly recreated 19th century Americana.

With a $250,000 budget, director Henry King shot the film on locations near his own home in the heart of the Virginia Blue Ridge Mountains. While filming in the hills among isolated mountaineers, the film company stumbled upon one of America's queerest religious colonies. The outstanding commandments of their faith were that no clothing would enfold their bodies, and the use of water, except as a beverage, was forbidden. Needless to say, these fanatics seldom mingled with neighbors or the film crew. They kept to themselves, isolated in a section of the mountains where they pursued their smooth and clothing-free ways, immune from safety razors, soap, or interference.

The company encountered life as it had been fifty years before, and even found an authentic old cabin that once belonged to Confederate guerilla raiders who hid while Union troops searched the surrounding country. The cabin was used for exteriors in the film.

One day while filming, Gladys Hulette played opposite Richard and was submitting to some hard treatment enacted as part of the story. Nearby, a wizened, old mountaineer stood watching the scene for some time. Puzzled, confused, and misunderstanding that the director's efforts to get the actress to cry were on behalf of a film scene, he approached the director, shook his fist, and warned, "If you want to abuse a woman, get someone of your own size. You can't make this one cry any more when I'm here!"

"We had a great time down in Virginia making *Tol'able David*," Richard told Emma-Lindsay Squier of *Picture Play Magazine*. "We were there for six weeks straight, about forty miles from a railroad, in the locality where Hergesheimer laid the story. Many of the natives had never seen a railroad train, and few of them knew what a motion picture was. They thought it was wonderful, and we had lots of them working in it, all the local celebrities — the Mayor, the Justice of the Peace, and the Sheriff. Some of them were mighty good actors, too."

When asked if he was going to follow this type of character in future films, Richard said, "I'm not going in for any particular type. Very few people can specialize and get away with it. No, I like versatility. And, above all, I want a good story. Not a story that's written around me, but one that I can fit into. I'd like to do

In 1921, Mary Hay, still in her teens, singing and dancing every evening and matinees in a musical comedy, visited Richard under a bank of Cooper-Hewitt lights to watch him work on the George Fitzmaurice production, *Experience*.

Arthur C. Miller at the camera filming a scene at the Long Island Studio of the George Fitzmaurice production for Paramount, *Experience* (1921). Seated at the table are Richard Barthelmess, playing the role of "Youth," Edna Wheaton, winner of a beauty contest, playing "Beauty," and director Fitzmaurice.

Director George Fitzmaurice filming Richard Barthelmess in a scene for *Experience* (1921).

Hergesheimer's *Java Head*. It is so colorful, and there are splendid dramatic possibilities for the part of the story that's laid in China."

When the film was released, Richard departed from his usual custom of not making personal appearances, and spoke at the Central Presbyterian Church at Montclair, New Jersey. *Tol'able David* was the first film thrown on the screen of the handsome new church auditorium. To honor the occasion, Richard consented to speak, and told of the circumstances connected with the filming of the picture. Until then, few films escaped the strict hands of the State censors or were allowed a presentation in churches.

Tol'able David was one of the best films of 1921, and ultimately a milestone in Richard's career. Director King spent only $86,000 of the $250,000 budget to complete the picture. The film won *Photoplay Magazine's* 1922 Medal of Honor as outstanding film of the year.

Richard's work in *Tol'able David* was unprecedented in his career up to that time. Through his portrayal of this intensely human story of the Virginia backwoods, he developed a new screen creed for his fledgling company.

"Simple, unextravagant stories, portraying life as it really is, are what the public wants today," he said, in an interview with *Screenland* magazine. "Nobody's perfect. All of us have faults as well as virtues. There is no superman, outside of the imagination of too fervid authors. The vamp, the double-dyed villain, and the infallible hero are dying out. We must portray humanity as it really is, if we are going to stand the acid test of popularity."

His role in *Tol'able David* was widely acclaimed as one of his best performances, if not his very best. Ernest Torrence, playing the most brazen of the three villains thwarting the boy and his attempt to deliver the mail, gave a performance that established him as one of the great villains of the silent screen.

The film's incredible success guaranteed that Inspiration Pictures would have a place in the industry, and for the first time, Richard found himself in control of his professional destiny.

"Well, it's a pretty big responsibility," he told one interviewer. "You have to know just where the money goes and attend to a thousand little details you never thought of when you were working under salary. But I like it, of course. I have a good release — First

National — and I can pick the kind of stories I want to do. On the whole, it's a great satisfaction — or it will be if this picture goes over, as I'm hoping it will. Mr. Hergesheimer seemed very much pleased the way we did it, and when an author gives his okay to his brain child on the screen, it must be good."

Tragically, a few years later in 1928, Ralph Yearsley, who played Saul Hatburn in the film, committed suicide when at the age of thirty-one.

For the next five years, Richard worked as both star and producer, handling all aspects of eleven consecutive film productions, while turning in competent and often acclaimed performances. Though none of these films repeated the success of *Tol'able David*, and they were not of the caliber of the Griffith films, Inspiration Pictures rolled off slick, polished, and entertaining productions that never disappointed his fans. With this series, he became one of Hollywood's biggest and most commercial stars.

While his status was on the ascent, others were already bringing their careers to a close. After appearing in thirty-nine films between 1914 and 1921, Marguerite Clark, who had helped Richard find his initial success in several of her early films, reached the number one position in the industry, according to the Quigly Publication Poll of motion picture exhibitors of 1920. Having achieved her goal of reaching the top, and after completing her final film, *Scrambled Wives* (1921), Marguerite married and completely left the film industry to enjoy a new life with her husband on their plantation in New Orleans. She was never tempted to return to the limelight.

The Seventh Day was Richard's thirty-third motion picture. It was made near New Harbor, Maine, when Richard was at the height of his popularity and busily turning out one film after another for his own company. The original title was *All at Sea*, and later was changed to the more mysterious title to reflect an initial image less confusing with that of a naval picture.

"I take the part of a young sailor on a fishing schooner," he told writer John Patton. "We had engaged for the sea scenes one of the largest fishing schooners that puts out of Portland. It was being fitted out especially for sword fishing. Captain Turner thought it would be a good idea and that I would absorb much atmosphere if I really went sword fishing. So, with a sailor to instruct me, we put

Director Henry King with Richard Barthelmess while filming *The Bondboy* (1922).

Director John S. Robertson and crew filming a scene with Richard Barthelmess and Dorothy Gish on location in Havana for the film, *The Bright Shawl* (1923).

out in a dory. Others of the crew were sprinkled all around the ocean in their dories. Finally, we spied a giant fish. The sailor showed me how to throw the harpoon and eagerly I waited the opportunity to pierce the fish right behind the head. I suppose my aim was accurate as I let go this huge javelin. After I saw the weapon sink into the fish and the fish do what you might call a run and then disappear, I congratulated myself on having, at my first trial, landed a swordfish." Richard soon developed a keen interest in deep sea fishing, which lasted throughout the rest of his life.

Richard loved being away from Hollywood, and since costume pictures were popular in the early 1920s, he found a story that enabled him to travel to an exotic location. In 1922, Joseph Hergesheimer, one of Richard's favorite authors, drew vivid characters for a costume story in his novel, *The Bright Shawl*. Edmund Goulding, who had written *Fury* and some of Richard's other films, adapted the story to the screen. To compliment his role as Charles Abbott, a carefully selected cast was assembled. It included the glittering talent of his popular co-star, Dorothy Gish, as "La Clavel," the fiery and vivid Andalusian dancer, who brought all Havana to worship at the whirling fringe of her gorgeous shawl, and who ultimately gave her life for the cause of Cuban liberty. Mary Astor portrayed Narcissa, a fragrant blossom of a woman, who captures Charles' heart. Jetta Goudal filled out the character of the vamp, La Pilar, and Richard's new-found pal, William H. Powell, appeared in a vivid character part. In addition, future star, Edward G. Robinson made an early appearance.

The Bright Shawl took Richard, cast, and crew away from Hollywood studios and manufactured sets in search of authentic atmosphere. The colorful romance was set in picturesque Havana, and to record the real-life settings, Richard, Dorothy Gish, and director John Robertson journeyed to Cuba. Exteriors were shot among old world locations including the historic El Morro Castle. Even the extras were drawn from a Spanish stock company playing in Havana at the time the producers arrived.

The parade of talent on the trip to Cuba went beyond the actors. Also with them was Everett Shinn, a famous artist, who arranged the artistic design of the scenes. At his command were all the natural scenic splendors and old architectural triumphs of Cuba. Most of

The friendship of Richard Barthelmess and William Powell grew out of a mutual dislike for each other while casting took place for the film, *The Bright Shawl* (1923).

the props used in the picture were authentic and historic, including hand-carved, Spanish oak doors that were taken from the celebrated castle built by Prince de Balboa. After the film was finished, these props were donated to the Spanish Museum in New York for preservation.

"The doors will not only have a historic value," said Shinn, "but will live for centuries as an art and will be a model for future generations. Not only were the doors an object of beauty, but also they were serviceable in withstanding forcible entry. All houses built in the early days of Cuba had to be constructed with the idea of resisting the pirates who made frequent incursions into the islands, being attracted by the stories of the great wealth of this garden spot of the South Seas. There are marks on these doors which prove that efforts to break them down by using a battering

Richard Barthelmess spent days practicing the dueling scenes during camera breaks while filming *The Bright Shawl* (1923).

ram had failed." In addition, centuries-old pottery believed to have been fashioned by the ancient Moors was procured and utilized in the film.

Richard literally followed in John Barrymore's shoes in *The Bright Shawl*. Barrymore turned over to Richard his specially built shoes, which served him in the play, *Peter Ibbetson*, and in other stage successes. They were made of the softest leather, with a very high heel that was constructed so that it looked like an ordinary heel, but in reality, was three inches higher. Richard was also given a costume that Barrymore wore in *Peter Ibbetson*, and it was also used in the film.

Mary Astor, with her usual candid simplicity, later wrote about *The Bright Shawl* in her book, *A Life on Film:* "We made tepid love in front of the camera and we rode a cushioned, flowered gondola in a reproduction on the back lot of the canals of Xochimilco...."

For his next effort, Richard finally attempted to save his marriage. He brought his wife onto the screen with a production that was tailored to fit her buoyant personality. The film was titled *New Toys*.

Mary explained his reasons for working with her: "When I was working on the stage and Dick on the screen, we really never saw one another at all. I would be working most of the night; Dick would be working all day. Then, Dick thought it would be good for me to do a picture with him. Last year, when he saw *New Toys* on the stage, we realized that it was exactly the story for us. In fact, people will doubtless say that it is the story of our real selves . . . as to whether I remain on the screen or not, remains to be seen. I doubt it. I'm not pretty enough to do very much in pictures. Most of the big ones on the screen are pretty, very. And I wouldn't be satisfied to be just one of the rank and file."

Mary's uncertainty was grounded in reality. She realized that her work in the new film was more of a precautionary measure Richard had devised to keep her in tow, and hopefully, to enable them to find some common ground that would help cement the shifting foundation of their troubled marriage.

While Richard's career was flourishing, he hoped to be instrumental in helping his wife achieve some new level of success. Like D. W. Griffith, Richard was sure that Mary had "*It*," that strange quality labeled by Elinor Glyn with the provocative two-letter word, an attribute also known as "screen personality." *IT* was nothing so obvious as beauty or a pretty face; *IT* had nothing to do with dramatic ability. *IT* was a certain trick of moving, a funny elusive way of smiling, and a gift for being amusing, interesting, distinctive, and attractive to both men and women.

At the age of twenty-three, Mary radiated the personality of a little brownie. In the artificial atmosphere of the stage and a studio, she was so completely without pose that she sometimes struck people as being defenseless. She had no self-conscious mannerisms, and no artificiality. It was this complete naturalness that Richard believed would put Mary across on the screen. He also hoped he would be able to save their marriage by spending more time together working on the film.

"It was the only thing to do," Mary later explained. "It was the

John Decker's 1924 caricature portrait of Mary Hay and Richard Barthelmess.

only way we could stay together. The separate career business didn't work out . . . it was really wretched. I was interested in my work, and he was interested in his. That's all right, I suppose, but we had no time for each other."

New Toys was intended to be a vehicle that would start Mary off in pictures. After it, their plan was for her to appear in other pictures without Richard. "In this first picture, I'd rather work with Richard than anyone else," Mary told Agnes Smith. "I can have the benefit of his advice and help. He knows his business, and I can learn more from him about screen acting than anyone I know of."

While Mary and Richard were working on *New Toys*, Richard met a young, distinctive woman who had a small role in the film. Katherine Wilson was a gracious brunette from a well-known family in Jacksonville, Florida. She had been educated at Rogers Hall, Boston, and at Madam Rieffel's Finishing School in New York. Katherine would come back into Richard's life a few years later in a profound way.

New Toys was another hit for both Richard and Inspiration Pictures. Mary had found it quite simple to give up her early successes in musical comedy — for a while, but with her appearance in this film with Richard came managers bearing offers — tempting offers — and more tantalizing successes on the stage.

Director John S. Robertson bending over Richard Barthelmess under the framework and in front of the cameras while filming *The Fighting Blade* (1923).

Richard made his next film without Mary. *The Fighting Blade*, produced in 1923, challenged him to look manly in satins and plumes as a lad of England in the days of Oliver Cromwell. As the gallant swordsman and chivalrous lover who joined the forces of Parliament for the sake of a woman, Richard labored as well as could be expected. His hair and costumes were closely patterned after a famous Rembrandt painting, and as their inspiration, the film's designers painstakingly copied every detail with startling accuracy. As an actor, Richard showed his convincing adaptability in the role of a courageous Dutchman, exhibiting self-assurance in every expression. Director John S. Robertson permitted the star to get the utmost from every scene, dwelling long enough on the romantic episodes to allow him to show his romantic and adventurous veins. Richard even endured a thrilling torture scene. Expressions on his face agonized audiences when his tormentors drove cruel wedges between the handcuffs on his wrists. His eyes narrowed, his jaw contracted, he bit his lips, and after the intense suffering, he rose to his feet, silent, contemptuous, and victorious. Though melodramatic in the extreme, the film pleased audiences at that time.

The Inspiration Pictures assembly line continued to grind out one film after another. For a change, *Twenty-One* featured Richard as a 1923 model youth. He discarded the plumes from recent costume pictures and the barefoot country boys from his past.

May McAvoy getting an assist from Richard Barthelmess with the make-up on her ugly nose for the pre-transformation scenes while filming *The Enchanted Cottage* (1924).

In a simple story of a misunderstood rich boy, who was poor because he was unloved, he again was directed by John S. Robertson, and again scored another hit with audiences.

With each new film, Richard tried to show versatility. In 1924, he began work on an odd film, a poignant fantasy about two bitter people looking for love. *The Enchanted Cottage* gave him a chance to twist and maim himself into a cripple. The story follows a lonely and unattractive man and woman when they enter a cottage, which then transforms the couple into glorious, glamorous new images that depict each as the other sees them.

John England, a writer for *Movie Weekly*, observed the filming one day at the ancient studio in Fort Lee, New Jersey, where director John S. Robertson was composing a scene under the glare of lights at the grave of England's Unknown Soldier. May McAvoy appeared in her characterization as Laura Pennington, complete with a misshapen nose and garbed in a tweed coat. England wrote:

> "Tears hovered in her eyes as she looked wistfully at the slab of stone set into the cathedral floor. Close held in either arm were a tiny blond-headed girl in Scotch kilts, and a young boy in Eton suit. She was garbed in that shapeless, shoddy tweed to which only the London Cockney is able to do justice. Something extraordinary had happened to the bridge of her nose since we last had seen it. We stood off in a corner, watching, while John Robertson gave directions. His whispers of instruction were inaudible. Their effect was immediate and impressive. Never have we seen a man master of a situation with so little effort. Then, Richard appeared, now frocked in an immaculate morning coat, bearing in one hand a silk hat, and in the other, weirdly enough, a heavy walking stick and an umbrella. He had suddenly grown older. There was a tired, ravaged convalescent look in his face. We peered inquisitively. Across his cheeks, beneath his chin and around his eyes, were heavy purple shadows. We glanced furtively again at the bridge of Miss McAvoy's

ordinarily adorable nose . . . " Filming continued on the scene in the graveyard, as the two actors completed work on this isolated moment for the picture.

When the film was released, critics were amazed at Richard's ability to turn from a handsome leading man into a man of pronounced unattractiveness. He succeeded in establishing himself as one of the best actors on the screen by shaping himself into a physically wrecked veteran with stooped shoulders, limping steps, twisted torso, and pathetic, hollow-cheeks.

At this time, rumors began spreading of an impending production of Shakespeare's *Romeo and Juliet*, which was to again star Richard with Lillian Gish. He planned to film the tale of the two lovers of Verona in actual Italian locations. Unfortunately, early talks produced a conflict with billing the two stars. At that same time, First National offered him a contract for more money than he had ever made with his own company, calling for three films a year at a reported annual fee of $375,000. Richard's primary motivation for being an actor had always been money and not any lust for glory or fame. With that offer, he reluctantly made the difficult decision to disband Inspiration Pictures and go to work for First National. The need for financial security, which was the driving force behind his decisions, led him to analyze his success carefully. He realized that the string of successes with Inspiration Pictures was tenuous. How long luck would hold out was a matter of opinion, but the safety of a princely, steady income was hard for him to argue against. Because of this decision, plans for the fascinating proposed production of *Romeo and Juliet* fell by the wayside.

Before work began in the spring of 1925 on his initial First National film, Richard and William Powell were feeling a "back to nature" urge, and they fled Hollywood for the wilds of a little island off the California coast. They planned a peaceful outing, but underestimated the hospitality of the natives. Mosquitoes, gnats, and flies saw that the visitors never had a dull moment. To make matters worse, the tide rose and all but covered the small island on which they were camping. Each morning brought the sun, heat, more bugs, and mounting discomfort. When they arrived home,

Bessie Love looking at a camera set-up for *Soul-Fire*, while director John Robertson and Richard Barthelmess observe.

Richard told Powell that the next time they took a vacation it would be on the corner of Broadway and 42nd Street.

Those escapes were brief. With fame came unwanted and constant contact with the public. Richard received letters by the thousands from young men wanting to get into the movies.

"There is a distinct place for the college man on the screen," he told one interviewer. "The college man comes specially-trained to meet the problems of living. University life has taught him self-reliance application and concentration. There is a place for the collegian in motion pictures, I mean particularly in fields other than acting. He should make a particularly good director. He has the mental background so necessary to his work. He should make a particularly successful executive because he has an excellent perspective upon the drama and literature. Of course, the college-trained man ought to make an excellent actor, too. There is only one thing against him

Marie Dressler, Addison Mizner, and Richard Barthelmess at the Cloister Inn, Boca Raton, Florida, January 12, 1926. Mizner was an architect of Boca Raton. His brother was screenwriter Wilson Mizner.

there. The University course takes up four valuable years of his life. Every big actor has come through a hard, long school of learning his trade. The college man, perforce, must try to succeed without learning this essential groundwork of acting. College boys frequently write to me about the prospects of succeeding in motion pictures. I always give the answer I have presented here."

In 1926, F. W. Murnau attracted a great deal of attention with *Sunrise*, his first American film. Much was made in the press and among studios about the new techniques used by the innovative German director. While Richard and others watched these developments with interest, the public could not have cared less. After much ballyhoo on the part of William Fox over his acquisition of Murnau, the New York showings of *Sunrise* were a disappointment at the box office. Los Angeles and Philadelphia fortunes fared better, but it never fully recovered from the stigma of its New York opening. Reviews were mixed and general attendance was poor. The glittering effects, gliding cameras, and waves of dissolves shown by the film's technique could not overcome the generally impoverished story line. The film ultimately was one of Fox's top grosser for the year. Regardless of the varying opinions by critics, the film sparked much discussion, and it was examined in-depth by nearly every publication of merit. It also heralded the biggest change ever to hit the motion picture industry: sound. Warner Bros. had already shown John Barrymore in *Don Juan* with a synchronized music score that used their Vitaphone process of sound on synchronized discs. Fox followed suit with their competitive Movietone process, which featured sound on film. Both systems were successful.

As a visionary, Murnau was sensitive enough to see into the future. "There will be other technical changes in the next ten or twenty years. The three-dimension movie will be the usual thing instead of the occasional effect. I produced an appearance of depth in the marsh sequence of *Sunrise* by a trick arrangement of lights and shadows. Other directors have experimented with sets in which the floors rise and fall, and the lines of doors, ceiling and furniture slant sharply according to the laws of perspective. But there is a simpler and less expensive device already in preparation which I may not explain now, but which will produce the same illusion of depth and distance as the old-fashioned stereopticon slides."

"Perhaps, too, there will be a radical change in the way motion pictures are projected. I understand one producer is experimenting in a method of showing a picture without a screen so that it looks as though the characters themselves were present in the room in which the audience sits! Television and the radio may bring the

Mary Hay in her dressing room at the theater where she scored a great hit in the musical comedy, *Marjolaine*.

movies of the future through the air into your own home at the turn of a key."

D. W. Griffith, considering the many changes taking place within the industry and the moving camera technique touted by Murnau, did not hold the German influence in awe. "Motion pictures haven't changed," he declared in a 1926 interview. "The technique of telling your story varies with passing vogues, but the photoplay remains essentially the same. It has remained unchanged since the Biograph days. Yes, I know, it has become the custom to say that the Germans are pioneers in a new technique. Why, they are doing the things that we discarded long ago. A certain primitive virility comes of that, but it is absurd to talk of a new technique. They do things long prohibited over here. Mugging, for instance. Long scenes played right at the camera. We did all that in the beginning. The fact that this primitive stuff has been dressed up with superb camera work has confused observers. The Germans' have a fine mechanical mind. They have perfected the camera. In fact, after the war, we found that they had gone beyond us in cameras and camera equipment. In lighting, too. But this new German technique is all bosh. We make better pictures in America."

In the autumn of 1926, Richard sensed the changes that were in the wind for the film industry. While film art was reaching a climax, his personal life was evolving into a downward spiral. The pressures of fame were the greatest disadvantage in his life. He and Mary could not compete with successes tugging each of them in different directions. Their dissimilarity in temperaments was too wide to resolve. Mary, impulsive and gay, was not ready for the slippers-and-hearth calm that Richard preferred. Richard, methodically thoughtful and serious, did not have her frivolity and humor. Although he was happy by nature, he did not like professional comedians or men who tried to be the life of a party with non-stop jokes. He and Mary were polar opposites. His dream of happiness with Mary soon degenerated into complete disillusionment. Reluctantly, they separated.

Advertisement for the Sidney Olcott film, *The White Black Sheep* (1926).

"She didn't, in the very nature of things, want a home, children, responsibility, or settling down," Richard explained to Gladys Hall, a sympathetic writer for *Movie Mirror*. "I felt very shabbily treated, very much injured. I shouldn't have been. The fault was that I didn't *know*. We were sweethearts, not friends."

The couple found the strain of adjusting their separate careers around each other was impossible. Mary left Richard to accept a dancing engagement at Ciros, a popular nightclub, and then sailed to Paris for another engagement dancing with Clifton Webb.

They divorced in Paris in January 1927. Richard lost a bitter battle for the complete custody of Mary, their four-year-old child. The dispute was submitted to the Rev. S. Parkes Cadman, a New York clergyman, as arbiter. He decided that little Mary was to be shared for six months each year with each parent.

In April 1927, Mary Hay went away and married Vivian Bath, an Englishman. When she passed through Los Angeles on her honeymoon, traveling the first leg of a journey to Singapore, she deposited her daughter with Richard, and then disappeared. The remainder of the Mary Hay story was without much fanfare. Within a year, she came back, appearing on Broadway in *Treasure Girl* at the Alvin Theater. Three years later, she co-wrote with Bruce Spaulding, Anthony Baird, and Nella Steward an original play called *Greater Love*, which premiered at the Liberty Theater on March 2, 1931, and closed after only eight performances. It would be the last time anyone in a New York theater would ever see Mary Hay.

Meanwhile, Richard's life and work had to go on. With his first film for First National, Richard enjoyed one of his greatest personal successes. In *The Patent Leather Kid* (1927), he turned in one of his best performances in a stirring war story about a cocky, second-rate prizefighter with a flair for patent leather in everything from his shoes to his hair. As Curley Boyle, a conceited, young boxer to whom the flag of his country meant less than the towel his trainer waves in his face, Richard played a young man unwillingly drafted into the army. Curly was a demon of a battler in fist-fighting combat, but proved to be a coward who was afraid to put on a uniform after his induction. He later redeemed himself while in a heated battle. The story swept him from a Broadway honky-tonk through the frenzy of his first fight game, climaxing with the living hell-on-earth of World War One.

The Rupert Hughes novel was hailed as a masterpiece of visualization when published. For its translation to the screen, a motion picture had seldom been conceived under more auspicious circumstances. To those responsible for the production, Richard seemed ideal for the part of Curly Boyle.

Enough time had passed since the real-life armistice in 1918 to enable audiences to look back and redefine what the war had done to them. The stupendous undertaking of the filming of the war scenes was done at Camp Lewis, Washington, with the full aid and cooperation of the US War Department. Advice from Col. Robert Alexander, who was then in command of Camp Lewis, assisted in the technical accuracy of the war scenes.

An odd difficulty presented itself during the pre-production efforts: no one could locate an actual copy of a draft card issued when conscription became the law during World War One. The scenario called for the card to be used in a close-up. The producers found that very few men had kept their official war summons, and a long search followed for an actual copy of a draft card before one was found and used in the film.

So much detail occupied the shooting of the war scenes that Richard A. Rowland, General Manager of First National Pictures, personally made several trips to the distant location to assist Al Rockett, Production Manager, and director, Alfred Santell, in their work.

A love story of sorts was woven throughout the picture. Molly O'Day, a young actress picked from 2,000 applicants for the part of the Golden Dancer who loved Curly, found that her career peaked as a result of this part.

3,000 US soldiers, 600 civilians posing as German soldiers, and $5 million worth of US Army guns, tanks, and equipment were used in the war scenes.

During the days when filming progressed, twelve cameramen perched as high as sixty feet in the air to cover the expanse of the battlegrounds. 175,000 feet of wiring connected the planted mines for the explosions. One particular shot of a procession leading up to the battlefield extended over a distance of five miles. In scope, the film was stupendous.

Richard Barthelmess and Al Santell observing Harry Redmond, the man at the explosives switchboard, while filming *The Patent Leather Kid* (1927).

To provide realism, more than fifty tanks charged in the grand advance over German trenches and shell-torn territory. Coupled with artillery barrages and airplane attacks, the heightened effect was a sensational recreation of the war.

Industry insiders were impressed with how Richard had matured as an actor. He won a Special Academy Award for his work in *The Patent Leather Kid*.

After production work was finally completed, there was a party for the opening on Broadway of *The Patent Leather Kid* that was held at The Ambassador Hotel in New York. Richard went through a dark period during this time after his divorce from Mary Hay. At the party, Richard greeted guests with a faint smile, but his eyes were deep, miserable pits that mirrored his hidden emotions. Most of the guests did not realize their host's unhappiness. Talk rose high and spirited, as Richard observed the array of glittering celebrities in the party: Billie Dove all in white, flipping her sweet, sophisticated bangs; a famous film critic sporting a grim expression that was devoid of amusement; a fragile blond newspaper woman with her companion; a beautiful woman executive compressing the tenderness which threatened to break through her official air; a young film editor, who was not a day over twenty-five with a lilt and joy abounding around his face. All these people drifted around and merged under the moonlight while Richard stood in the wings with a face that was masked in discontent and crowned by brows like two furious caterpillars.

He wondered if a great love would exist for him in this decade of superb indifference to everything idyllic. The days of Mary Hay were behind him. She belonged to bygone memories of swimming together in the turquoise waters of Mamaroneck Cove where they first met, and with the irrevocably gone weeks they had spent at the old Griffith studio. The heartbreak of their marriage had been wrapped away like a dead child's shoes and placed at the back of his heart, only to be recalled when the future demanded toleration, sympathy, and a patient viewpoint when pressed for a comment. He wondered if he would ever stumble across a woman who would incite a second passion that penetrated the years of his impending maturity. He longed for someone to accompany him while he was at the pinnacle of his power and the apex of his art.

For a time, Richard, Ronald Coleman, and William Powell vowed that they would never marry again. Although terrifically pursued by the feminine sex, they reveled in their bachelorhood. Dick harbored a profound aversion to ever having any future wife that was under the grip of theatrical ambitions. He had had his fill of actresses and wanted a real woman, but there were still many available and stunning actresses pursuing him.

1927 photo of Richard with his daughter, Mary Hay Barthelmess.

"It has the spirit of youth," Richard said in 1926 of his newly acquired Rolls Royce. "It's long, rangy lines, great power, and vitality buoy me up when I am the least bit enervated after hours of screening."

These vows were short-lived for the three bachelors. Richard kept his personal life as separate as possible from his on-screen labors. He showed his love for good friend, William Powell, and his new bride, Carole Lombard, on their return from a Honolulu honeymoon. When their boat passed through the Golden Gate in San Francisco, Richard escorted it to its pier along side his boat that was loaded with many notable Hollywood film celebrities on board. The newlywed couple later joined the party, which lasted until they sailed into the Los Angeles harbor after a voyage of 500 miles.

Nearly a week later, there was a big surprise in store for Richard's fans: they learned that he had become engaged to Katherine Young Wilson, a distinguished Broadway actress he had meet some time before while filming *New Toys*. Katherine was known in Manhattan theatrical circles as the girl who had made a hit on Broadway as the heroine of Dreiser's *American Tragedy*. She had also appeared in *Love 'Em and Leave 'Em*. Announcements ran in many national newspapers proclaiming their official engagement. She was very pretty, a talented trouper, and a delightful young lady characterized by great simplicity. He sent out to the jeweler's for the rarest of diamonds in order for his fiancée to have her choice of stones. They hoped to be married in the autumn of 1927.

The wedding never took place. By March 1928, friends wondered whether their romance was over. The wedding had been indefinitely postponed, and for a time, that was the only comment either would make about it.

Public speculation about the next woman to enter his life seemed to swirl around Richard's every move. Film magazines began to recall his previous leading ladies as they pried into the feminine side of his personal life.

In an article that was allegedly written by Richard for *Motion Picture Magazine*, he pointed out, "There are stars, I am told, who prefer players opposite them who will be shadowy figures upon the final film. Personally, I want, first of all, an actress who can act. In every picture I do, about two-thirds of the way through, I begin to feel that my leading woman is stealing my picture. I like that because it makes me work all the harder. It becomes a race — and that is just what a star needs. A star is faced on all sides with the temptation to do things the easiest way. It seems to me the ideal leading woman has charm, ability, and a sympathetic response. Of course, no personal feeling really enters into the scene — but the ideal leading woman must respond quickly and surely to the moods of the moment. Then, too, I like a leading woman whom I can respect as an artist. She must be a star, either actually or potentially. Naturally, it would not be fair to make direct comparisons, but I honestly believe Dorothy Gish to be one of the best actresses I have ever worked with. I believe, too, if she had had Lillian's opportunities, she would have been as great a star, or even greater. The public has never realized Dorothy's potentialities. She has marvelous sense of comedy. She has a tremendous sense of dramatic values." Richard went on to project admiration for Dorothy Mackaill, who played with him in three pictures.

In 1927, Richard played the part of a young daredevil Cavalry officer in *Ranson's Folly*. Many exciting experiences and narrow escapes occurred during the making of this film. During the filming of a spectacular fire scene, a number of horses became terrorized by smoke, and plunged into the group of actors and crew.

On another occasion, as preparations were under way to film scenes near Lookout Mountain, a landslide swept down on the livestock corral, nearly burying the horses, mules, cows, sheep, and goats. The quick action of the keepers rescued the animals, but saddles, harnesses, and other equipment were irretrievably buried in the rock and rubble, netting a loss of thousands of dollars to the company.

Famous true-life characters from the Indian nations represented themselves in *Ranson's Folly*. Chief Eagle Wing of the Klamath Tribe, and Chief Big Tree of the Iroquois Tribe played important support roles in the film about the US Army on the Western frontier during the Indian wars.

In *The Noose* (1928), Richard gave a superb performance in a heart-gripping melodrama as the son of a bootlegger. In a moment of anger while he is in charge of a booze-running truck, the bootlegger slays Montagu Love, the leader of the bootleg ring. Audiences were stung by the realistic depictions of New York nightlife, a side street honky-tonk, and a shot ringing out above the blare of jazz music. The kid he played in the story faced "the noose" rather than betray his mother's shameful secret, while his mother, who could have saved him, could not bring herself to tell the terrible truth. In graphic detail, the film depicted the horror of a final death march to his execution. He scored a great personal hit in *The Noose*. The theme of capital punishment rang true with audiences, and once again, the Academy of Motion Picture Arts and Sciences recognized his work in the film as one of the outstanding portrayals by an actor in 1928. He was nominated for "Best Actor" for his work in *The Noose* (1928), but when the winners were announced, he lost the award to Emil Jannings.

One fan wrote to a magazine after seeing the riveting film: "After my experience of the other evening, I feel as though anyone who could see *The Noose* and still believe in capital punishment should have a taste of it personally. I always have been bitterly opposed to the taking of life, whether lawfully or unlawfully, and now I hate it a hundred-fold. I wish I could forget the old lady who sat beside me in the theater at the showing of *The Noose*. Wish I could forget the choking cry, 'Oh, God! My son!' that came from the quivering lips as Barthelmess began his death march. And most of all, I wish I could forget the look of agonized pain on that anguished face as the bent, gray-haired man led her out . . . ."

By 1928, the era of silent films was coming to an end. In August, Richard's silent film, *The Little Shepherd of Kingdom Come*, was playing side-by-side in theaters that were showing *The Lights of*

New York, the first all-talking, full-length picture that was also pleasing big crowds across America. An article in the *Sheboygan Press* stated, "Earl Burnett's popular Biltmore Hotel Orchestra furnishes the dance music for the night club scenes in *The Lights of New York*, the initial effort of a Vitaphone talking motion picture with spoken dialogue and sound effects throughout. Much of the rapid action of this story of New York night life centers around the café in which Helene Costello dances, and where her lover is charged with murder." The noise and music from talking pictures was taking the entire theater-going world by storm, and the death bells for silent movies were ringing loudly. It was the end of an era.

Uncertainties over the future of sound films reverberated throughout Hollywood. Some thought that the new technology was nothing more than a gimmick. Others prophesied that it was the way of the future. For the time being, Richard sidestepped the controversy and proceeded to make his next film as a silent picture. He tackled the difficult and showy job of playing opposite himself in *Wheel of Chance* (1928). Painstaking camerawork pitted him visually against himself playing a slick, black-headed, polished lawyer, who grew up believing that his twin brother had been killed in childhood. Later, as a prosecuting attorney, he is reunited with his long-lost brother on the day of the trial when he learns the red-haired, uncouth gangster is the twin brother he believed to be dead. In *Wheel of Chance*, Richard played the dual roles with distinction. This showy type of dual-performance interested critics who thought his delineation of the differing characters was admirable.

By the end of 1928, it had become clear that silent films were going the way of the horse and buggy. Panic had completely taken over the film industry. Terrified actors who had never spoken on a theater stage were suddenly forced to stand immobile in front of hidden microphones and attempt to recite memorized dialogue that replaced the silent film printed subtitles. They met with varying degrees of success. Some went on to greater acclaim, while others saw their careers grinding to a halt. Emil Jannings, who had recently won an Academy Award for Best Actor, had a thick German accent, so he simply packed his bags and moved back to his homeland.

Richard Barthelmess filming *Scarlet Seas* (1928).

Dorothy Gish, Richard's co-star in a number of silent pictures, had spent her youth on the stages of American theaters. She made one attempt at a talking picture, and then left films altogether to return to working on the Broadway stage. Others, like Constance Talmadge and Jack Pickford, simply quit working in films altogether. Within just a few months, other silent stars wished that they could burn down the sound stages that had been hastily erected at every studio in Hollywood. The entire industry was in chaos over the conversion to sound, and no one was sure of what they were doing.

Richard made his final silent picture, *Out of the Ruins*, and then he quietly and confidently faced the talking picture challenge and went immediately to work on his first attempt. Tests were done that proved he had a pleasing voice, and two pictures were planned to be made with the new technology. No one could have foreseen that Richard's voice was going to erupt into one of the most outrageous public relations nightmares of his entire life.

Chapter 7
The Silent Stars Go By

Scarlet Seas (1928) was Richard's first talking picture. The primitive recording equipment Warner Bros. used was cumbersome, and the film producers knew little of the sound-blending techniques that would later become standard. There were unforeseen oddities that resulted. When the finished film was shown, the sound of knocking on doors came through the auditorium speakers like sledgehammer blows. The film score tended to overpower the actors' voices in some scenes. Producers scrambled to come to grips with the new demands of talking pictures and the unyielding fickleness of the public. They demanded fresh faces.

"The average life of a film star is five years," Richard remarked to writer Samuel Mook. "The talkies will bring in a complete new set of stars. When the talkie turmoil subsides, the old favorites will still reign supreme." His prediction proved to be partly true, for Richard was one of those who retained his popularity during Hollywood turbulent transition to talking pictures. Unfortunately, there were many others who found that their careers abruptly ended. Broadway actors were recruited to fill the ranks because they could talk. Some succeeded, but some failed.

Once the initial turmoil subsided and many of the stage actors had been sent back to New York, only a few of the new imports found a successful place in Hollywood for their careers. Many of the old favorites eventually waned with the public. Ruth Chatterton and Ann Harding were two who came from the stage and found a niche in films, while Thomas Meighan, Lillian Gish, Mary Pickford, Norma Talmadge, Douglas Fairbanks, and John Gilbert were forced to realize that their vogue had passed.

Richard Barthelmess with his second love, Katherine Wilson, a distinguished Broadway actress from a well-known family in Jacksonville, Florida, In 1927, their engagement was a big surprise, but after three years, the wedding was indefinitely postponed.

Richard steadily advanced in motion pictures because he was not afraid of having a capable cast beside him. He gave a wide, open stage to his fellow players, doing his utmost to get as much of their talent as possible in their scenes.

In an article appearing in the *Decatur Daily Review*, August 19, 1928, it was reported that only 800 of the 20,000 movie theaters in the United States had been equipped for the exhibition of sound pictures. "Practically all the big picture producing companies are now at work on pictures with sound and music. Most of these companies will have to make pictures to fit both kinds of houses, those wired for sound pictures and those not equipped. The sound equipment wiring costs about $15,000, so the bill for changing the theaters over for the new picture business will be enormous. Officers of the leading companies recognize that the task of producing pictures is becoming greater and that with the sound pictures a demand for story, acting, and directing was never greater. These same officials also declare that the picture will remain the thing."

An article in an August 1928 *Decatur Daily Review* showed how the sound revolution was affecting many top stars. "The voices of Gloria Swanson, John Barrymore, and Ronald Colman may be heard in their next pictures released through United Artists," the newspaper reported, "but the voices of Mary Pickford, Norma Talmadge, Dolores del Rio, Vilma Banky, Charlie Chaplin, and Douglas Fairbanks will not be heard." The announcement came from Alexander Lichiman, Vice President and sales head of United Artists. The article seemed to suggest that the company was willing to go forward with those actors who were confident in their ability to speak, but would continue with silent film production for a time with those other stars less willing to gamble on the untried technology. Whether they wanted to or not, they would all soon take their first steps. D. W. Griffith had recorded the voices of one thousand soldiers singing "La Marseillaise" in the din of battle. He used the Movietone process for a short film titled *The Love Song*. What became of this interesting experiment is not known, as Griffith never released a 1928 film by that name containing such a sequence.

Griffith opened his first talking picture, *Abraham Lincoln*, on October 25, 1930, to critical acclaim, but the public's reception was modest. The film returned a slight profit, but Griffith found that making it was a "nightmare of the mind and nerves," and he departed for a favorite hideout in Mineral Wells, Texas, when the shooting was barely completed. He left the final editing to others. The following year, he made his final film, *The Struggle*, and then when he was fifty-six-years old, he was tired out and ready to stop directing. *The Struggle* was made cheaply and hastily in a rented Bronx studio, and despite a script by old hands John Emerson and Anita Loos, and some scenes that were sharply etched with realistic touches, the film failed to succeed with audiences. He never made another film.

Lillian Gish, Richard's co-star in *Broken Blossoms* and *Way Down East*, said in her autobiography, "I was upset at the changes that were taking place in our working world. Talking pictures had been born. Al Jolson, the man whom Mr. Griffith had wanted to bring to films a few years earlier, had sung in *The Jazz Singer*. When I returned to Hollywood, I saw that every studio was being transformed with soundproofing, which made it airtight. Under the hot lights, the poor actors had to wear rubber suits under their costumes to keep them looking dry during the filming." She prepared to make her talkie debut in *The Swan*. Mary Pickford lent her a bungalow on the United Artist lot where she slept whenever she had to be on the set early. In spite of her professional best, the film turned out slow and dull. Lillian left films and retreated to Broadway, starring in *Uncle Vanya*, *Hamlet*, and other fine plays.

The film industry underwent a complete upheaval. By January 1929, it was expected that a thousand theaters in the country had been equipped for sound pictures, beginning with the largest cities like New York. One by one, smaller cities converted as time and money afforded. In the meantime, the industry cranked out both silent and sound versions of many of their pictures. The silent versions were nothing more than the sound picture with subtitles added to replace the sound track. They tried to create the illusion that nothing had changed, but audiences could tell the difference.

Richard was a man without illusions. He could take his screen work and analyze it from start to finish with cold-blooded candor, without letting his personal likes and dislikes influence his judgment. "When you are in the midst of a production," he said, "you lose all sense of perspective. Either the new picture is great or you find yourself, unconsciously, comparing it unfavorably to past vehicles. But looking back at your pictures after a lapse of time, you can view them dispassionately. Have you ever noticed, for instance, when a person lights a cigarette in the dark how the match casts shadows and high lights, illuminating prominent features? Well, that's how it is with pictures. Time is the match that makes their faults and merits stand out in bold relief."

Richard's pleasing voice translated well into sound films. In *Weary River* (1929), he played a singer of a popular song of the same name as the film. He gave a very effective performance. On

In 1931, when Professor Albert Einstein made a tour of the Warner Bros. Hollywood studios, he examined a Vitaphone recording apparatus with Richard Barthelmess.

first viewing, everyone at the studio thought they had done a great job, and the producers felt sure that audiences were going to enjoy hearing Richard "sing." They made full use of the possibilities of the talking picture technology and were proud of their efforts. Publicity went out advertising that the film would present a talking and singing Richard Barthelmess. Prospects looked good for the film.

Around this time, Professor Albert Einstein made a tour of the Hollywood studios, and examined a Vitaphone recording apparatus with Richard. The visit was dutifully recorded in an historic photograph picturing Richard standing beside the brilliant man while he was observing the machinery. It is not certain whether Einstein was told that the use of sound in a film had not been fully explored at the time filming was completed on *Weary River*. Writers and directors had not yet worked out a smooth blend to the new medium. Everyone connected with *Weary River* crossed their fingers and anticipated an overwhelmingly positive response from audiences and critics. It was opened in New York.

Mordaunt Hall wrote in the January 25, 1929 edition of the *New York Times*, "Richard Barthelmess was heard as well as seen last night from the screen of the Central Theater in a First National Vitaphone picture called *Weary River*. The chief attribute of this banal jailbird tale is that it has some interesting prison sequences, and perhaps there are those who may enthuse over Mr. Barthelmess' rendition of a song, also known as "Weary River." He does sing it quite well, but it would take a far better singer and a much better song to atone for the lack of imagination and suspense in this photoplay, which is one of those that slip from silence to sound every now and again."

Then, disaster struck.

Ads for *Weary River* proclaimed superlatives about the quality of his singing voice, which was said to be heard for the first time in this film. During the first days when the film was released, audiences believed it, but then someone leaked out the fact that his singing had actually been dubbed by another artist. The public felt cheated. Widespread derision echoed from coast to coast. The revelation was true. Richard could not sing well enough to put across the title song and Warner Bros. had substituted another performer's voice for his vocals. The fatal mistake that the studio made was in crediting Richard with the vocals. They thought that doing this was no different than crediting action stars with performing dangerous stunts that were actually performed by doubles. They did not realize the reaction the public would have to his apparent singing. Fooled into believing it was actually his voice heard warbling the vocals, people clamored for more musical vocals from the actor. They wanted him to make records, go on radio and sing, and make concert appearances. Mortified that he was unable to provide them with live musical performances or records, he was compelled to truthfully come out in the press explaining the process of dubbing and quell the demands for more of his singing. It was like trying to stamp out a fire with one foot.

To Samuel Mook, a writer for *Picture Play*, Richard explained: "I have been severely criticized for permitting Johnny Murray to double for me in singing *Weary River*. It was impossible to omit the singing and still have a picture. Unfortunately, I cannot sing. Had I attempted to, it would have completely destroyed the illusion of

Richard Barthelmess was said to "sing" as a wistful crooner in his 1928 talkie, *Weary River*, a role that stirred fans in an unexpected manner.

the film, because no one would have believed that a person who sings as I do could have built the reputation for himself that the convict did. Far from trying to trade on Murray's talents, his doubling for me was the best thing in the world for him, because it was the means of his getting a contract with the studio."

Richard went on to explain, "The fans understand that many of the high dives and parachute leaps they see in pictures are performed by doubles. They know that pictures of people balancing on the edge of buildings supposedly high in the air are really filmed about three or four feet from the ground. They never mind any of those things because they add to the illusion, so why should they object because I had a voice double for the same purpose?"

"As to the advertising 'Hear Richard Barthelmess sing and talk,' the sales department was responsible for that," Richard claimed. "I had nothing to do with it. The only thing I could do was the thing I did do as soon as I discovered it, and that was, first, to tell the press that I had not done the singing and, second, to make them cut it out of the advertising."

This back-pedaling quelled the furor. He never sang in a movie again either. From then on, he stayed with the tried and true formula of solid stories with strong acting.Richard's work often took him into stories with dramatic depth, and for his next pictures, he wisely stayed away from musicals and comedies because getting laughs had already proved difficult for those directors fashioning comedy films in a talking pictures. They were stumped over how to determine proper pauses after gag lines. Comedy was proving to be the most difficult form of entertainment to be put into talking motion pictures because of the impossibility of timing the laughs, according to Victor Moore, comedian, in a 1930 interview with the *Decatur Herald*. "There is no sure way of determining how long an audience will laugh at a comic situation seen or heard on the screen," Moore explained. "Therefore, there is always the danger of laughter making important succeeding speeches inaudible. On the other hand, if the actors use pantomime for seconds after the gag line, they may appear ridiculous if a cold audience refuses to laugh." Speaking from his experience of more than thirty years as an actor and director, Moore declared there was only one way of timing funny situations: take a completed picture to some out-of-the-way place, show it to an audience for a week, determine how they react, and then remedy defects by filming rewritten scenes when required. "This was not necessary in the days of silent comedies, when the audiences could yell with laughter and still follow the meaning," Moore said. "Yet I know that Charles Chaplin, one of the greatest actors and directors of the film industry, always gives his productions several extended previews and sometimes radically revamps them before release."

Richard often used film magazines as a way to communicate with his fans, and for years, he had a reputation among writers for being one of the most difficult stars to interview. The press hounded him, and when cornered, he invariably failed to offer them the exciting

Richard with six-year old daughter, Mary Hay Barthelmess sailing on his schooner in 1929.

Off Catalina Island aboard the Barthelmess yacht, *Pegasus*, in 1929 were Richard, Jessica, Beatrice Lillie, Florence Vidor, and Jascha Heifetz.

and funny anecdotes they wanted. As a result, he often came across as aloof, uncommunicative, disinterested, and to some writers, rude.

When Carroll Graham, a writer for *Picture Play*, asked him how he could account for these bad impressions, Richard replied, "How do I know? I treat people from the press as I treat everyone else. I think the interviewer is more to blame than the other person in such cases. More depends on the writer than on the subject of it. How can anyone talk to a stranger, a person you've never met before without being self-conscious and strained? I can't talk about myself — neither could you — it's impossible. One of the pleasantest interviews I've ever had was just before I left the Coast. The writer got me talking about Bill Powell, and she got me to talk about him. That's entirely different. Bill is a subject I could discuss, because he's one of my best friends. I told her about the first picture we made together — it was *The Bright Shawl*, made at Fort Lee and Havana. When it opened in New York, all the critics said, quite truthfully, that the whole picture belonged to him. I called him up next morning and said, 'You've stolen that picture right out from under me!'"

"'Yes,' he said, 'I expected to,' and hung up."

Unlike other stars, Richard never went in for any kind of sensational publicity, and never attempted to force himself down the public's throat by posing for lurid advertisements or making pseudo-sensational statements for the wire services. He seemed to avoid the press as much as possible.

He explained to writer Carroll Graham, "When I was coming East, I was awakened at an unearthly hour in the morning when the train stopped at a little town. Somebody was beating on my door. I got up, sleepy and unshaved, pulled on a robe and stuck my head out. A woman was out there, and the first thing she said was, 'What do you think of the Movietone, Mr. Barthelmess?'

"I said, 'I don't work for the Movietone; I work for the Vitaphone. Besides all that, who are you?'

"She was from some paper in the town, and she asked me a lot of questions I was too sleepy to answer very well. I think she was pretty indignant when she went away. Now I ask you, how civil could you be under those circumstances? And I've probably made an enemy for life."

Richard Barthelmess filming *Young Nowheres* (1929).

Despite the rudeness of some press members, he continued to be written about in newspaper and magazines wherever he went. He did not go out of his way to make a good or bad impression. Naturally modest and reticent about talking to himself, he was not publicity mad, as some actors were, and consequently, never went out of his way to get himself featured in a story. Some writers interpreted this lack of enthusiasm as disinterest, or thought that he was uncommunicative. He preferred to concentrate on his work.

The effort paid well, for in his next motion picture, he achieved one of his biggest successes.

The Dawn Patrol (1930) was one of Richard's outstanding efforts in a sound film. Once again, audiences saw him in a thrilling battle tale. By 1930, he had been a star for nearly two decades since his debut on the screen in 1916, and he was one of the few old-time favorites who survived the upheavals in the industry without losing one iota of his popularity. He withstood the blinding glare of unwanted spotlights, and he had his feet set squarely at the top of a business that rated as one of the most precarious in the world. Through the early years of the 1930s, as other stars abdicated their positions, many fortunes were made and lost, reputations were dazzled and faded, and companies changed their names or folded, yet Richard managed to keep his position. He was one of the few actors who could sit in conferences and argue stories just as readily as an author, and who could discuss directorial points with the greatest of directors. From the purchase of a story to the final cutting, he was interested and involved, and placed a sure hand on each film as it developed. No phase of the production escaped his interest and concern.

"Funny thing — I almost made it with Jack Gilbert," said Howard Hawks of *The Dawn Patrol* in *The Grey Fox* of Hollywood. "Gilbert hadn't made a talking picture, but he was the biggest star we ever had in silent pictures and Louis B. Mayer got me to bring Gilbert in and talk to him. Well, Gilbert went back and told Mayer he'd make the picture without any salary and that's all Mayer wanted, because he told Gilbert he wouldn't let him do it if he *paid* to make the picture. He wanted to humiliate him. I got Mayer by the front of the coat and bumped his head up against the wall and said, 'Don't ever make me part of your dirty little schemes again.' I didn't stand too well with Mayer for a while."

Ronald Colman was Hawks' original choice for the leading role of the ace Captain Courtney in *The Dawn Patrol*. When Colman bowed out, Richard was quickly brought in to play the part, the film being similar in theme to Richard's earlier World War One film, *The Patent Leather Kid*, in which he enjoyed one of his greatest successes.

Richard championed for Douglas Fairbanks, Jr. to play the role of Scotty in *The Dawn Patrol*. Unfortunately, Jack Warner and John Barrymore had already received Fairbanks' promise to appear in their sound remake of *Moby Dick*. Fairbanks idolized John Barrymore, and anticipated a once-in-a-lifetime experience working with the famous actor.

Fairbanks remembered in his autobiography, "For me, the idea of working with and learning from my old hero thrilled me more than the picture itself . . . Barrymore kept insisting — which was wonderfully flattering — that I appear with him. But he was finally overruled by my old friend from Poverty Row days, Darryl Zanuck . . ."

Richard encouraged Fairbanks to gently decline the opportunity to appear in the Barrymore film. "When *The Dawn Patrol* was finally released in mid-1930," Fairbanks recalled, "I was delighted that my original hopes for *Moby Dick* had been overruled. Barrymore's new version turned out to be not nearly so good as his original silent one. But *The Dawn Patrol* became a spectacular, worldwide success."

In Brian Connell's book, *Knight Errant — A Biography of Douglas Fairbanks, Jr.*, Richard is quoted as having said, "Howard has his heart set on young Fairbanks playing one of the three principal roles. I'd known Doug since he was a boy, so I went to him and asked which part he thought would be better for him. He leaped at the chance in *The Dawn Patrol*. I told him to call Jack, tell him the problem, and see if he would release him. Which he did."

Richard later recalled an amusing incident during preparations for this production. "Young Doug in those days was a fancier of Barrymore. He affected the same rather Byronic collars and he wore his hair rather long. This was a military picture, so Howard told him to go and get his hair cut. He did, and when he came back Howard took one look at him and said: 'Now go and get your hair cut.' So he had two haircuts, but this time he had it almost clipped off."

When *The Dawn Patrol* began production in February 1930, Howard Hughes was in the final stages of producing his somewhat similar film, *Hell's Angels*. The film industry had rapidly converted to sound during the elongated production of Hughes' film, and he was embroiled in the painstaking task of converting it from a silent film to one with sound, adding new cast members, switching directors, and rewriting the script to include dialogue.

Hawks began hiring many experts who had labored on the beleaguered Hughes film, including Elmer Dyer, the chief cameraman, and Harry Reynolds, an aviation technician. When Hughes learned of this, his competitive suspicions were aroused, and he tried to sabotage the production, buying up all the World War One fighter planes he had not already purchased, even though his own film had completed aerial photography. Then, Hughes strongly objected to certain scenes that he felt had been shamelessly lifted from the scenario of *Hell's Angels*. A bitter series of lawsuits followed, and First National was forced to file for a restraining order to prevent Hughes from interfering further with *The Dawn Patrol*.

According to Todd McCarthy, in his book, *Howard Hawks The Grey Fox of Hollywood*, Hughes swore in more than ten court manuscript pages about how *The Dawn Patrol* "had copied every detail portrayed in the picture, in addition to copying the dramatic characterization, sequences, motivation and the greater part of the dramatic incidents connected with the final bombing sequence."

Despite the dust that Hughes stirred up, the production began in March 1930, filming the English airdrome sequences, and continued until late May of that same year. The remaining climactic scene of the daring raid on an ammunition dump in Germany was shot despite Hughes' objections some days after the eventual premier of *Hell's Angels.*

This early sound effort was remarkable for its natural dialogue in a year when so many other "talkies" featured the self-conscious vocalizations of inexperienced silent performers struggling with the new medium. According to author Todd McCarthy, Howard Hawks explained, "Actually *The Dawn Patrol* was the first dramatic talkie made without a lot of overacting. It was very quiet. During the shooting I had thirty or forty communications from the front office saying I had a marvelous chance to make a good scene and didn't do anything with it. It was just a different way of playing it, you see. I was saying that they had been emoting too much and by underplaying we got away from that . . . ."

The Dawn Patrol premiered on July 10, 1930 at the Winter Garden in New York. The first week's attendance smashed previous house records, and ultimately proved to be one of First National's biggest hits of the year. So convinced were the executives at First National of the film's success, Howard Hawks was signed to a three-picture contract paying $25,000 per film.

Douglas Fairbanks signed his first long-term contract with Warner Bros. as an immediate result of his notices in this film, and was quickly put into the Leslie Howard film, *Outward Bound*, which was followed by a part in the classic gangster film, *Little Caesar*.

The Dawn Patrol won the 1931 Academy Award for Best Original Story. Screenwriter John Monk Saunders, a World War One flying instructor and one of the most sought-after writers in the film business, wrote the story from his own recollections of the war. Hawks claimed years later to have conceived the story, but Saunders alone earned the official screen credit and the Oscar. For the next eight years, Saunders contributed many other successful screenplays, but by 1938, his career was all but over. Two years later, after extensive care at Johns Hopkins for a nervous disorder, Saunders was found dead at his beach house in Fort Myers, Florida at the age of forty-two. He had committed suicide by hanging.

While many silent film stars were disappearing, Richard found his popularity cresting after his moving work in *The Dawn Patrol*. When asked what it meant to be a star, *Hollywood Magazine* reporter, Jan Vantol, had to prod him to even venture his opinion.

"Just what does it mean to be a star?" Richard asked, after pondering her question for several moments. "That question takes a good deal of territory, doesn't it? It is not an easy one to answer off hand. It means certain things to me, yet perhaps, it means something entirely different to the whiskered gentleman who is eating his lunch over there on the other side of the room," Richard said, pointing to John Barrymore in character makeup and relaxing on the set of his film, *Svengali*.

"Let's put it this way," rephrased the interviewer, "in your individual case what is the one outstanding advantage of being a star?"

Richard smiled and answered, "That's better — much better. To my way of thinking the one all-important offering of stardom is security — financial security, I mean. There are other advantages, of course, but they all pale into insignificance when compared with that one vital consideration."

Richard added, "I think that the saddest feature of Hollywood life is the host of old-timer stars who have lost their place on the screen and now have absolutely nothing to show for their huge earnings. There are many of them in just that situation. And they might just as well have retired with sufficient income to insure that they would live in comfort and ease. I've always regarded my profession as a business, and risked being called frugal in order to save my money. I was twenty-one years old when I started in pictures, but even then, I had set my heart on winning financial security. I realized that I could earn more money as a motion picture actor than I could in any other line of work. I couldn't see the use of earning it if I did not invest it properly."

"Most stars prefer to talk about the satisfaction of giving an artistic performance and rather minimize the financial consideration," noted the interviewer.

"With the possible exception of a few individuals, that is just a lot of hooey," Richard stated bluntly. "You may depend upon it — almost every actor in Hollywood gives a great deal more thought to his weekly pay check than he does about his art. Naturally we want to be good actors, but the fundamental reason for our desire to excel is, after all, a financial one."

Richard was not without aspirations for artistic achievements. Despite his claims that the driving force behind his work was financial security, he had a surprising, long-standing desire to play the role of Rip Van Winkle, a desire that he never fulfilled. By the 1930s, the public's fascination with movie stars had boiled to an obsession. He knew they would never accept him in a character role, however much he wanted to portray one. Handling the public had also become a wearying fact of life for him. People followed him wherever he went. This loss of personal privacy was a constant irritant that he could not escape.

"The moment that I am recognized as Richard Barthelmess, the screen star, I am overwhelmed by the curiosity of the crowd, which apparently regards me with the same interest that would be accorded a dancing mouse or any other strange animal," he lamented.

Richard enjoyed sharing the spotlight of public interest. Instead of resenting the presence of reporters when arriving at a hotel, he was always delighted by their attention, *when they were expected*. He was flattered rather than annoyed by the recognition of the crowd, but he often steeled himself for the usual comments people would fling when first seeing him. The five-foot ten, 152-pound actor complained, "It is extremely annoying to hear flappers say, 'I didn't know he was short — I thought he was taller!' Or, 'Look, there's that crooked smile! He really has it!' Or 'That's really his shiny black hair. I thought maybe he made it up that way for pictures!'"

Adolph Zukor, in a comment quoted by Scott Eyman in his book, *The Speed of Sound*, said the depression was deeply affecting the American motion picture industry. "It may be that people wanted to forget their troubles by going to a picture, and of course the 'talkies' had been a big shot in the arm. At any rate, in 1930, the profits of the Paramount – Publix Corporation were $18,000,000, the highest ever. Our assets had risen in less than two decades from the practically none at the Twenty-sixth Street studio to $300,000,000. People spoke of the motion picture industry as 'depression proof.' Yet I knew too well its hazardous nature to expect complete escape form the ills besetting others."

"The year 1931 was not so good as its predecessor," Zukor also recalled, "yet profits stood at $6,000,000. Then the bottom dropped out. The loss in 1932 was a staggering $21,000,000. Paramount stock dropped rapidly."

The Lash (1930) returned Richard to a role that was reminiscent of his earlier role in *Scarlet Days* (1919). As a revenge-seeking Spaniard, he rode ahead of a gang of Robin Hood-style avengers. *The Lash* was filmed under the title, *Adios*, and was based on a novel of the same name by Lanier Bartlett and Virginia Stivers Bartlett. Costume pictures were the rage in 1930, and this superbly colorful tale of old Mexico brought Richard into a tale of a fiery Don Francisco who turns bandit. He looked great in the short jackets and flared trousers called for by the role, and the picture earned generally good reviews.

Mary Astor recalled in *A Life on Film*, "I went to Warner Bros. for one picture, still free-lancing, for a picture with Richard Barthelmess, a great silent star who had survived because of a warm,

An unexpected thrill not in the scenario turned the cast and crew of *The Lash* (1930) into an amateur fire department. One of the buildings in the village set burst into flames, and director Frank Lloyd kept the cameras grinding to get the sudden outburst into the film footage.

soft voice and a personality that matched. *The Lash* was probably one of the weakest pictures he ever did, and he was no longer young enough to play a dashing, Robin Hood bandit. He was a short, stocky man, and had to wear a girdle to pull in a slight paunch, and he used to cuss because it made him 'short of breath,' when what he was really cussing about was the inevitable encroachment of middle age."

While filming *The Lash*, Frank Lloyd led cast and crew out to Calabasas, some fifty miles outside of Hollywood, for location photography. 1,500 head of cattle were set to stampede through a makeshift village created by the property men from First National in the climactic cattle stampede. The director perched high atop a ten-foot wide platform built from the side of the hill overlooking the enormous expanse of the valley on which the stampede was to take place. Cameras were mounted beside him, and the cameraman fussed with equipment as the lens aimed straight at an enormous piece of crystal clear glass on which were painted tiny houses and other background images. Through these effects, the real background blended seamlessly into a more picturesque image of the Mexican town, artistically composed to give the illusion of homes nestled among the hills.

The company spread out over half a square mile with riders stationed at various points over the hills. Prior to rolling the cameras, the cattle hid from the blistering hot California sun by hugging the trees to keep cool. Lloyd barked orders through a field telephone hooked up to loudspeakers positioned over the terrain, while Richard and Arthur Stone posed mounted on horseback ready for the scene. Dick rested on a spirited and beautiful black horse named Midnight, a steed supplied by Curley Eagles.

Cowboys busied themselves herding the cattle into position to move as directed, and as their efforts brought the animals into camera view, the cast and crew stood poised to move on command.

When everything was set, Lloyd gave his signal through the field telephone. Pedro Leone, an expert rider appearing in films for years, picked it up from his position atop a distant hill, and began the scene by charging at the cattle. In one take, Lloyd captured the stampeding herd as they thundered down the slopes, crashing into the mock villages erected under their counterparts painted on the glass in front of the camera. The pursuing riders whooped while a motley crew of colorfully garbed Spaniards appeared from nowhere in chase. A carefully timed fire exploded from one house nearest the camera, erupting into a sheet of flames in a grand sight, and become more headstrong when billowed by the prairie wind. These action sequences were cut into the finished picture, which was then given the new title, *The Lash*.

On release, one magazine said of the film, "This is the same old Spanish-California story — the bandit/hero robs the rich to give to the poor. Richard Barthelmess, however, does add some glamour to such a role because he is a sincere and earnest actor. There happens to be a very thrilling cattle stampede, which provides the exciting moments, and Mary Astor adds another good performance to her already long list."

By 1931, centuries-old stage traditions were rapidly dying under the influence of motion pictures. Whereas, in its beginnings, the humble motion picture copied the stage in acting techniques and in the grouping of scenes before the cameras, time had turned the tables fully in the opposite direction. For example, Stuart Walker,

William Powell, Carole Lombard, and Richard Barthelmess at a 1931 tennis match.

who was the stage director of the Little Theater for twenty years, joined the Paramount Studios during the transition to talking pictures. He noticed the changes taking place.

"For centuries, it was believed that a player could not speak dialogue while moving," Walker explained to an interviewer writing for the *Reno Evening Gazette*. "As late as 1912, William Farnum, while engaged in a stage fight, halted the action, strode downstage to deliver a speech, and then returned to the battle. His opponent obligingly waited until he was through talking before re-attacking him. Many of our present day stage stars will not permit another member of the cast to move while they are talking. They consider movement a ruse by the others to catch the audience's eye and 'steal' the scene on the presumption that the audience watches the movement rather than the speaker."

By the early 1930s, stage stars often talked while walking, a direct result of the influence of the screen on the theater. Those actors who were crossing back and forth between the theater and motion pictures brought with them the refined techniques they had learned while emoting for the camera. Richard, having spent the bulk of his professional career only in motion pictures, took the changes in film technique in stride. He adapted well to the new requirements of talking pictures, and continued to impress audiences with the ease of his apparently effortless appearances. By 1931, he had become closely identified with war and aviation dramas, and he actively sought out that type of story.

The Last Flight (1931) again pictured Richard as an aviator. "This is the most unusual picture I have ever made," he remarked while filming. "It is a story of four aviators' lives *after* the war. It is a down-to-earth, human tale done with utter simplicity. It will be either a great attraction or a dismal flop."

The story followed a war-wracked aviators involved with an odd-acting girl, Nikki, as they struggled to regain their composure in Paris after the War skidded to a halt at the Armistice. The stories of Nikki by John Monk Saunders had been serialized in *Liberty Magazine* with great popularity, and Saunders was at that time married to Fay Wray with whom Richard had just filmed *The Finger Points*. The odd film might have been great, were it not for the pedestrian direction, but the delightfully drifting screwball played by Helen Chandler helped lift the film above the ordinary.

There were four other sterling actors in the cast: Johnny Mack Brown, David Manners, Walter Byron, and Elliott Nugent. Any one of them was potentially capable of stealing the picture. Richard believed that filling out this film with competent, qualified professionals increased the likelihood of an audience's pleasure with his own work. He was touchy about this issue, not out of insecurity, but because he found that they helped put the story over.

Richard had an innate shyness at the core of his character, and he learned to make it pay. He disliked wearing make-up, and he was most happy in roles where he could wear little or none. He always shied away from posing for gag picture or stunts for the purpose of publicity. These feelings came from being on the "top of the heap" for so long. Maintaining his popularity through good pictures, even though it was proving to be impossible to avoid the occasional bad picture, was a strong testament to his commitment to excellence. With the industry in the doldrums, he was more careful than ever in his choice of roles.

In *The Finger Points*, Richard worked with Fay Wray, who was then beginning her career as a contract player for Paramount. She

Richard Barthelmess filming *The Finger Points* (1931).

recalled in her autobiography that Paramount began loaning their contract players to other studios after the stock market crash in October 1929. Her husband, John Monk Saunders, wrote the script for *The Finger Points*. "It was probably because of John that I was loaned to Warner Bros. for *The Finger Points*. It was his script. Richard Barthelmess was the star and Clark Gable had a very small part. There was talk on the set about the interesting quality of the tall young Gable playing a gangster . . . I remember nothing about *me* in *The Finger Points*. Richard Barthelmess, yes. Even he, not as an actor, but as a person. Contained, controlled, insecure even though he had been a great star in silents. He was an original; it is not possible to say, 'someone *like* Richard Barthelmess.' The youthful quality remained with him always . . . ."

In 1932 during the depths of the depression, economic doldrums fell hard on Hollywood. Many stars were asked to renegotiate their contracts, and Richard was no exception. Before starting his next film, he agreed to make his next three pictures for what he would previously have been paid for two. World conditions were dismal, and he wisely chose to continue working with a guarantee of three more films than face the possible loss of his contract due to studio cuts. This effort on his part earned him a great deal of admiration from Warner Bros. executives, and it had much to do with his continued work during the depression.

His next picture was *Cabin in the Cotton*. The story followed a southern plantation cotton planter named Marvin Blake, an under-dog tenant farmer, who is befriended by a planter and then finds himself torn by loyalty to his class and an obligation to their enemy, also his benefactor. Marvin falls in love with the headstrong and naughty daughter of the plantation owner, a role played by the up-and-coming Bette Davis. There was one passage in which the little hussy does a coy strip in front of him by way of coquetry.

"I'd like to make love to you, but I just washed my hair," she sniffs while batting her huge eyes at Marvin. This line quickly became famous for Bette when the ensuing years amassed legendary quotes tied to the actress' work. She claimed it was the favorite of all her film lines.

Davis struggled with her director during the making of *Cabin in the Cotton*. Michael Curtiz reluctantly helmed the picture, and frequently embarrassed Davis within earshot of the crew. "He fought Zanuck over her casting," Richard later recalled in *Fasten Your Seat Belts*, "probably thought Ann Dvorak or some other directly sexual type would have been more right for it — and he couldn't admit it when he saw he was wrong. Mike Curtiz was a mean one. I was the star of the film, so I could walk away from him and hole up in my dressing room, but Bette was a contract player and had to put up with him, and put up with him she did. Indeed, she would taunt him in return at times. She knew Darryl Zanuck believed in her and that Curtiz couldn't remove her. And she gave that performance all she had."

While Richard retreated to his dressing room, Curtiz forced Davis to perform to a cold camera that represented the star. He berated her fledgling inability to turn on electric passion to the merciless, staring lens of the camera. In spite of the hardships, her role in this film was a breakthrough performance that earned her much critical praise.

Richard admired her talent, too. Lawrence J. Quirk talked to the star in 1960, and heard him tell of his admiration for her passion at the youthful age of twenty-four. "I was thirty-seven or so at the time, and had forgotten a lot more than she was in the process of discovering — and I don't mean acting. I admit I was never noted — onscreen or off — for being a hot lover-boy. That was not my thing, not my gift, if that is the word for it, but she was so exciting and seductive that she would have aroused a wooden Indian. More important, she was an excellent actress who, I knew even then, required only the right director and the right script to shine along with the best of the stars of the time. When *Of Human Bondage* came along a couple of years later, I was not at all surprised at the sensation she made. It was all there in *Cabin*, but the story and the director were not right for her."

While making *Cabin in the Cotton*, Bette was nearing the end of her twenty-six week contract with Warner Bros. Her performance is full of attention-drawing effects, including repeated clinching and unclenching of her fists, twisting of her hips and shoulders, and boldly thrusting herself at the camera. These effects aroused the desired reaction from Darryl Zanuck. On June 16, 1932, a week after completing *Cabin in the Cotton*, her option was picked up for five more years. Waiting in the wings for her was the triumph she was to have in *Of Human Bondage*.

By the mid-1930s, some fans were beginning to wonder what had happened to Richard Barthelmess. He was still held in great admiration, but there seemed to be such a long time lapsing between pictures that it was becoming increasingly easy to forget him. Cinemas were filled with films spotlighting new stars like Clark Gable, Robert Montgomery, and others, and they were eclipsing him. The spotlight was moving away.

At the same time, the great love of his life was finally moving in.

In 1934, Richard met Jessica Stewart Sargent of Los Angeles while on the *S. S. France* en route to Paris. "We met on shipboard, bound for Europe," he recounted. "We were both married at the

Official marriage portrait of Richard Barthelmess and Jessica Sergeant.

time, or rather, we were not yet divorced, either of us. There could be no question of marriage between us and, as a matter of fact, the last thing either of us wanted at the time was marriage with anyone. We were out for a trip and freedom and a good time and to forget things that had hurt. Naturally, we turned to the person or persons with whom we could have the most fun. We turned to each other."

For Richard and Jessica, their attraction was not originally a matter of emotion. The basis for their camaraderie was a bond of friendship and congeniality that was unconfused by sex. They had fun together, enjoyed doing the same things, meeting the same

Richard Barthelmess with Jessica near their home on Malibu Beach.

people, and most importantly, they liked to talk together. For the immediate future, there was no thought of marriage between them. By the time they finally did begin to discuss matrimony, they were two close friends who liked as well as loved each other. "We liked each other first," he thought back, "and loved each other afterward. Jeremy Taylor once said, 'True love is friendship set on fire.' That is the perfect motto and the perfect description of our marriage, to the last letter."

Jessica and Richard came together evenly, each carrying the same amount of baggage from the past, first marriages that failed, and one child. Jessica's son, Stewart, was separated by two months in age from Richard's daughter, Mary. The children inherited their parent's congeniality.

"You can't very easily divorce *friends*," he said. "First marriage is a dream. Second marriage is a deed. One is a fantasy apt to explode, like a bubble, in your face. The second is a fact, which you know all about. The trouble with most young people and, so, most young marriages, is that they have not been brought up to *expect physical attraction*. They have never been taught that physical attraction is an appetite, like hunger or thirst, liable to be encountered many times during youth. Result being that the first time they meet up with the elemental impulse very strongly they believe that it must be love and must mean marriage. The French do this sort of thing much better. There, a man has one, two or more mistresses before he finally marries and settles down. When he does, he marries a woman who makes him feel not only that he wants to kiss her — there are so many women whom it would be pleasant and even thrilling to kiss — but also that he wants to share life with her, all of it."

Dick valued the security of insurance, sound investments, real estate, and bills paid-in-full. "Which all indicates that I should never in the world have married a cute little girl who was a dancer and not, by any stretch of anything but a love-fevered imagination, a potential housewife and mother," he later agonized in an interview with Gladys Hall. In "Jessie," Richard found the woman of his dreams.

They were married on April 20th in Reno, Nevada. This matrimony was different than his first love with Mary Hay. Richard resolved to refrain from intimacy with any woman involved in acting. Like many in the divorce-ridden world, Richard wanted a chance for happiness, a stable home life, and a second marriage with a woman who prized wifely duties more than a professional career.

They went on a honeymoon under the balmy breezes and glamour of Palm Beach, Richard all togged out in a lightweight, white beach shirt, and Jessica wearing a flowery beach dress with a broad-brimmed hat. Both sported sun-kissed tans, and posed for countless pictures with the ever-present press.

The bachelors of Hollywood may have never forgiven him for deserting their ranks, but after seeing the happiness the new Mrs. Barthelmess brought him, they forgave him and gloried in their newfound romance. Richard adopted Jessica's son, Stewart, and

Richard and Jessica on board their yacht, *Pegasus*.

along with his daughter, the charming family group sailed for Norway, Sweden, Finland and Denmark on a Midnight Sun cruise.

When they returned to California, Jessica adjusted to all the circumstances of being an actor's wife. She had never known a Hollywood star prior to meeting Richard, and found herself a complete stranger in a strange town with strange ways. She quickly melted into his circle of friends, and became pals with Kay Francis, Ronald Colman, and Bill Powell. Richard's friends became her friends, and she was never suspicious or resentful of the demands of his work. She harbored no jealousy over his lovemaking to actresses in the movies, knowing full well it was no more personal than any other business gesture and not even half so private.

Jessica was careful to avoid making evening engagements for Richard when he was in the middle of making a film. She knew the value of sleep to a camera face, and was self-sufficient enough to settle into an evening alone reading a book without considering it a hardship.

With his new home life, Richard made a public plea for privacy. To one of his favorite writers, Helen Louise Walker, he said, "I insist that my life outside the studio should be my own affair . . . if they would not make us public figures — but they do. We become symbols of something or other and people demand that we set examples. I maintain that it is not a part of our job. The thing makes prisoners of us. We cannot go to public places without attracting attention. We must be constantly on our guard to avoid offending somebody. Our homes, then, become sanctuaries — the only places where we can be ourselves. I will not have my home invaded by the glare of publicity . . . please don't think I am a sorehead. Please don't quote me as wailing about the penalties of fame and all that sort of rot. I am simply trying to protect my happiness and secure the privacy to which every man is entitled."

For Richard, the disillusionment in his plea was real. This grim attempt to protect his private life sprang from bitter, recent experiences. He deliberately dropped from public view for several seasons. Publicity, on which his career had been built, was the "goose that lays the golden egg," and the egg was put away on a high shelf in the back of his life. Shrinking away from public view hurt his career irreparably, but it gave him the satisfying personal life that he craved.

Esther Ralston recalled in her autobiography about being taken to the Barthelmess home by William Powell after dinner one night. "We were ushered into a large bedroom, and since I had never met the Barthelmess family before, I was startled to see Mrs. Barthelmess calmly ensconced in bed with several large dogs lying beside her. Mr. Barthelmess sat us before a roaring fire and we chatted sociably with him and his wife until it was time to go home."

Ever since D. W. Griffith opened his eyes to all things Oriental back when they were making *Broken Blossoms*, he loved to immerse in that culture. He and Jessica took time away from his work to travel to Shanghai to watch the Sino-Japanese fireworks,

Richard Barthelmess and Anita Page do their best imitation of comedian Jimmie Durante.

accompanied by their friend, Ronald Colman. More time was spent away from the cameras battling a court action to recover $72,225.00 from two brokerage firms charged with diverting some of his investment income in stocks to other uses. Richard and Jessica both appeared in court and won the case. At another time, the couple took a respite from their work and travels to visit Baden-Baden, a favorite spa of Hollywood stars.

To enjoy their new lives together, Richard diverted some of his remaining fortune to the building of their dream home on a choice piece of beachfront property resting on the pink sand dunes between Santa Monica and the Malibu.

With the front door facing the ocean and its back against the California mountains, the mansion stood securely facing China, standing as it was in the middle of a wilderness of Spanish haciendas. Old English influences abounded in its design, marked with simplicity and lack of ostentation. When John Gilbert first stepped into the new abode, he opened his eyes wide and declared, "Why, it's crisp and white as lettuce!" What Gilbert meant is unclear. By then, he was lost in frequent bouts with alcoholism, and the unfortunate actor died a short time later on January 9, 1936.

Richard Barthelmess horseback riding with Jessica in 1933 while on vacation in the Indian country where he planned to shoot the film, Massacre.

The Barthelmess house was a white, two-story, framed farmhouse, with a green shingled roof, and a huge, whitewashed chimney that matched the foamy caps on the ocean waves. Three garages faced the ocean highway, and the house was designed around a courtyard in the old New England manner. Sixteen rooms filled the interior, and the exterior was over planted with olive and pine trees, flowers, and judiciously placed shrubs. Every room was fitted with an entrance from an outside balcony. At its heart was a massive living room with the monster fireplace in which great logs roared in serene competition with the sound of the ocean waves.

In the midst of this opulence, the depression of the 1930s was taking its toll on the studios and their grosses. An historic meeting took place at the Writer's Club. The following report appeared in the March 11, 1933 *Hollywood Citizen-News*:

> "The motion picture industry had an earthquake all its own last night. The shocks recorded at the various group mass meetings were reverberations of indignation and protest over various resolutions and proposals submitted for a fifty percent cut in all salaries during the coming eight weeks.
>
> About 200 important actors and actresses attended a mass meeting held at the Writer's Club. After a long and stormy session they appointed Walter Huston as their representative on the Academy Emergency Committee established to investigate conditions. Lawrence Grant was named as alternate for Huston, who is on his way to Hollywood from a mountain cabin.
>
> An advisory committee of five also was named to work with Mr. Huston in the coming negotiations. The five unanimously selected last night were Robert Emmett O'Connor, Lewis Stone, Charles Bickford, Wallace Beery and Alan Dinehart. They were chosen as representing the best fighting blood of the actors' contingent.
>
> The dissension of the big contract players last night did not seem to be inspired by selfish motive. The high salaried actors were fighting to protect the small salaried and freelance groups. They were working together as a fraternity of actors.
>
> A dramatic climax came when John Miljan announced he would donate $2000 any time for a fund to be given to studio workers in need of aid,

but he would not be stampeded into accepting a resolution he regarded as unfair.

'I resigned from Equity two years ago because I refused to be stampeded,' shouted Miljan, 'and I refuse to be stampeded now. I am resigning from the Academy!'

With these words he stalked out of the meeting amid loud applause.

Wallace Beery demanded to know who would receive the benefits of these salary donations. He asked if those of the industry really in need of money would get his salary if he donated it. Receiving an unsatisfactory reply, Beery also left the meeting. Lewis Stone was another who raised vigorous doubts and objections, although he declined to accept appointment to the Emergency Committee.

Fredric March, Robert Emmett O'Connor, Richard Barthelmess and James Cagney were other speakers. Reginald Barlow presided at the meeting with Conrad Nagel, Sam Hardy and Lawrence Grant flanking him. Barlow had difficulty keeping the people in order.

It was the feeling of those present that the proposed pay slash would work a great burden on the free-lance actors. If this group should agree to a fifty per cent slash for eight weeks, it was pointed out, deductions of their salaries might be prolonged over many months or even a year, since they do not work steadily.

The depression affected nearly everyone, and Hollywood stars were not immune to the losses suffered by people who were not in the film industry. In November 1931, the *Reno Evening Gazette*

Dutch Petit, Richard's stand-in and double, appeared on the set of many of his 1930s motion pictures.

reported imminent reductions to movie star's salaries. Up to that time, film actors had been relatively untouched by the depression. Studios lost millions of dollars while their stocks plunged, but the high salaries lavished on some actors continued. According to David O. Selznick, players, directors, writers, and executive who had been earning from $1,000 to $5,000 weekly could expect to work for half that amount and like it. "Of course, there will be a few outstanding persons who will continue to receive enormous salaries," Selznick said, "and they will be entitled to them. If a good actress, for example, can add a tremendous amount to the receipts of a picture simply by her presence in it, it is only right that she should receive a commensurate salary. But salaries throughout the industry as a whole must be reduced. They are out of proportion to the present earning capacity of the industry. Naturally, the salaries will rise again as business conditions improve. But I doubt if they will reach their present peak just as it is doubtful if the picture industry ever again will enjoy the period of prosperity it went through two and three years ago."

In June 1933, Richard was reportedly "between pictures." Having just completed work on *Central Airport*, he reveled in time spent with his wife and children. His days were spent on the sunny

Stewart, Jessica, and Richard in the early 1930s.

boat deck of his yacht, swimming in the chilly waters, lunch, long walks, and horseback rides. Evenings were frequently spent with pals, Bill Powell and Carole Lombard, Ronald Colman, and Ernest Torrence and his wife.

Richard contemplated the changing times in the country and the changes within the film industry as it slowly recovered from the aftermath of the conversion from silent pictures to talking pictures. At the same time, *he* was changing. He had reached the apex of his career, and had to face the fact that he was no longer the misty-eyed

Richard and Jessica with his daughter, Mary Hay, and Stewart, her son by a first marriage, just before they sailed for Norway, Sweden, Finland, and Denmark in 1932.

youth the public had once loved. A fresh, new crop of leading men had charmed the studios and the hearts of the public. Charles Boyer, Gary Cooper, Buster Crabbe, Bing Crosby, Clark Gable, Cary Grant, and Robert Taylor were just a few of those who were playing the outstanding "leading man" roles at the major studios. At Richard's studio, Warner Bros., Humphrey Bogart and James Cagney typified the anti-hero prevalent at that time. Richard was finding it increasing difficult to compete for the best parts. There was change in the wind, and he felt it.

G. W. Pabst (seated) directing Richard Barthelmess and Jean Muir in *A Modern Hero* (1934). Richard had to stand on a box several inches thick to increase his height to make him appear taller than his co-star.

Chapter 8
Goodbye to Youth

After nearly twenty years as a Hollywood star, Richard revealed candidly to Gladys Hall "I have said good-bye to youth. I am no longer young and I know it. I have stood at the crossroads. I've looked behind me and I've seen down that long bright road the figures of *Tol'able David*, of the boys who were in *Broken Blossoms* and *Way Down East*, and others, retreating into the past. I've waved good-bye to *Tol'able David*. I know that he is gone forever."

Fay Wray recalled in her autobiography that around this time that Richard ". . . foolishly had plastic surgery to remove bags under his eyes, leaving him with one grotesquely pulled lower lid." The calamity was soon corrected, and he fortunately regained his celebrated good looks, but it did not much matter. Hollywood had turned the spotlight on younger new stars, and Richard was wise enough to know that the parade had gone by.

Few stars stood the pace of work as steadily as he had. He was at a place in his life where he could look back over the rapidly changing landscape of the town and the industry. "Hollywood is a much more vital place than it used to be," he said in a 1933 interview. "There is more intelligence, but also more economic pressure. Much of the color is gone. There is more work and less play." He went on to explain, "Hollywood is more interesting, but less spectacular. Not even the Brown Derby has the atmosphere that you used to find at the Sunset Inn or at the Vernon Country Club." The club still stood in 1933, keeping a lonely vigil over the sparkling Pacific at Santa Monica. Now virtually deserted, the dance floor once was graced by Corinne Griffith dancing her way into the attention of producers. The times were changing. "We didn't consider that

Richard Barthelmess, ill at ease in a 1930s musical.

Jessica, Richard, and Alice Faye at the premier of *The Grapes of Wrath*.

picture-making was work. Things were done in a more leisurely and probably in a more slipshod manner. With Griffith, we made up the continuity as we rehearsed, and often rehearsed for eight or ten weeks . . . those days are gone forever."

By 1933, even the great director, D. W. Griffith, was unable to work in the industry he helped build. "No one has taken Griffith's place," Richard remarked. "In fact, I doubt if anyone will. He will be more appreciated as the years go on. Perhaps I shouldn't say it, but Griffith will, I think, only be fully appreciated posthumously."

Time was taking the old silent stars down odd turns in the roads of their lives. They were disappearing at a fantastic, unbelievable pace. Richard recalled one ironic turn of events in the life of the greatest star of them all: "Three years ago, in New York, I was walking in Central Park with Mary Pickford. Some kids on skates came up and asked me for my autograph — and didn't know Mary . . . *Mary Pickford, who had more publicity than any woman alive.* You'd think no one could ever forget Mary Pickford. Then, a year ago, I was sitting in a café in Budapest with Bill Powell and some people came up and asked him for his autograph, *and didn't know me,* in spite of the $60 million dollars worth of publicity I had."

When asked if he regretted the passing of the "old days," Richard admitted, "Yes, everyone who knew them does. But we have to admit the new days are better. Pictures are better, and better minds are engaged on them. They'll be better next year than this, if we weather the present financial storm — and , of course, we will!"

(LEFT TO RIGHT) **Stewart Barthelmess, Mary Hay Barthelmess, Mary Pickford, and Richard Barthelmess at a 1938 party.**

Still a star after all those years, he continued to happily greet admiring ladies of all ages who still gazed at him with appreciative eyes. Richard had said goodbye to youth, but he found himself faced with a tough decision about whether to continue to play assigned roles or freelance and carefully pick occasional, memorable opportunities.

"I knew," he confessed to Gladys Hall, "several months ago that I stood at the crossroads. My pictures were terrible. *I* was terrible. I was miscast and ridiculous. People were laughing at me, not weeping with me. The reviews matched the pictures. I was dying — and I knew it."

The crossroads pointed in four directions and he had to make a choice. One fork pointed to a retreat from his career into a cocoon of complete seclusion, memories pressed into scrapbooks, and the close love of his family. "I've had everything," he remarked at that time. "I've nothing to complain about. I've made a small fortune. Some of it is gone now, but there is enough left for me to live comfortably on, keep my family comfortably. I am completely happy. My original ambitions are fulfilled. People are apt to think of me as morose, melancholy because I have a sort of Buster Keaton pan — but that is just the face. The heart beats to jazz often enough." He thought if he followed that path he would go to the South Sea Islands and live the life of a lotus-eater, feeding upon memories. The idea had its appeal, but it was only a dream of youth.

The second fork led to a new and possibly shaky career as a producer and director. He had already gone down that road for some time, and seriously considered moving away from facing cameras to a seat behind the equipment. "I believe I am a producer at heart," he said. "In the old Inspiration Picture days, in the days when I was working with Griffith, I had a lot to say about my parts and about the way I should play them. We were individuals then and not cans of soup turned out by a factory. And I've always been keenly interested in developing talent other than my own. Quite a few people who became prominent in pictures took their first starry steps in pictures of mine — Dorothy Mackaill and Bill Powell, Ernest Torrence, Madge Evans, Loretta Young, and others."

For a time, Walter Camp and Richard discussed reforming a producing company. After conferring with Joseph Schenck, he

Richard Barthelmess with Mr. and Mrs. Ronald Colman greeted by two leading Japanese actors in 1932 when they visited the Nikitsu Studios in Japan.

steered away from the plan. The depression brought failing grosses to most studios, and that road seemed decidedly unwise.

The third fork led to the loss of empowerment that he would suffer by signing with some other studio to act in stories that were not of his personal choosing. "If I took that fork, I knew rigor mortis would set in!" Richard lamented.

The last road led to free-lancing, and this was the path that he chose to take. For his remaining years, he had enough money saved to provide for his life, and he vowed to go forward with only those projects that interested him. "I came back to Hollywood and I took that fork of the road. And now, I have finished *Four Hours to Kill* at Paramount."

For Richard, if life did not begin at forty, then it certainly opened widely at that age and led to richer, riper, and more worthwhile work. "I shall work now — more than ever before — for the joy of working. I have never taken pictures for a racket. Always, I've been intensely serious about my work. I've been grateful for the things my work has given me. Money doesn't interest me any longer. I want enough to pay my taxes, to educate our two children,

Richard Barthelmess on the radio in 1933.

to buy Jessie a new coat now and then. But there won't be enough money in all of Hollywood to make me play a part unless I believe it. Unless I know it's truly a part suited to me."

The new technology of television was beginning to loom on the horizon. When questioned about its impending emergence and whether he could see himself a part of pioneering efforts to create the new medium, Richard said, "I don't see why not. I would be greatly interested in the idea, at least."

In 1934, Richard was a guest on the Rudy Vallee radio program. He dabbled in radio for a time, and publicity reports went out that he was to star as a host of his own series. Nothing came of the plan, and Richard struck out for other studios to resume his freelance film career.

Four Hours to Kill (1935) brought him to Paramount to play a murderer, which was a complete change of pace. This new film intrigued audiences with the story of a murderer doomed to hang. While handcuffed to a detective, the two have four hours to kill before the train departs to take him to his hanging. They attend a theater show where he sees the wife of Noel Madison, the man who testified against him. He brushes closely to the manager in the lobby of the theater and deftly takes the manager's gun. After he calls Madison to tell him his wife needs him at the theater, and quietly waits in a phone booth to shoot Madison on arrival at the theater. Madison arrives, Barthelmess is discovered, and then shot.

Four Hours to Kill presented a new Richard Barthelmess in a thrilling murder mystery, an excellent vehicle chocked-full of five subplots and an anti-hero character. Initially titled *Shanghai Orchids*, the original director was Howard Kawks. In order to direct *Scarface*, Hawks had signed a multi-picture deal with Howard Hughes' Caddo Company. His insecurities surfaced just after finishing Warner Bros.' *Tiger Shark*, and he broke rank with Warner Bros. to move to MGM. There, he clashed with the forces of studio policy and the star system, and decided to leave the film business altogether. First National-Warner Bros. felt he still owed them one film, and proposed that he direct Richard in his next film, tentatively titled *Shanghai Orchids*. After reading the script, he refused, and the directing chore fell to Mitchell Leisen.

Richard in 1935 with sailing buddies (LEFT TO RIGHT) **Warner Baxter, William Powell, and Ronald Colman.**

By 1936, Richard's film career seemed to be skidding to a halt. Although his personal reviews for his two films made that year were fine, he wanted to live in New York, and an intriguing proposition came to return to the stage, something he had not done since his youth.

That year, Richard took the brave leap to Broadway and appeared in the original cast of *The Postman Always Rings Twice*. He made a striking debut on the stage as a California vagrant who takes a job in a gas station because he took a fancy to the peculiar beauty of the wife of the station owner.

Brooks Atkinson of the *New York Times* thought the new play was as good as the novel by James M. Cain on which it was based. "It turned up callously at the Lyceum last evening with Richard Barthelmess as the snide killer and Mary Phillips as the killeress," he wrote. "Nearly everything that the stage can do for such an impetuous exercise in crime, Mr. Cain and his theater associates have done with considerable technical skill, and many of the twelve scenes sputter with garish excitement."

Platinum-haired Jean Harlow with Clark Gable and Richard Barthelmess in 1936.

Regarding Richard, Atkinson also wrote, "As the reckless lover of a gas station strumpet, Mr. Barthelmess does a blameless job in his first starring appearance on Broadway. He is pleasantly forthright, although he lacks the rasp and bite that are needed to make Frank Chambers a credible adventurer. He is up against some excellent actors in his stage debut . . . ."

Richard later recalled, "After making *Four Hours to Kill*, I tried the theater. I didn't like it. I tried travel. We went abroad to live for a year. I was there nearly two years, thanks to a long illness. Loafing didn't seem to agree with me. I wondered about producing again, getting my fingers in the movie pie somewhere. I bid up to $100,000 for the movie rights to *Dead End*. Goldwyn outbid me. There were other stories that interested me from a production standpoint. One was *Golden Boy*. I tried to get that — but Columbia had just closed a deal for it. I finally came back here to put the kids in school, and started playing golf, which would take up so much of my day that time wouldn't hang heavy on my hands. But I still had time to wonder, 'Where am I going from here?' Time to think. It was ridiculous that anyone with my experience should cease to have any acting value. As a leading man, yes. But somebody has to

Richard Barthelmess with Ann Dvorak, taking direction from Alan Crosland while filming *Massacre* (1934).

(LEFT TO RIGHT) **Arthur Byron, William Lynn, Richard, and James Melton with Bette Davis in 1936 at a party in New York at the Ritz.**

play those Lionel Barrymore roles some day. It was fantastic that, at forty, an actor's career should be behind him."

It took another year for Richard to find his next "important part in an important picture." At that time, he commented, "I'm not in it for another bath of Fame. I'm not in it for big money. I'm not looking for anything except diversified roles. Important roles in important pictures. I don't want to be a star. I don't want to be a glamour boy. The only recognition I want is as a leading character actor. Let's hope I get it!"

In 1936, he received an honorary degree from Trinity College in Hartford, the university he attended but from which he left to appear as an actor in films. After closing *The Postman Always Rings Twice*, Richard, Jessica, and the children set out together to enjoy the thrill of travel, and they spent the summer of 1936 touring England, Ireland, Scotland, and Wales. By autumn, the children were settled in English schools, and Richard flew with Jessica for a month-long visit to Switzerland.

For more than twenty-five years, the boyish matinee idol of the silent film era had brought great sighs from women in movie houses throughout the country. He was the clean-cut American hero, not strikingly handsome, but good-looking, masculine, unassuming, and modest. His shy, crooked smile and sleek black hair brought him an average of 6,000 fan letters a month at the height of his career.

Although the industry had changed officially to talking pictures, silent films were still golden as late as 1938. The successful return engagements on a national scale of Rudolph Valentino's *The Sheik* and *Son of the Sheik* had stirred up a great deal of talk about the possible revival of other silent films. Although domestic production of silent films had stopped nearly ten years earlier in the United States, they continued to be made in Soviet Russia, France, Japan, and India. Of the world's 90,000 theaters, more than a third lacked sound equipment. Russia alone had 27,000 soundless screens in 1938. France had about 1,000. There were scatterings of silent film houses all around the world. In America, there was also an audience of millions of people showing silent films in non-theatrical settings such as churches, schools, civic centers, hospitals, and in the growing home market.

The home-movie market for silent films had become more than a hobby; it had been accountable for the medium's second lease on life. More than 200,000 people owned 8mm or 16mm projectors, and a surprisingly large proportion of them were renting silent films to augment their weekly family outings and personal filmmaking. Companies were marketing prints in smaller gauge formats to feed the demand, and many silent films were still available for viewing. Popular titles at that time were the Pearl White serials, Richard Barthelmess and Dorothy Gish in *The Bright Shawl*, Lillian and Dorothy Gish in *Romola*, and Elmo Lincoln in *Tarzan of the Apes*. The comedies of Charlie Chaplin, Laurel and Hardy, and the Keystone Cops were enormously popular, as were all of the D. W. Griffith Biograph dramas with Mary Pickford and Lillian Gish.

Charlie Chaplin stated that that demand for his comedies in the non-theatrical field was in direct ratio to their former popularity with theater audiences. The Y.M.C.A. film bureau officials said their silent films were shown to about 5,000,000 people annually. At least another 5,000,000 people rented pictures released by Kodascope, Willoughby, Bell & Howell, and from public libraries. It seemed that silent films would flourish indefinitely, as long as copies were made available to non-theatrical venues.

In the legitimate film theaters of 1939, it was another story. When film magazines wrote about Richard, they now used words that labeled him as "once a movie star," and "you remember the name. Perhaps you even remember the man." Richard returned to films in a Columbia picture called *Plane No. 4*. The role was a comeback of sorts, for Howard Hawks was set to direct the aviation story, which would star Jean Arthur and Cary Grant. It was Richard's first appearance on screen in five years. After three and a half years of self-sought retirement, the suddenly launched "come-back" presented him in a strong role as a disgraced flyer earning redemption during a crisis.

Columbia publicized his return as an "event," and trotted Richard out to dine with Monty Prosser and Howard Hawks at a Columbia press banquet. Richard donned an aviator's head goggles to pose for publicity photos. The studio publicity mill began to grind out reams of copy proclaiming, "Barthelmess is Back!"

Richard Barthelmess and William Powell with Diana Lewis, Powell's newlywed, in 1940 at the Cocoanut Grove where the bride met many of her husband's old cronies for the first time.

One of his co-stars was Rita Hayworth, and the film took her on a drastic change of career direction. Shooting began the day before Christmas 1938, and Columbia intended the film to be its blockbuster for the year. Howard Hawks had complete control over all aspects of the production. Rita lobbied for and won the role of "the other woman."

According to Hawks, in the book, *Rita Hayworth, The Time, The Place, and The Woman*, the film was based on a true story gleaned from a bush pilot with whom he flew on a trip to Mexico, an incident about another pilot and his girl. Hawks also witnessed another incident with a fellow who bailed out of an airplane, leaving his partner to crash. When his peers blackballed him, the repentant parachuter went to horrendous lengths to redeem himself. Hawks merged the two stories into a ten-page treatment and Harry Cohn approved the story for production.

Frank Capra and Loretta Young with Richard at the premier of the film, *The Doctor Takes a Wife*.

The finished film, released as *Only Angels Have Wings*, was given its preview on May 11, 1939 to an ecstatic Los Angeles audience. The same reaction repeated when the film premiered in New York. For Rita Hayworth, her performance proved to be a revelation; for Richard, it was the final important one of his career.

When asked why he wanted to get back into the grind of film production since he had no need for the income and his career had lasted longer than most, Richard commented, "I was lonely. Yes, I have lots of friends, that's true, but you see they're working in pictures. They're in the swim. I was just an outsider. Oh, we tried to talk of other things and get back on the old footing, but I could see they had gone on and left me. So, I had to get in, too, to be where they were, so we could all be fellow workers again. I couldn't stay on the outside any longer."

Had he not been living in Hollywood, and had his two children not been comfortably enrolled in schools there, he probably would not have gotten back into the harness of being a star in a film again.

He signed a new contract with Columbia calling for two pictures a year, with the option of taking outside assignments. The contract specified "important parts in important pictures." Richard had enough of straight romantic leads and was anxious to step into more mature, meaty, character parts. He still harbored a desire to portray General Grant. He regretted missing the chance to play the role performed by Paul Muni in *The Good Earth*, which would have ideally suited him because of his strong identification with Oriental films like *Broken Blossoms* and *Son of the Gods*.

"The point I'm trying to get across is that I'm still reasonably young and, if I have to, I can look younger," he said to Roger Carroll in *Motion Picture Magazine*. "But I can also look older, if I have to. I can still be romantic, if need be, but I can play other parts, too. There are big roles that cry for actors who can be romantic, but are ready, willing and able to be something else. Look at some of the things that Spencer Tracy and Paul Muni have done in *Captains Courageous, Boys Town, Zola,* and *Pasteur*. There could be more roles like those, if there were more actors to play them. That's where I hope to fit in."

Richard Barthelmess having dinner with Claudette Colbert in 1940.

Richard broke his usual vow to avoid all public appearances, and in his attempt to restart his downed career, he attended the Hollywood premier of *The Grapes of Wrath* as part of a personal appearance tour.

For his next picture, Columbia found the role of J. B. Roscoe perfect for Richard in the George Brent film, *The Man Who Talked Too Much* (1940).

On September 25, 1940, Marguerite Clark, Richard's co-star in many silent films, passed away in New York of pneumonia. After making her last film, *Scrambled Wives* (1921), Marguerite had spent nineteen years dividing her time between her home in New York and her husband's plantation in New Orleans until his death in 1936. She had permanently moved back to New York for the four years just before she passed away.

Also in 1940, Richard took part in a screen test at Twentieth Century-Fox. It was not *he* who was tested, *but his daughter*, Mary Hay Barthelmess, now grown up, beautiful, and vivacious. Very proudly, Richard played with his back to the camera, feeding his daughter lines from John Barrymore's part in *My Dear Children*, as Mary played the part of the daughter. At the age of seventeen, she had real talent, and hopes ran high that she would find a place in the film industry as a second generation star. The following year, before the film studios could invite her to join their ranks, she began rehearsals for *Letters to Lucerne*, a play by Allen Vincent and Fritz Rotter that was placed in the main hall and dormitory of a girls' school in Switzerland, near Lucerne.

In 1942, John Wayne and Randolph Scott starred in a remake of The Spoilers, the classic Rex Beach melodrama. The story of a saloon owner and a crook attempting to steal a gold mine got the full treatment in this lusty presentation by Universal. Audiences were too young to remember the terrific fight scene in the silent version of Jack London's gusty tale of Alaska in the gold-rush days, and were content to view the battle royal between Wayne and Scott. The two stars recreated a full-blown version of the famous brawl, giving audiences their money's worth in the tale of violent passions in the Nome of the 1900s. Marlene Dietrich was prominent as the seductive barroom queen of the Alaskan mining town, adding beauty and color to her role, and Richard was featured in the role of the

Mary Hay Barthelmess at the time she was starring in the play, *Letters from Lucern*, and making her screen test.

"Bronco Kid," a treacherous card dealer in love with her. William Farnum, who appeared in the original 1914 movie, played a key role in this remake.

That same year, producer Cliff Reid made one of his last RKO productions, *The Mayor of 44th Street* (1942). The producers brought Richard in as the third lead in the role of Ed Kirby. Scriptwriters Lewis R. Foster and Frank Ryan attempted to mix a raw underworld melodrama with bandleader Freddy Martin's "sweet swing" music; the outcome was about as involving and stimulating as a game of solitaire. The film was based on a story that appeared in a *Collier's* magazine article, and though several songs were woven into the thin story, the outcome was undistinguished. With the rising conflict in Europe, Richard all but lost interest in continuing with his film career. It was his final performance on screen.

When he finished his work at RKO in *The Mayor of 44th Street*, he headed east in time for the opening of his daughter's stage debut. *Letters to Lucerne* opened on December 23, 1941, at the Cort Theater. She received good notices, but the play closed after a run of only twenty-three performances. After a few other attempts, Mary lost interest in pursing a film career, and despite her screen test, she never appeared in a motion picture.

Soon after, George M. Cohan, who had featured Richard in his 1917 film, *Hit-The-Trail-Holliday*, died of cancer in New York on November 5, 1942. That same year, Cohan was immortalized in the James Cagney film, *Yankee Doodle Dandy*.

Winifred Allen, who played with Richard in the 1917 *For Valour*, died on January 3, 1943, in Rochester, New York. Between 1915 and 1924, Winifred starred in eleven silent films, and she never made a sound motion picture. She was already forgotten by the time of her death.

When World War Two began, Richard made a momentous decision. Answering the call to arms, he walked away from Hollywood, put his career behind him, and enlisted in the US Navy as a Lieutenant Commander. While in service, he had the gratifying experience of swearing in his son, Stewart, who had also enlisted. For Richard, it spelled the end of his film career. Like others, he chose to defend his country rather than stay at home and selfishly pursue personal interests. While he was away, older audiences almost forgot about him. A new generation sprang up to fill audience seats, and they had never even heard of him or seen him in any motion picture.

Charles G. Sampas, writing in the *Lowell Sun* in October 1945, lamented, "This modern generation. We were talking with a group of lads at the Square the other evening about movie stars. The topic was about the quality of pictures, and I mentioned Richard Barthelmess. 'Who?' the lads asked. 'Richard Barthelmess.' 'Never

RICHARD BARTHELMESS, left, former film star, and his son here stage a two-man meeting in New York City of the Mutual Admiration society. Barthelmess is a Navy lieutenant commander and is flag lieutenant and aide to Vice Adm. Herbert F. Leary. The son, Ensign Stewart S. Barthelmess, has just received his commission in the Navy.

Newspaper photo and caption of Richard with his son during World War Two.

heard of him!' That's the way it is, I guess. We're old — and we just don't realize it. The Young at Heart, eh?"

Sampas, again writing in the March 1945 *Lowell Sun*, published a letter from a reader:

> "Dear Mr. Sampas: Being an old Lowellite, I often get *The Sun* and, of course, the first thing I read is your column to catch up on the 'scuttlebutt' of Lowell. Even though we are a few miles away, we often reminisce . . . I was reading your column today in the Friday night's *Sun*, and you mentioned you wondered where Richard Barthelmess was, and that prompted this letter. I am with the Navy Department at 90 Church Street, New York City, and often see Richard Barthelmess, now a Lieutenant Commander in the US Navy, in and out of the building. He is now attached to the Commander, Eastern Sea Frontier, at Church Street. He is well-liked by everyone."

After the war ended, Richard was transferred to Norfolk, Virginia, bearing a commendation for his excellent work. He then returned to his country home on Long Island, comfortable as a wealthy man, and harbored no wish to return to the screen. After appearing in seventy-nine motion pictures, fifty-seven of which were silent, Richard moved into his autumn years living in satisfied retirement. Over the following years, he turned down several offers to return to movies, feeling no compelling need to reaffirm the enduring fame that had come his way so early in life. After four decades of motion picture successes and a permanent niche in Hollywood history, he had accomplished all that he had set out to achieve, and above all else, he had the financial security that was his original motivation for getting into films when Alla Nazimova first invited him to appear with her in *War Brides*.

On July 13, 1945, Alla Nazimova passed away in the Los Angeles Good Samaritan Hospital after suffering a brief bout with coronary thrombosis. A favorite for two decades, the Russian-born actress was sixty-four, and had successfully returned to pictures after an

(TOP) **Grown-up Stewart Barthelmess on the town with Sonja Henie,**

(CENTER) **with Henie, Skitch Henderson, and Anita Colby, and**

(BOTTOM) **with Henie at the 1946 opening of Stables in Palm Springs.**

absence of more than fifteen years. Her last picture was *The Bridge of San Luis Rey*.

By this time, D. W. Griffith was sometimes called the "father of the film industry." He had grown old, and upstart producers said his usefulness was at an end. In his later years, he lived at the Knickerbocker Hotel in Hollywood. Griffith did not need money, and he was not destitute. He lived comfortably on an annuity he had wisely set up many years earlier. In the art form he largely perfected, there was little left for him. He was seen wandering around Beverly Hills and Hollywood, roaming from tavern to tavern, visiting old friends, and watching the industry's new films with wistful admiration. Frances Marion told a heart-breaking story in her autobiography about passing Grauman's Chinese Theater one night when a star's footprints were being recorded in the cement. She saw Griffith hovering on the edge of the crowd and looking bewildered and lost. No one had ever asked for his footprints, and in fact, no one had ever filled his shoes. She saw the security guards push him back behind a rope. They were unaware that the man they were shoving had virtually started the film careers of those stars that were already imprinted in the cement at their feet.

On Friday July 24, 1948, Griffith died. Charles Brackett, President of the American Academy of Motion Picture Arts and Sciences, read the eulogy at a memorial service given at the Hollywood Masonic Temple. Actor Donald Crisp, who appeared in *The Birth of a Nation* and many other important productions made by Griffith in his heyday, delivered a eulogy. There were hymns sun by the Bob Mitchell Boy Choir, and an invocation by the Rev. Emil Brinistool, Methodist minister and lifelong friend of Griffith. The body lay in state over the weekend in a mortuary chapel, and on the following Tuesday, final services were held.

A monument to him should have been erected at Sunset Boulevard and Vine Streets, but the new generation of Hollywood insiders had little interest in the pioneers who had paved the way for them. Instead, on May 14, 1950, Mary Pickford, Lillian Gish, Mae Marsh, and Richard Barthelmess, four famous stars of the silent screen who loved him, joined forces and accompanied a small group of people to gather to dedicate an honest and dignified memorial to him in the Griffith family cemetery at La Grange,

(TOP) **D. W. Griffith near the end of his life.**
(BOTTOM) **Richard and Jessica in their later years, sedate residents of Southampton, Long Island.**

Kentucky. He was buried under a seven-foot Georgia marble stone near the white frame church where he attended Sunday school as a boy.

During the following years, Richard amassed substantial real estate holdings, and in 1955, he sold his fifty-acre beachfront estate, The Dunes in South Hampton, to Henry Ford II. Richard said that he had only one regret after he stopped acting: selling his production company in the 1920s to accept a lucrative contract with the First National Film Corporation. Richard was justly proud of the films he personally produced during those years under the banner of his company, Inspiration Pictures. By 1955, many of the few remaining prints and negatives of those films were decaying in the dark of the Warner Bros. vaults. No one anticipated the enormous interest these films would have in the coming decades, and many of them were forever lost.

By the late 1950s, many of the early stars were falling from the forgotten skies of the silent cinema. There were those, like Richard, Harold Lloyd, Charlie Chaplin, Mary Pickford, Carlyle Blackwell, and William Farnum, who had gained great wealth and retired in splendor. Other movie luminaries, such as Mae Murray and Clara Bow, became like imploding novas, last seen in a burst of bazaar publicity, and then callously forgotten until their death notices were posted in the nation's newspaper. Gloria Swanson, Pola Negri, and a few others flared again in one or two memorable performances, and then quietly passed into oblivion. Others eked out an existence where they could. Marie Osborne, known as "Little Mary Sunshine," one of the first child stars, was now working as a stand-in for Ginger Rogers and other stars. Mae Marsh was playing unaccredited bit parts in John Ford pictures. Most of them, like quietly passing dinosaurs, were helpless as their careers ebbed into extinction years after their faces and names had become little more than footnotes in film history books.

Theda Bara, star of forty-four films, including the 1917 *Camille* with Richard, died on April 7, 1955, of abdominal cancer at the age of sixty-nine in Los Angeles, California. "During the rest of my screen career, I am going to continue doing vampires as long as people sin," she once said. "For I believe that humanity needs the moral lesson, and it needs it in repeatedly larger doses." Theda did not see her vow fulfilled. By 1955, she was little more than a face in an Encyclopedia Britannica article that capsulated all that people mistakenly thought was bizarre and antiquated about silent movies. All but three of her films had decayed and were forever lost.

Mary Hay, Richard's first wife, quietly died on June 4, 1957, in Inverness, California at the age of fifty-five. No one noticed her passing, and scarcely a newspaper bothered to mention the death of the forgotten woman who once danced nightly in front of hundreds of adoring fans, the idol of the New York smart set.

Richard Barthelmess as fans remember him best.

In 1958, Richard developed throat cancer and, over the next five years, underwent several operations. He eventually lost his voice. With Jessica at his bedside, he died of cancer on Sunday, August 17, 1963, at his summer home at 800 Park Avenue in New York City. He was sixty-eight years old, and in his last days, he had been reduced to communicating in pantomime as he had done in so many films in his youth. Immediately after his death, his will was filed for probate in court. His property, including substantial real estate holdings on both coasts, was bequeathed to his widow, to his surviving adopted son, Stewart, then living in Paris, and his to daughter, Mrs. Mary Hay Bradley, then living in San Rafael, California.

Florence Reed, who played Lucretia Borgia in Richard's 1917 film, *The Eternal Sin*, died in East Islip, Long Island, New York, on November 21, 1967.

One night, not long after she appeared on Broadway in *I Never Sang For My Father*, Lillian Gish received a summons from Rapallo, Italy, that her sister, Dorothy, Richard's co-star in several silent films, was stricken with bronchial pneumonia. Within hours,

Richard Barthelmess photograph, which appeared in many newspapers accompanying his obituary.

Lillian was on a trans-Atlantic flight to her sister's side, but by the time she arrived on June 4, 1968, Dorothy had died. "Even when our work separated us, there was a kind of extra-sensory perception that bound us together," Lillian recalled in her autobiography. "I think of the first words that Hal Holbrook uttered in *I Never Sang For My Father* — out of context, perhaps, but with a special meaning for me: 'Death ends a life, but not a relationship.'"

Dorothy left behind an estate valued at nearly $1 million dollars. It was bequeathed to her sister and the Actors Fund of America. Lillian received all of Dorothy's personal property and income from her trust fund. According to Dorothy's probated will, upon Lillian's death, the funds would revert to the actor's organization.

Billie Burke, with whom Richard first appeared in films as part of *Gloria's Romance*, died on May 14, 1970, at her home in Los Angeles.

Anna Q. Nilsson, star of Richard's fifth film, *The Moral Code*, quietly passed away on February 11, 1974, at her home in Hemet California.

Evelyn Greely, Richard's costar in *Just a Song at Twilight*, died on March 25, 1975, in her home at West Palm Beach, Florida.

Gladys Leslie, who played opposite Richard in *Wild Primrose* (1919), quietly passed away on October 2, 1976, in Boynton Beach, Florida.

Olga Petrova, star of *The Soul of a Magdalen*, the 1917 film in which Richard played her son, Louis Broulette, died on November 30, 1977, in Clearwater, Florida.

Carol Dempster, Richard's costar in several films, finished *The Sorrows of Satan* in 1926, and never made another film. She died on February 1, 1991, in La Jolla, California.

Lillian Gish, who made film history with Richard in *Broken Blossoms* (1919) and *Way Down East* (1920), died of heart failure at her home in New York on February 27, 1993. She outlived all of them, making her final film, *The Whales of August*, in 1987.

One of D. W. Griffith's favorite quotations applies well to Richard and his life in pictures: "What you get is a living. What you give is life."

Part 2: Filmography

Richard Barthelmess played credited roles in at least seventy-six motion pictures, and appeared in unaccredited roles in at least three others. For each film, advertising played a major role in selling the film to the public. Like the circus, stage-plays, and vaudeville shows that preceded motion pictures as a form of amusement, movies were dependent on the successful results of careful promotions. Early posters and lobby cards from the pre-1920 era testify to the use of poster art and photography from the very beginnings of the medium. Many posters were works of art, blending lurid colors with photos and graphics to lure the public and their coins into the theaters. Newspaper line art was a simpler form of advertising, using black and white graphics along with sensational descriptions to attract attention. Still picture photography of the scenes captured the dramatic moments, and these pictures were distributed in the advertising art, as postcards, in magazines, newspapers, and mounted at theaters. Fortunately, many examples of these promotional items have survived for the films of Richard Barthelmess.

The earliest examples of poster and advertising art dating prior to World War One are extremely difficult to find. In paper drives during World War One and World War Two, thousands of these artworks were recycled. After the war, remaining prints were often tossed into garbage cans, their future aesthetic and monetary value unknown to the careless hands sweeping them into extinction. In the 1960s, interest in the art form surged as movie aficionados rediscovered the art of the silent film, and collectors began to appreciate advertising and poster art as treasures. Soon, a thriving trade mushroomed into popularity.

S. Barret McCormick, writing in *Motion Picture News*, July 13, 1918, explored the use of salesmanship in print advertising. "The finding of the marketable element and the presenting of an appealing sample to the prospective purchaser," he pointed out, "and advertising is the only sample of an attraction that the public receives before buying. It is the fragrant whiff from the cologne bottle that Madame gets before she decides on a certain perfume. So atmosphere becomes an essential quantity in photoplay advertising. It is the frame to your sales argument, the dress of your salesman in print. It must convey a mental impression of the product either through subtle insinuation or bold proclamation."

Advertising atmosphere was either presented pictorially or through printed word, and usually with a combination of the two elements. Illustrations spoke with a universal tongue, attracting the attention and interest of a ticket buyer, and the written word clinched sales with a convincing argument of the necessity of spending money on a ticket to see a film.

This Filmography reproduces lobby cards, theatrical posters, or newspaper ads circulated at the time of the original release of Richard's films. They give a strong flavor of the art of the times as it was used to fan the flame of interest in a motion picture.

In addition, the films of Richard Barthelmess are represented by production notes and contemporary reviews that give a feel for how the films were perceived in their time by the leading reviewers of the *New York Times, Variety,* and a host of other local magazines and newspapers from around the country.

Where possible, photographic scene stills are shown, giving a glimpse into the pictorial values of each film. For those films that are now lost, these photographs are the only surviving examples of the production.

After a few brief appearances as a youth on stage, including a role in *Mrs. Wiggs of the Cabbage Patch* (1913), Richard Barthelmess began his film career as an extra. His first giant step toward engaging in a full-fledged career in what was then a new art was with an appearance with Billie Burke, one of the brightest stars of the stage and screen.

GLORIA'S ROMANCE (1916)
KLEINE
PRODUCER: GEORGE KLEINE
DIRECTOR: COLLIN CAMPBELL AND WALTER EDWIN
CAST: Billie Burke, David Powell, Frank McGlyn, Henry Kolker, William Roselle, William T. Carleton, Frank Belcher, Jule Power, Richard Barthelmess, Lois Freeman, Helen Hart, Adelaide Hastings, Rapley Holmes, Frank McGlynn, Sr., Maurice Stewart, Henry Weaver

Peggy (1916) was the actress' first motion picture. Billie Burke romped through the unusually entertaining picture with all the camera knowledge and assurance of a screen veteran. For her next picture, a serial called *Gloria's Romance*, she gathered around her the best writer, director, and cast possible. Richard Barthelmess played a role in several of the twenty episodes.

Rupert Hughes, author, historian, musician, and soldier, first wrote directly for the screen with this serial. Unfortunately, his story was changed so much by the studio it was almost unrecognizable in its final form. Hughes saw only the first two episodes at a gala performance on Broadway. Critics panned the serial, and the audience was bored. Not even the music of Jerome Kern saved it. Improvements were hastily made in the remaining episodes, and they proved to be more popular with general audiences.

According to a reviewer in the *New York Times*, after watching the unreeling of the first episode at the Globe Theater on May 22, 1916, "An interesting experiment was begun last night at the Globe Theatre with the first exhibition of the first chapters of a new movie serial, entitled *Gloria's Romance* with Billie Burke as the star. This installment of the story will be kept on the Globe screen for two weeks, and then other chapters will follow. The movie serial idea is not new, but heretofore they have always been shown in regular picture theatres and not offered as an attraction in a regular playhouse . . . Mr. And Mrs. Rupert Hughes are the authors of the story, which Miss Burke has acted for the screen. The role they have provided for her is that of a young hoyden, whose enthusiasm for excitement gets her into all kinds of scrapes. In the first two chapters she has a lively enough time to satisfy even her adventurous nature. Gloria is spending the season with her crabid father at Palm Beach, when one night she gets up out of bed and goes to the veranda of the hotel to watch the older folks dance within. Here the idea of going for a joy ride in her brother's car seizes her, and she jumps in and opens the throttle."

"A few minutes later she is floundering in the surf, whither the car has flung itself when the steering post broke. From the beach to the Everglades with their interesting denizens of alligators, crocodiles, and Seminoles is but a few steps, and soon Gloria is having adventures with the wild animals and humans of the glades . . . Miss Burke proved herself a good screen subject in her first picture several months ago. She is winsome and girlish-looking, and when she dons the clothes of a boy she is altogether cunning. She does not look as young as her short frocks are intended to make her, and she would be more of a vision if her frocks were longer, but one should not demand everything . . . Jerome Kern, master of insinuating melody, has composed a score for the serial, and last night he conducted the orchestra."

The twenty, two-reel episodes were released at weekly intervals:
Lost in the Everglades released May 5, 1916
Caught By the Seminoles released May 15, 1916
A Perilous Love released May 22, 1916
The Social Vortex released May 29, 1916
The Gathering Storm released June 5, 1916
Hidden Fires released June 12, 1916
The Harvest of Sin released June 19, 1916
The Mesh of Mystery released June 26, 1916
The Shadow of Scandal released July 3, 1916
Tangled Threads released July 10, 1916
The Fugitive Witness released July 17, 1916
Her Fighting Spirit released July 24, 1916
The Midnight Riot released July 31, 1916
The Floating Trap released August 7, 1916
The Murderer at Bay released August 14, 1916
A Modern Pirate released August 21, 1916
The Tell-Tale Envelope released August 23, 1916
The Bitter Truth released August 23, 1916
Her Vow Fulfilled released August 23, 1916
Love's Reward released August 23, 1916

A reviewer in the *Daily Kennebec Journal,* wrote of the sixth chapter, "Mystery piles upon mystery as the plot develops and Gloria finds it wonderfully fascinating work to unravel one complication after another. How she eventually succeeds in solving the riddle, how she finds what really happened to Francois and determines which man of the two is really worthy of her heart and hand, hold one spellbound to the very end of *Gloria's Romance,* which requires twenty feature chapters for the telling."

Billie Burke, star of *Gloria's Romance* (1916).

Gloria's Romance newspaper advertisement as it appeared in the *Indianapolis Star*.

Romeo and Juliet (1916)
Metro
Director: John W. Noble and Francis X. Bushman
Cast: Francis X. Bushman, Beverly Bayne, Horace Vinton, John Davidson, Eric Hudson, Edmund Elton, Leonard Grover, Fritz Leiber, Olaf Skavlan, Robert Cummings, Adelle Barker, A. J. Herbert, Edwin Boring, William Morris, Joseph Dailey, Adella Barker, Helen Dunbar, Genevieve Reynolds, Ethel Mandell, Barry Maxwell, W. H. Burton, W. Lawson Butt. Richard Barthelmess appears as an unaccredited extra.
Synopsis: Romeo and Juliet, two youths from rival families in medieval Italy, fall in love despite the tension between their families. After secretly marrying, circumstances prevent their union from blossoming. Thinking that Juliet has died, Romeo drinks poison and dies next to her in a tomb. Juliet awakens, discovers her lover dead, and stabs herself to death. The warring families vow to settle their differences.

The January 1917 *Photoplay* reviewed the film, calling Bushman's performance the best of his career. "We have the Metro organization to thank for a sun-painting of the great Veronese love-tragedy," the reviewer wrote. "From time to time the little fluttering hearts whose musky notes grace the whittled pine desk of our blind, deaf, ninety-year-old answer-man make much wailing to-do and whatnot over this department's abuse of Mr. Bushman. Abate, gentle cardiac earthquakes, for as Romeo this department found Mr. Bushman not only in the best role of his career, but doing the best acting he has ever shot into the transparencies. Medically, we might term Mr. Bushman the acting hypochondriac. He has always been thinking of himself and his pretty clothes and his sweet biceps and grand smile, and forgetting his character. He may have been 'scairt' into doing a superb Romeo by the overwhelming splendor and tradition of the soulful Italian lad; nevertheless, the fact remains that he is a super Romeo, performing with discretion, dignity, an unusual amount of reserve, and astounding sincerity."

Jerome Hart wrote in the March 1923 *Motion Picture Classic* that the film suffered in the translation to silent movies. "The solitary screen production known of *Romeo and Juliet* to the writer is that made a few years ago with Francis X. Bushman and Beverley Bayne.

The story lost a great deal for those who knew it and loved Shakespeare's matchless lines, although it had its picturesque and vital moments. Miss Bayne was a very pretty, but rather colorless Juliet, while Mr. Bushman was a handsome but mature Romeo. So much is inevitably lost in transferring Shakespeare to the screen that one feels about such an attempt much the same sort of annoyance that many of us experience at witnessing the 'expressionistic' Shakespearean productions of Mr. Arthur Hopkins."

Francis X. Bushman and Beverly Bayne in *Romeo and Juliet* (1916), in which Richard Barthelmess appeared as an extra as one of the people in the streets of Verona.

WAR BRIDES (1916)
SELZNICK
PRODUCER: MARION WENTWORTH
DIRECTOR: HERBERT BRENON
LENGTH: 8 REELS
CAST: Alla Nazimova, Charles Hutchinson, Charles Bryant, William Bailey, Theodora Warfield, Nila Mac, Robert Whitworth, Gertrude Berkeley, Ned Burton, Charles Chailles, Richard Barthelmess, Alex Shannon
SYNOPSIS: The story follows Joan, played by Nazimova, and her reaction to a wartime edict that women shall marry soldiers to bring forth more children as future food for cannons. Rather than submit to this decree, she makes an impassioned plea to the King, fails to touch a responsive chord, and then kills herself. The theme brought forward the awful waste of war, and conveyed a message felt by millions of mothers at the time the film was released when World War One was on everyone's mind. Finally, the story pointed to an ideal, which could only be brought to pass by womankind: the end of war and the dawn of everlasting peace could be brought forth by all mothers if they refused to support warmongers and their destructive aims.

A reviewer in the *New York Times* wrote of Nazimova's first success in a motion picture: "Alla Nazimova was seen for the first time as a screen actress last night at the Broadway Theater in a film version of Marion Craig Wentworth's dramatic playlet, *War Brides*, in which she acted in vaudeville during the early part of the war . . . Mme. Nazimova justified the great interest thus manifested by showing that she had adapted her talents to the new medium with unusual success. In the language of the studio, she screens well, which, translated, means that she is a good subject for motion photography . . . the film abounds with striking photography."

Edward Weitzel wrote in the *Moving Picture World* that the young men who play her sons, including Richard Barthelmess ". . . justify their mother's price in them."

A reviewer in the *Washington Post* wrote of Nazimova and the film, ". . . a role throbbing with pathos, compelling in its appeal and gripping in its tragic intensity. And with such a character to portray, Mme. Nazimova displays an emotional sincerity which those of us who have sat admiringly watching without being moved by her latter-day achievements . . . with fire, force, and feeling, a really great actress is once more revealed in her conception and delineation of Joan, the wife of a soldier. The scene is a peasant's cottage, the home of Joan's mother-in-law. The mother has already furnished three sons to the army, and a fourth is preparing to march away, while the only daughter wishes to enlist in the Red Cross ranks, but she is persuaded by her mother and a hot-blooded suitor that her higher duty as a patriot is to become a "war bride," following the example of other girls of the village, so that she may bear a man-child for her country. It is at this point that Joan enters the cottage. She is a short, crude creature, who stands with her feet planted far apart, her shoulders bent not merely by sorrow, but as if they have borne many burdens, her gestures awkward, her fingers blunted by toil. Around her neck she clutches a black shawl, her head is bare, her black hair pulled severely back from the forehead. It is from this woman who has suffered and is suffering, that there pours a seething flood of eloquence and invective against war and the pitiful war brides."

War Brides newspaper advertisement as it appeared in the *Sheboygan Press.*

Three scenes from *War Brides* (1916) starring Alla Nazimova as Joan, a woman who kills herself rather than cooperate with an edict that, in times of war, women shall marry soldiers to bring forth more children as future food for cannons.

SNOW WHITE (1916)
FAMOUS PLAYERS — PARAMOUNT
DIRECTOR: J. SEARLE DAWLEY
SCREENPLAY: WINTHROP AMES
LENGTH: 6 REELS
CAST: Marguerite Clark, Dorothy Cumming, Lionel Braham, Creighton Hale, Alice Washburn, Richard Barthelmess
SYNOPSIS: Jealous Queen Brangomar, seething with envy for the princess, Snow White, makes the girl work as a scullery maid. When Prince Florimond falls in love with Snow White, the jealous queen plots to have her murdered. To carry out her scheme, she commissions Berthold, the hunter, to kill her. Instead of this, Berthold takes her into the safety of the forest where lives with seven dwarfs. The queen learns that Snow White is alive, and tracks her down. Assuming a guise, the queen tricks Snow White into taking a bite of a poisoned apple. The girl seemingly falls dead, but recovers in the arms of the prince. In a twist of fate, Hex, the witch, who years before made Queen Brangomar beautiful, turns the queen into a peacock.

In *Motion Picture News*, George Shorey wrote, "In this play, Miss Clark is charming beyond words to describe. She fits exactly into the role of the Princess Snow White, and Creighton Hale as Prince Florimund is a likely match for her charm and beauty."

Edward Wagenknecht wrote in *Fifty Great American Silent Films 1912-1920*, "*Snow White* was the Christmas attraction from Famous Players Film Company in 1916. Marguerite Clark has performed the tale on stage for Winthrop Ames at the Little Theater at Matinees and Saturday morning performances while she was starring with John Barrymore in *The Affairs of Anatol*. Picturing Santa Claus emerging from a chimney at the beginning emphasized its seasonal quality. The gifts he left came to life and transitioned the story into fairyland where the Snow White story unfolded."

A reviewer in the *Iowa City Citation* wrote, "Marguerite Clark, second to none in popularity among the stars of the screen, is the star of the Famous Players adaptation of the popular fairy tale, *Snow White*, which is the Paramount Picture at the Englert Theater this week. This is not the first time that Miss Clark has played the charming role of Snow White, as she was the star of the stage version of the same tale, which created a veritable sensation at the Little Theater in New York under the direction of Winthrop Ames. The photoplay version of the Grimm Brother's fairy tale was produced under the direction of J. Searle Dawley whose artistic handling of *Little Lady Eileen, Mice and Men,* and other of Miss Clark's starring vehicles, arouses great expectation for this adaptation of a favorite fairy tale."

Snow White newspaper ad as it appeared in *Chillicothe Constitution.*

Marguerite Clark in *Snow White* (1916), in which Richard played the Prince. Walt Disney was so taken with this production as a youth that he chose to remake it as his first full-length animated feature.

Just a Song at Twilight (1922)
Dixie Film Company
Director: Burton L. King and Carlton S. King
Scenario: Henry Albert Phillips, based on *Just a Song at Twilight (Love's Old Sweet Song)*, a popular 1884 song, written by J. Clifton Bingham and James L. Molloy.
Length: 60 minutes
Cast: Evelyn Greeley, Pedro de Cordoba, Richard Barthelmess, Charles Wellesley, Nellie Grant, Frank Lyon
Synopsis: This story of long-lost relatives presumed dead follows Richard Barthelmess as George Turner and his attempt to find his father, Carlyle Turner. Word comes that Carlyle is still living, and his son goes in search. He finds work with Stephen Winter, a rich, former business associate of his father, and also begins a romance with his daughter, Lucy.

When George's step-father learns of his adopted son's romance, he expels the boy from his home, and soon regrets his actions. In a dream, he revisits earlier days when he vied with George's father for the affections of Lucy Lee, and recalls eloping with the girl. Lucy broke his heart when she realized her true love was for Carlyle, and in a flash of jealousy, he falsified murder charges against his rival. Carlyle was thrown in jail, after which Lucy died of a broken heart. Suddenly waking from his nightmare, he confesses to George, and has Carlyle pardoned in a surprise reconciliation. Lucy finds the way clear to marry George.

A reviewer in *Variety* wrote, "It is a pretty, heart-interest tale, well acted and photographed, with excellent direction throughout. But, the titles are not always sufficiently explanatory — especially in the first reel — to enable one to follow the story with the proper degree of certainty. This could be easily remedied. The drama is described as retrospective in that the second, third, and fourth reels are a flashback of what transpired eighteen years previously, taking the form of a dream in which the conscience of the man who committed a wrong is awakened to a realization of evil and his efforts to make every restitution possible."

The Moral Code (1917)
Erbograph
Director: Ashley Miller
Screenplay: Henry Albert Phillips and Ashley Miller
Length: 5 reels
Cast: Anna Q. Nilsson, Walter Hitchcock, Richard Barthelmess, Florence Hamilton.
Synopsis: Gilbert Gerard, a man of high morals, marries Gracia Brown to save the honor of his family after Gary Miller, an unscrupulous nephew, has disgraced Gracia. Gracia is unable to understand her husband's high moral standards, and refused to accept the sacred marriage vows.

Gilbert meets another woman, Jean Hyland, and falls in love with her. When Gary returns, Gilbert convinces Gracia to run away with him. When Jean overhears the conversation, she tries to convince Gracia to thwart their plan and remain faithful to her husband. In spite of her entreaties, Gracia and Gary plan to elope, forcing Gerard to realize that he is not responsible for the actions of his nephew. He orders both lovers from his home, files for divorce, and marries Jean.

A reviewer for the *Fort Wayne News* wrote, "This is a powerful screen presentation of a very real, vital problem of everyday life in England and America, where regulation of the marriage relation is in accordance with laws and traditions of the past, not the living present."

The Eternal Sin (1917)
Herbert Brenon Film Company
Director: Herbert Brenon
Screenplay: George Edwardes-Hall with adaptation by Herbert Brenon
Length: 6 reels
Cast: Florence Reed, William E. Shay, Stephen Gratton, Henry Armetta, Richard Barthelmess, Florence Hamilton, Alexander Shannon, A. G. Parker, M. J. Briggs, Edward Thorne, Elmer Patterson, Anthony Merlo, William Welsh, Juliet Brenon, Henrietta Gilbert, Henry Armetta, Jane Fearnley, Charles Ray Howard

Florence Reed, the star of *The Eternal Sin*, won a considerable reputation on the stage long before she appeared in the movies. She played opposite Walker Whiteside in *The Typhoon*, and later was featured in *The Yellow Ticket*, a melodrama that ran for some time at the Eltinge Theater in New York. Then, she was in an all-star revival of *A Celebrated Case*. During the 1917 season, she played a temptress in a spectacular production of *The Wanderer*. She enjoyed particularly strong roles, and has this type of role as Lucretia Borgia in *The Eternal Sin*.

SYNOPSIS: Lucretia Borgia has a son, Gennaro, who grows to manhood unaware of the identity of his mother. Lucretia has married the Duke of Ferrara. One horrible day, five conspirators, the fathers of Gennaro's dearest friends, kill her brother. Lucretia discovers their deed, and has the old men tortured to death.

Gennaro and his companions journey to Lucretia's domain. There, she sees her grown son for the first time. Her husband, the Duke, sees them together, and thinking he is one of his wife's lovers, poisons Gennaro. Lucretia discovers his act and administers an antidote, which saves his life. Bent on revenge, Lucretia schemes to poison the five friends of her son for the sins of their fathers. All are poisoned at a dinner. Her son arrives uninvited and unwittingly takes some of the food with the poison. Again, Lucretia begs him to take the antidote, but her refuses. In a fury of revenge, Gennaro stabs his Lucretia. As he lies dying, he learns that she was his real mother.

Variety said the film was "Gorgeous and thrilling." The premier at the Broadway attracted an audience that blocked Broadway for half an hour before curtain time. The review went on to note, "No more imposing galaxy of professionals had been seen in one production in some time."

According to a review in *Variety*, "The acting was at all times distinctive and almost flawless. Even the camera man was inspired with the splendors of his opportunities and admirably caught the right textures of soft shadings and blending lights at precisely the articulations necessary for dramatic effect and emphasis . . . ." The review went on to praise Richard in the role of the son of Lucretia Borgia, who, in the story, is trapped by Lucretia's husband thinking he is capturing his wife's secret lover. Lucretia finds herself face to face with the problem of either, confessing her past, permitting the murder of her son before her eyes, or tricking him to freedom. "The suspense of the pictured drama up to this situation is insistent and of cumulative intensity," the review commented. Florence Reid as Lucretia was said to be too young for "an offspring even so youthful as the handsome, tense and always sincere son attractively played by Richard Barthelmess."

The Eternal Sin newspaper advertisement as it appeared in *The Mansfield News.*

Richard Barthelmess, Florence Reed, and William Shaw in Herbert Brenon's *The Eternal Sin* (1917).

THE VALENTINE GIRL (1917)
FAMOUS PLAYERS
DIRECTOR: J. SEARLE DAWLEY
SCENARIO: J. SEARLE DAWLEY, BASED ON A STORY BY LAURA SAWYER
LENGTH: 5 REELS
CAST: Marguerite Clark, Richard Barthelmess, Adolphe Menjou, Frank Losee, Kathryn Adams, Maggie Holloway Fisher, Edith Campbell Walker, Charles Sutton
SYNOPSIS: This film was a "personality vehicle" for the popular star, Marguerite Clark, and as such, brought a mere thread of a plot to serve as an excuse for a series of pretty scenes featuring the star in her most artless and child-like moods. In the first half of the picture, she plays Marian Morgan, a little girl of twelve, and managed to both look and act the age with astonishing skill and naturalness. She appeared as the one guileless figure in a luxurious gambling house of which her father is the head. The lovely girl finds the children living next door refuse to play with her because of her inherited association with vice. In her loneliness, she invents imaginary playmates for herself out of the pages of her history book, and gravely poses as every imaginable character from Queen Elizabeth to Joan of Arc.

After her father's arrest and imprisonment, she is adopted by a clergyman's family and grows to womanhood in the shadow of the village church. There, she meets again her childhood sweetheart, and concludes the story in a pretty romance. A raid on the gambling house and a rescue form shipwreck in a picturesque beach scene serve to speed up the saccharine story. The Valentine idea is woven throughout the entire story with an appropriate accompaniment of candy hearts, forget-me-nots, and other sentimental symbols portrayed against dainty and sentimental symbols.

Richard appeared as her childhood sweetheart, and director Dawley made sure he was shown in an unusually attractive manner.

A reviewer in the *Fort Wayne News* wrote, "Delightful, wholesome and refreshing is the proper way to describe *The Valentine Girl,* the newest Paramount production starring the darling of the screen, Marguerite Clark, at the Jefferson again today. This feature pleased immensely the overflow audiences yesterday, and the smiling faces as the patrons left the theater were a sure indication that they had been agreeably entertained. Dainty little Miss Clark always assures us a good picture, but in *The Valentine Girl*, she goes even beyond the limits of what is expected. In short, to sum it up quickly, this is a splendid offering, out of the ordinary, above the average, and entirely satisfying."

Variety said the film, about a little girl transplanted into a home of wealth, and growing up into a beautiful young woman with a cloud over her life, was one of Marguerite Clark's most pleasing productions. "The piece is full of dainty charm," the review said, "and some fine double exposure work is shown, together with beautiful exteriors and wets which are beyond the ordinary for richness. It is a high class production, above the usual Paramount standard."

The Empire Theater distributed to patrons this advertising card for the J. Searle Dawley film, *The Valentine Girl* (1917).

Frank Losee, Marguerite Clark, and Maggie Holloway Fisher in J. Searle Dawley's *The Valentine Girl* (1917).

The Soul of a Magdalen (1917)
Metro
Director: Burton L. King
Story and Scenario: Lillian Case Russell
Length: 5 reels
Cast: Olga Petrova, Wyndham Standing, Richard Barthelmess, Mahlon Hamilton, Mathilde Brundage, Violet Reed, Gene Burnell, Francis Walton, Boris Korlin, Frank Moore, H. Cooper Cliffe
Synopsis: Olga Petrova was presented by Metro in this vehicle that gave her the opportunity to pose as a young girl who has a hard struggle with the world in her efforts to support her sick mother and invalid brother. Although her career is perfectly innocent, the girl deliberately blackens her own character in order to save her sweetheart's sister from making a false alliance.

When the film was first released, it ran into censorship problems. In an article in the *Mansfield News*, it was reported, "*The Soul of a Magdalene* has been held up by state censors. It is an Olga Petrova feature of the 'easiest way' type, which apparently makes the 'way' too realistic. There's too much Magdalene and not enough soul in it to suit the state board...."

Two months later, the same publication reported, "According to announcements today, Olga Petrova, who a few months ago joined Paramount, has severed her connections. Neither the company nor the star have stated just what they will do next."

In a related item, it was also reported that *The Soul of a Magdalene* was being scheduled for previews, apparently having soothed the ruffled feathers of State censors.

The film suffered at the hands of censors. *Variety* said in its review, "It is not stated who cut, assembled, or wrote the captions for this feature, but whoever did the job should be taken out to some quiet alley sometime between midnight and dawn and left there for the police to find in the morning, and if the job was well done, it would be a case for the coroner. Seldom, if ever, has there been a picture so badly butchered during its final stages as this one . . . the director managed to eke out a fair production, although some of the lighting and business was not just what it should have been, but even at this, the picture would have gotten by on the strength of its star, had not the final stages of assembling and titling been so frightfully mishandled." The performances were said to have been weak from the leading man and heavy right on down to the smallest bits. No prints are known to have survived.

The Soul of a Magdalen newspaper ad as it appeared in *The Mansfield News*.

Eugene Brewster, Olga Petrova, and Richard Barthelmess scouting locations at the time of the making of Burton L. King's *The Soul of a Magdalen* (1917).

THE STREETS OF ILLUSION (1917)
PATHÉ / ASTRA FILM CO.
DIRECTOR: WILLIAM PARKE
SCENARIO: Phillip Bartholomae from a story by Andrew Soutar
CAST: Gladys Hulette, Richard Barthelmess, J. H. Gilmore, William Parke, Jr., William Dudley, Warren Cook, Doris Grey, Kathryn Adams, Gerald Badgley, William P. Burt, Logan Paul, William Yearance, William Marion
SYNOPSIS: Beam, a pretty girl, watches her only brother, Robert, enlist in the war. After he has gone, she struggles to support her blind father, and their financial condition forces her to rent a vacant room in the house. Beam hears from friends that her brother has deserted, but refuses to tell their father. Instead, she regales him with cheerful stories of her brother's heroism.

Richard Barthelmess plays Donald Morton, a wealthy young man who helps the impoverished family. Beam's brother suddenly returns, and while she is concealing the boy in an upstairs room, Donald arrives and discovers her in an embrace. Beam lies, saying he is a new boarder. When a real boarder assaults the girl, Robert rescues her. The blind father hears his son's voice, and is overjoyed the hero has returned and saved his daughter. At that moment, Robert's commanding officer covers his desertion by trumping up a furlough, and then arrives to notify the boy to report back to camp. Robert returns to the army with his honor intact, Donald learns that Beam has been faithful to him, and all ends happily.

A reviewer for the *Fort Wayne News* wrote, "... Gladys Hulette's best picture yet ... a charming little girl who is also an artist. She has made a big reputation on the screen, and has also been featured on the stage, and her pictures are produced under the direction of a man who is becoming known as one of the master directors of the business, William Parke. He has had his own theatrical companies and he knows what he is doing. That is why he and Miss Hulette make one hit after another."

Richard Barthelmess, Gladys Hulette, and J. H. Gilmore in the Pathé film, *Streets of Illusion* (1917).

CAMILLE (1917)
FOX
PRODUCER: WILLIAM FOX
DIRECTOR: J. GORDON EDWARDS
SCENARIO: Adrian Johnson, based on a play by Alexander Dumas fils
CAST: Theda Bara, Alan Roscoe, Walter Law, Glen White, Claire Whitney, Richard Barthelmess, Alice Gale
SYNOPSIS: Camille, a Parisian courtesan, falls in love with a promising young man, Armand Duval. The young man's father secretly visits the girl, begging her to leave the boy and keep him from ruining his success as a career man. Reluctantly, she agrees to his demand, and after writing him a letter, ends the relationship and returns to the gay life in Paris. Once there, illness and poverty overwhelm her. Armand returns to her, learns of her pact with his father, and reclaims his love, only to find her die in his arms.

A reviewer in the *Sheboygan Press* wrote, "... this unusually beautiful photo-drama is wonderfully interpreted by the incomparable Bara. The story of Camille is familiar. It deals with the life story of a lovable adventuress, whose real womanly qualities are brought out under the influence of her love for Armand Duval, a young French student. There are many vivid scenes, which will fascinate the picture-loving public. Miss Bara is particularly fascinating in her latest picturization."

Another reviewer from the *Sheboygan Press* wrote, "Theda Bara, the William Fox star, is the offering ... this picturization gives Miss Bara's abilities the fullest scope, and she is at her best. Her play of emotions, as she picturizes the life of the famous French grizette, is vivid and real. Only Theda Bara can put just the brilliant touch to her own conception of *Camille*. *Camille* is very vicious, very beautiful and a very celebrated member of the French underworld, with a string of wealthy lovers, and all the usual ways of a woman of her class. She is woman enough to really fall in love once and for all. But at the end of it all, she dies a tragic death, leaving only the remembrance of her brilliant if unpleasant reputation and her love for Armand."

"Theda Bara," wrote a reviewer from the *Indianapolis Star*, "it is said, had always desired to play the famous *Camille* from the time of her ascendancy as a screen star, and William Fox, after months of preparation, gave Miss Bara her desire. He surrounded her with a large and capable company and with spectacular scenic effects, and produced the great play ... Miss Bara's work is forceful and convincing, and her supporting company is entirely capable."

BAB'S DIARY (1917)
FAMOUS PLAYERS
PRODUCER: ADOLPH ZUKOR
DIRECTOR: J. SEARLE DAWLEY
SCENARIO: Martha D. Foster and Margaret Turnbull from a story by Mary Roberts Reinhardt
LENGTH: 5 REELS
CAST: Marguerite Clark, Richard Barthelmess, Nigel Barrie, Leonora Morgan, Frank Losee, Isabel O'Madigan, Helen Green, Guy Coombs, John B. O'Brien, George O'Dell

Camille newspaper advertisement as it appeared in the *Fredericksburg News*.

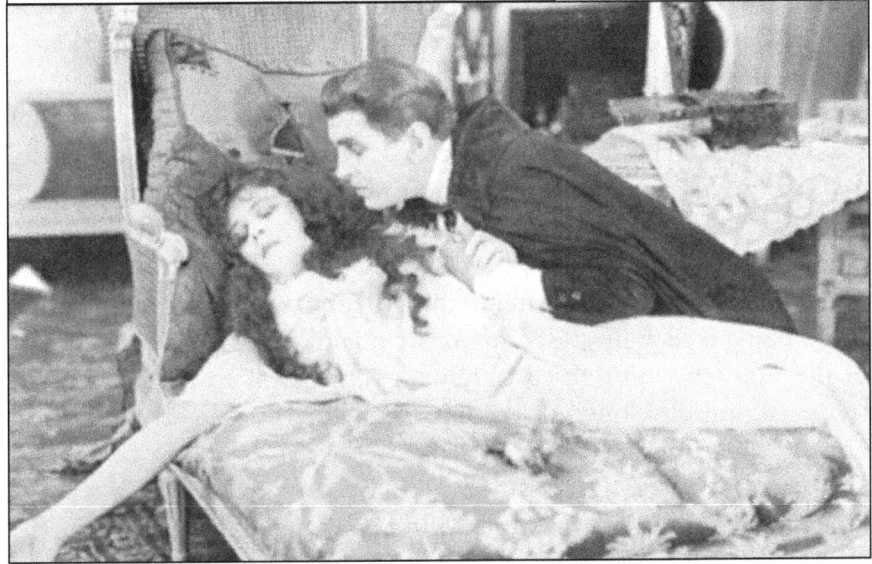

Theda Bara as Marguerite and Albert Roscoe as Armand in William Fox's *Camille* (1916), in which Richard played as an extra. *Variety* said Bara was "altogether too voluptuous and healthy" for the tragic heroine.

SYNOPSIS: Bab returns from a boarding school for the Christmas holiday. She finds her family excited about the impending wedding of her older sister, Leila, to Carter Brooks. In the uproar of preparations, Bab finds herself shunted aside and treated as a little girl. To remedy the situation, she takes a photograph of a popular matinee idol and invents a story that he is her own suitor, Harold Valentine.

When her sister's brother, Carter, recognizes the actor in the photo, he turns the tables on Babs, and invites the actor to visit their home during a party. When he arrives, Bab, bewildered and frightened, decides she must recover the letters she wrote the actor. She quietly leaves the party, blunders into the young man's apartment, sets off a burglar alarm, and is arrested. She is returned home, and after learning a lesson about deception, is sent back to boarding school.

Variety, in their review of the film, said the film deserved a tribute for handling a subject of light texture in a very artistic manner. "*Bab's Diary* radiates youth," the review noted. "It is light, adventuresome, gay, and one fairly swings along with the picture as its scenes reveal and diffuse the spirit of they to whom the world is big and bright and shining, who bask in the silver lining, caring naught of the clouds that enshroud it. Paramount has provided everything essential to ensure a faithful production. . . ."

A reviewer for the *Iowa Citizen* wrote, ". . . a novelty that is unique in its interest."

The *Newark Advocate* reported large crowds filled the auditorium for showings. Their reviewer wrote, ". . . Miss Clark is truly delightful and we might say it's one of the best pictures that she has appeared in so far — it is the sort of a picture that is sure to pull 'em away from the fireside. Miss Clark is always clever, but the writer can't remember having seen her in anything better than the present picture she is being screen in. Based upon the quaintly misspelled statements of the sub-deb who refused to remain subservient to the older sister, we see action developed in this picture, which is delightfully farcical and, at the same time, is kept from being too broad to be refined and capable of being classified as light comedy. *Bab's Diary* is a chuckle film, one of the smiley kind that makes you feel like the world is worth while again, no matter how grouchy you might have been when you arrived at the theater."

BAB'S BURGLAR (1917)
FAMOUS PLAYERS
PRODUCER: ADOLPH ZUKOR
DIRECTOR: J. SEARLE DAWLEY
SCENARIO: Adrian Johnson and Margaret Turnbull, based on a story by Mary Roberts Reinhart
LENGTH: 5 REELS

Bab's Diary newspaper advertisement as it appeared in the *Indianapolis Star*.

Richard Barthelmess as Tommy Gray smokes his first cigar, and Marguerite Clark as "Babs" thinks he has been poisoned in *Bab's Diary* (1917).

CAST: Marguerite Clark, Richard Barthelmess, Nigel Barrie, Frank Losee, Leonora Morgan, Isabel O'Madigan, Helen Green, Guy Coombs, George O'Dell, William Hinckley, Daisy Belmore

SYNOPSIS: Bab Archibald returns home on vacation from her boarding school. Her father deposits $1,000 in her bank account, and admonishes her to budget the money wisely, as it is the entire allowance she will have for the next year. Determined to be a spendthrift, Bab's buys a car, which she accidentally smashes through a fence and into a milk wagon. She is arrested for speeding, and after settling her fines, leaves with a total of sixteen cents remaining from her thousand dollars.

To recoup her finances, Bab takes a job as a cab driver. After delivering one customer to his destination, Bab discovers he has left behind a floor plan of her family home. She assumes the man is a burglar planning to rob the family. She waits at the house, and when she sees him through the window, locks all the doors and summons the family by firing a revolver. Racing to the rescue, the family explains the man is her sister's suitor coming to elope.

Variety, in its review, wrote, "It isn't the easiest thing in the world to sustain interest in a comedy for a full length feature, but the *Bab* series, judging by the way the audience receive them, seem to be doing so. The usual high grade Famous Players casting, production and photography."

A reviewer for the *Newark Advocate*, wrote, "Marguerite Clark is a winning Bab. She charms the audience at the Strand Theater as a Sub-Debutant. Altogether it is one of the freshest and most entertaining stories in which Miss Clark has ever trained her charms on an audience. *Bab's Burglar* is a story particularly adapted for screen production, and it makes delightful entertainment."

NEARLY MARRIED (1917)
GOLDWYN PICTURE CORPORATION
PRODUCER: SAMUEL GOLDWYN
DIRECTOR: CHESTER WITHEY
SCENARIO: Lawrence McCloskey from a story by Margaret Mayo
LENGTH: 6 REELS
CAST: Madge Kennedy, Frank Thomas, Mark Smith, Hedda Hopper, Richard Barthelmess, Alma Tell
SYNOPSIS: Betty Griffon is all set to marry Harry Lindsey. When she learns that her brother, Dick, is to be late for the ceremony, the wedding is delayed. After waiting a while, they are finally married, but immediately learn the brother was late because he has been injured in an accident. Betty refuses to leave on her honeymoon until her brother is fully recovered. When Harry objects, Betty says he is insensitive. She demands a divorce, and Harry hires his friend,

Marguerite Clark and Richard Barthelmess in *Bab's Burglar* (1917).

Tom Robinson, to testify as a correspondent. The couple reconciles just as a separation is granted. They realize they love each other and decide to remarry, but are prevented by a clause in the divorce papers forbidding Harry from marrying again. Love triumphs in the end, as they circumvent the New York law and are legally married in nearby New Jersey.

The most difficult type of film to sustain through a feature-length production is a farce. *Variety* said *Nearly Married* was one film demonstrating that such a thing was possible. "The complications are so fast that you are never once tired," the review stated. "You just smile and laugh alternately for a little more than an hour and when it is all over you feel that you could stand a little more just as good." The review went on to say it was "admirably acted, produced, directed, and photographed."

A reviewer in the *Mansfield News* wrote, "There's an unusually good comedy at the Majestic today where Madge Kennedy's latest screen effort, *Nearly Married*, which was taken from the stage success by Edgar Selwyn, is being shown for the final time. Miss Kennedy will be remembered for her work in *Baby Mine*, which was shown several weeks ago but in some ways, *Nearly Married* proves superior. It puts the little star of Goldwyn in a most entertaining and satisfying role and for actual entertainment will be found difficult to duplicate."

A reviewer for the *Coshocton Tribune* wrote, "*Nearly Married*, as the second starring vehicle of Madge Kennedy, is a worthy successor to *Baby Mine*, being a rapid-fire comedy with action from start to finish, and a swift succession of thrilling situations calculated to entertain a nation. The various happenings, involving a young bridal couple who become separated within a couple of minutes after the wedding ceremony, is performed."

FOR VALOUR (1917)
EASTERN TRIANGLE
DIRECTOR: ALBERT PARKER
SCENARIO: Robert Shirley from a story by I. A. R. Wylie
CAST: Winifred Allen, Henry Weaver, Richard Barthelmess, Mabel Ballin
SYNOPSIS: A young Canadian woman, Melia Nobbs, works in a theater to support her brother, Henry, and her invalid father. Her brother finds work, but gives in to the temptation to steal some cash from his employer. His theft is discovered, and when he faces arrest, his sister resorts to desperate measures to save him from ruin. While the star of the show for which she works is on stage dancing, she steals a similar amount from his belongings. Melia offers the money to Henry, but insists that he enlists in the army. Henry agrees, and no sooner does he go off to war than Melia is nabbed for the theft at the theater. Her father disowns her, and Melia faces prosecution. She refuses to reveal the reason for taking the money,

Nearly Married newspaper ad as it appeared in many newspapers around the country.

Madge Kennedy and Richard Barthelmess in *Nearly Married* (1917).

and is sent to prison. Henry bravely fights in France, suffers a battle wound, and returns wearing the Victoria Cross and minus one arm. He visits Melia in the prison hospital and finds her weak, worn, and overworked. Melia sees the medals her brother proudly wears, and realizes her sacrifice was for him and her country.

"*Variety* reviewed the film, and commented, "*For Valour* was well cast with Winifred Allen and Richard Barthelmess taking the leads in a story about a poor Canadian family lifted from the common place through the trials of war. Richard played Henry Nobbs who dons a uniform and goes overseas. In an engagement of battle, he drags his officer back from 'no man's land,' though he himself is sorely wounded. Because of his bravery, he loses an arm, but is given a lieutenant's rank and thus goes back home to his family."

Richard would win great acclaim some ten years later in a similar role in *The Patent Leather Kid*. Alan Dwan was a supervisor on the crew of this film. In 1928, director G. B. Samuelson remade the same story starring Dallas Cairns.

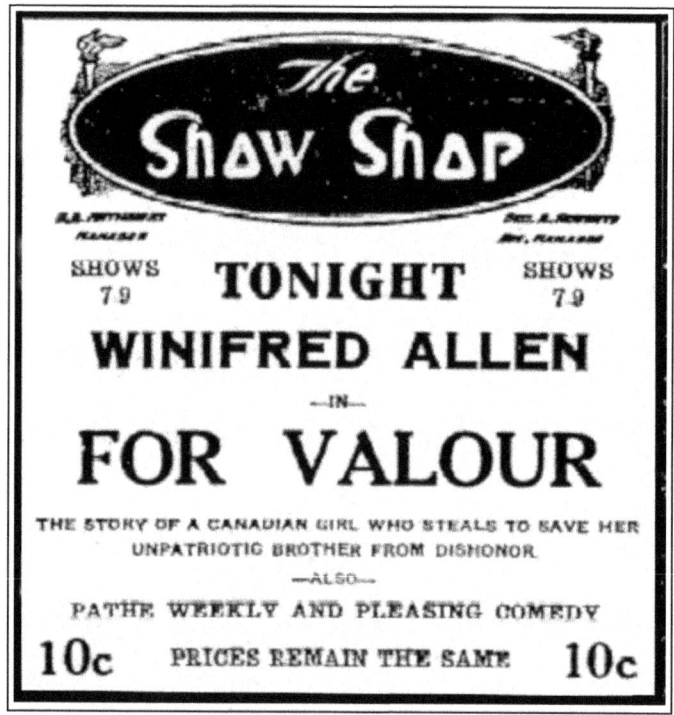

For Valour newspaper advertisement as it appeared in the *Middletown Press*.

Three scenes from Albert Parker's *For Valour* (1917), starring Richard Barthelmess, Mabel Ballin, Winifred Allen, and Henry Weaver.

THE SEVEN SWANS (1917)
FAMOUS PLAYERS
PRODUCER: ADOLPH ZUKOR
DIRECTOR: J. SEARLE DAWLEY
SCENARIO: J. Searle Dawley from the story by Hans Christian Anderson
LENGTH: 5 REELS
CAST: Marguerite Clark, Richard Barthelmess, William E. Danforth, Augusta Anderson, Edwin Denison, Daisy Belmore, Richard Allen, Jere Austin, Joseph Sterling, Frederick Merrick, Lee F. Daly, Stanley King, Gordon Dana, Jules Raucourt
SYNOPSIS: In a mythical kingdom, the Queen of the Bouncing Ball conspires to take over the land of the Seven Dials. With the aid of a witch, she transforms the seven princes of the kingdom into swans, and leads them far away from the court. Princess Tweedledee learns from the moon fairies of the fate fallen to her brothers, one of the princes, and goes to his aid.

The Princess finds the seven swans, and resolves to stay with them. While there, Prince Charming discovers her and falls madly in love. The moon fairies reappear and reveal that she can change her brothers back to human form if she will weave seven robes of nettle and cover the swans with them. They caution her of one condition: to make the magic work, she cannot speak to a human being. Prince Charming is puzzled by her refusal to speak to him during this time, and assumes she has lost her love for him. The Princess stays true to the condition of the magic and enforces the required dumbness. She returns to her native land, is accused of being a witch, and is sentenced to death.

Prince Charming comes to her rescue, at the last minute. The seven robes of nettle are quickly finished, thrown over the seven swans, and the Princes regain their human form. They all live happily ever after.

". . . the artistic quality of this picture is enhanced by excellent production direction, and photography . . . a study of infinite charm," wrote a reviewer for the *Washington Post*.

A reviewer from *Variety* admired the film, writing, "The production end of the feature is truly magnificent, and the direction and picturizing are very beautiful. Although released during the holiday time, when it is supposed to make a special appeal, the picture will be saleable in any season and may be depended upon to attract business to special children matinees."

Marguerite Clark and Richard Barthelmess in J. Searle Dawley's film of Hans Christian Anderson's *Seven Swans* **(1917).**

Sunshine Nan (1918)
Famous Players-Lasky-Paramount
Producer: Adolph Zukor
Director: Charles Giblyn
Scenario: Eve Unsell, based on *Calvary Alley*, a novel and story by Alice Hegan Rice
Length: 5 reels
Cast: Ann Pennington, Richard Barthelmess, Johnny Hines, Helen Tracey, Charles Eldridge, J. A. Furey, Mrs. Lewis McCord, Frank Losee
Synopsis: Nance Molloy lives in a home in a dingy alley near a cathedral. She is known for her cheerful disposition, in spite of the squalor of her surroundings, and her friends affectionately call her "Sunshine Nan."

A little rain falls in her life, however, due to her fondness for fighting with the cathedral choirboys. She and her pal, Dan Lewis, interfere in a family fight, and are blamed in part for the fracas. Both are sent to a reform school for five years.

Five years later, when Nance is reformed and released, she gains employment as a stenographer in the shoe factory owned by her father. Dan, also released, takes work in the factory's chemical department. While there, he invents a unique dye process. Another employee steals the formula and presents it to Nance's father as his own. Nance discovers him in the lab copying the formula, and a fight follows. Dan joins the struggle, which becomes violent, and chemicals are accidentally spilled. The lab erupts into a blaze of fire, Dan rescues Nance, and the plan to steal the formula is foiled.

When Nance and Dan are married, the town folk change the name of the alley to "Cathedral Court."

A reviewer for the *Lima Daily News* wrote, "Ann Pennington carries a pleasing personality that means much to the success of her characterization of Nan Molloy in her latest photoplay, *Sunshine Nan*. She not only gives the role a humorous finish, but also quaint touches of pathos that speak well for her versatility. While the story is a light one, it is admirably staged and directed. John Hines and Richard Barthelmess are prominent in support of the star."

Sunshine Nan newspaper ad as it appeared in the *Bridgeport Telegram*.

RICH MAN, POOR MAN (1918)
FAMOUS PLAYERS-LASKY-PARAMOUNT
PRODUCER: ADOLPH ZUKOR
DIRECTOR: J. SEARLE DAWLEY
SCENARIO: J. Searle Dawley from a novel by Maximilian Foster and a play by George Broadhurst
LENGTH: 5 REELS
CAST: Marguerite Clark, Richard Barthelmess, George Backus, Frederick Warde, J. W. Herbert, Augusta Anderson, Donald Clayton, William Wadsworth, Ottola Nesmith, Mary Davis, Winter Hall

Synopsis: Following the death of her mother, Betty Wynne takes work as a scullery maid in a boardinghouse. There, she meets one of the lodgers, Bayard Varick, and they fall in love.

Henry Mapleson, another lodger in the boardinghouse, is so enamored of Betty that he forges a document suggesting she is the long-lost granddaughter of millionaire, John Beeston. Betty is introduced to the old millionaire, now reduced to coldhearted bitterness, but he is soon softened by her sunny disposition.

Bayard harbors a long-standing belief that the millionaire ruined his father's business in a sour deal years earlier, and he refuses to visit Betty while she is in the rich man's house. Betty believes he no longer loves her, and agrees to marry the millionaire's cousin. Bayard discovers the truth of the forged document, speeds to the millionaire's estate, and reclaims his sweetheart. In a surprising turn of events, Bayard is revealed to be the millionaire's long-lost grandson.

Variety, said *Rich Man, Poor Man* was ". . . one of the best constructed dramas ever manufactured by a skilled playwright."

A reviewer in the *Trenton Evening Times* wrote, "Conveying the message that riches without love is a mockery . . . both the star and picture sustained expectations. Aside from the excellent characterization of Bab Wynne by Miss Clark, that of Frederick Warde, a crusty, drab and heartless multimillionaire, was a work of distinction. The photoplay was admirably displayed, and the musical accompaniment was artistic. Miss Clark's support was in every respect adequate. The other principal role was in the hands of Richard Barthelmess . . . ."

HIT-THE TRAIL HOLLIDAY (1918)
COHAN-ARTCRAFT
DIRECTOR: MARSHALL NEILAN
SCENARIO: John Emerson and Anita Loos, based on the play by George M. Cohan
CAST: George M. Cohan, Marguerite Clayton, Robert Broderick, Richard Barthelmess, Pat O'Malley, Russell Bassett, William Walcott, Estar Banks
SYNOPSIS: Billy Holiday, a bartender in a New York pub, is a teetotaler, but he serves drinks with a smile to a parade of steady customers. After watching the endlessly comical effect liquor has on people, he quits his job and decides to preach his new belief in abstinence to the entire world. Edith Jason, played by Marguerite Clayton, and her brother, Bobby, played by Richard Barthelmess, are agreeable to his ambition, but find his methods are too unorthodox. Undaunted, Billy continues his crusade, determined to overcome all obstacles until there is no one left who drinks.

Broadway star, George M. Cohan made his film debut in this picture. *Variety* said the film, made from a scenario by Anita Loos and John Emerson, the witty writers of comedies for Constance Talmadge and Douglas Fairbanks, had "a number of human touches such as a trip uptown on the subway, the stopping to drop a penny in the vending machines for a piece of gum, which strikes home to New Yorkers if not to picture patrons in other communities . . . it is almost a comedy, and should please wherever shown. The star registers excellently, and is supported by an admirable company of players. The titles cannot help but entertain."

A reviewer for the *Lincoln Daily Star* wrote, "If you want to travel a trail of laughter that is one continuous joy ride from curtain to curtain, hit the trail . . . and see George M. Cohan's newest comedy . . . it's a laughing journey all the way. The new piece is a typical American comedy in Cohan's best vein. It introduces a number of quaint country-folk characters, the best bartender in all Yorkdom, who, in his new environment, takes sides with the Prohibition Party and organizes a temperance campaign that puts the boozers to rest. This particular Billy Holliday route is all laughter."

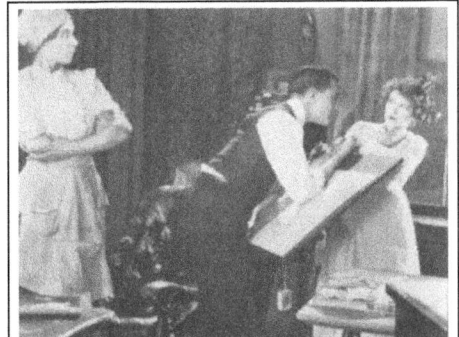

Richard Barthelmess and Marguerite Clark in *Rich Man, Poor Man* (1918).

Hit-the-Trail Holiday (1918) starred George M. Cohan (BOTTOM), and featured (TOP) Marguerite Clayton, Russell Bassett, and Richard Barthelmess with Cohan in a film about a bartender turned temperance champion.

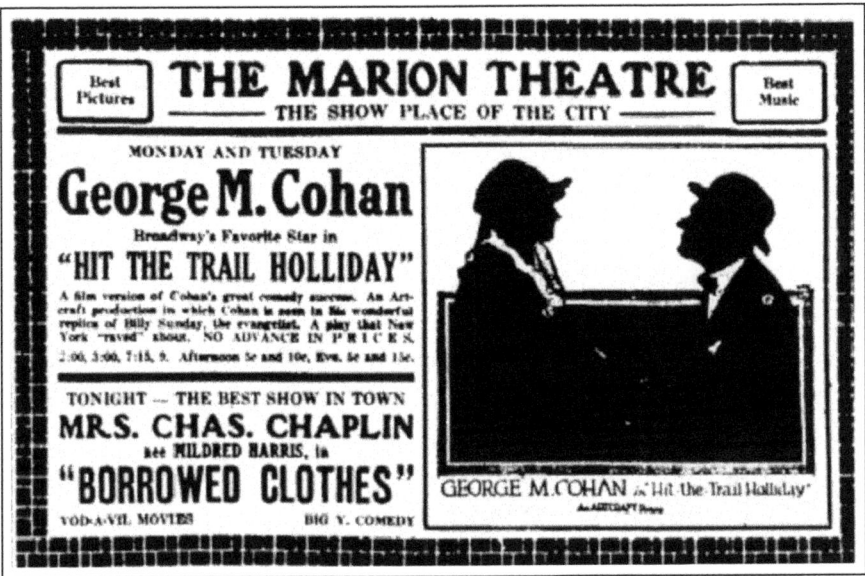

Hit-the-Trail Holiday newspaper advertisement as it appeared in the *Marion Star*.

WILD PRIMROSE (1918)
VITAGRAPH INC.
PRODUCER: ALBERT E. SMITH
DIRECTOR: FREDERICK A. THOMSON
SCENARIO: A. Van Buren Powell, based on a story by Joseph Franklin Poland
LENGTH: 5 REELS
CAST: Gladys Leslie, Richard Barthelmess, Eulalie Jensen, Charles Kent, Claude Gillingwater, Ann Warrington, Arthur Lewis, Bigelow Cooper
SYNOPSIS: Primrose Standish, the daughter of a wealthy Northerner and his untutored Southern wife, grows up in the care of her uncle because her father chose to desert the family. She is unaware that her father left his wife shortly after her birth to take up with a haughty but cultured woman.

Primrose is well reared by her uncle, and becomes a refined and educated young lady. As the years pass, Standish longs for his daughter and sends for her, but he is unaware of the deep resentment she feels for him. In a surprising turn of the tables, Primrose decides to visit her father in the guise of an uncouth mountain girl.

While shocking her father with outrageous behavior, a young man, Jack Wilton, who has been Standish's ward, falls in love with her. His attraction is from afar, for years earlier, in a moment of drunken infatuation, he married a dancer named Marie.

Financial reversals mount for Standish, and Newton, a broker to whom he owes money, demands the hand of Primrose in marriage as repayment. Standish rejects Newton, and reveals her true self at a ball. She offers to solve her father's financial problems by giving him some of her rich oil lands. After Standish has repaid Newton, his secretary recognizes Marie as his long-lost wife. Jack, suddenly free from his first hasty marriage, is free to follow his heart and marry Primrose.

A reviewer for the *Oxnard Courier* wrote, ". . . one of the best Miss Leslie has had since she became a star."

Variety's reviewer wrote that the story of this Vitagraph feature ". . . excels more in the manner of unfolding than in the plot itself. The company is unusually good, especially Gladys Leslie as Primrose and Richard Barthelmess as Jack."

Wild Primrose advertisement as it appeared in the *Sandusky Star Journal*.

The Hope Chest (1919)

Paramount-Famous Players
Producer: D. W. Griffith
Director: Elmer Clifton
Scenario: M. M. Stearns, from a story by Mark Lee Luther
Length: 5 reels
Cast: Dorothy Gish, Richard Barthelmess, George Fawcett, Sam De Grasse, Kate Toncray, Carol Dempster, Bertram Grassby
Synopsis: Sheila Moore, the daughter of an ex-vaudeville actor, Lew Moore, is forced to work as a waitress in the candy shop of a chocolate manufacturer. While behind the counter, she delights customers with her comical antics and charms Tom Ballantyne, the son of the proprietor. They fall in love and soon marry, but Tom fear's his parents will object, so they keep their marriage a secret. Sheila's father insists they inform Tom's parents, and the young couple agree. Unfortunately, when Tom breaks the news, his parents react with the expected anger, and Tom, equally angry at their attitude, leaves home.

Sheila remains in their home as their ward on the condition that she keeps the marriage and her vaudevillian heritage a secret. When she visits her family in a theater, the Ballantynes discover her. In a moment of exasperation, Sheila vents her anger at the snobbish family, and returns to her father's home with Tom in tow. In the end, the two families reconcile.

"*The Hope Chest* is an amusing photoplay which must be considered mostly farce if considered as anything at all," reviewed the *New York Times*. "Dorothy Gish is as eloquent with face, hands, arms, and every motion as ever. She is altogether a fascinating young person, and has a rare gift for putting life into the characters she assumes, even when they are impossible. In *The Hope Chest*, she is adequately supported by George Fawcett, Richard Barthelmess, and others."

Variety wrote, "Dorothy Gish is in her happiest vein in this five-reel Paramount feature taken from the story by Markee Lee Luther . . . Richard Barthelmess is the hero son of the millionaire chocolate manufacturer, and gives a very likeable performance. He is a good looking young chap, has a fine screen appearance, and can act."

Two scenes from Elmer Clifton's *The Hope Chest* (1918) starring Dorothy Gish, Richard Barthelmess, and George Fawcett.

The Hope Chest newspaper advertisement as it appeared in the *Mansfield News*.

BOOTS (1919)
FAMOUS PLAYERS-LASKY
PRODUCER: D. W. GRIFFITH
DIRECTOR: ELMER CLIFTON
SCENARIO: M. M. STEARNS
CAST: Dorothy Gish, Richard Barthelmess, Fontaine La Rue, Edward Peil Sr., Kate V. Toncray, Ramond Cannon
SYNOPSIS: President Wilson has a planned summit meeting with King George in London. A Bolshevist group, headed by Mme. De Valdee, follows this upcoming meeting and plots to assassinate the world leaders. When the meeting place is announced, Mme. De Valdee is sent in disguise to pose as a sculptress while the planned conspiracy develops.

Boots, a maid at an old inn, is in love with a boarder, Everette White. She loves to read romantic books, and is blissfully unaware that Everett is actually a detective for Scotland Yard assigned to infiltrate the Bolshevist conspiracy and watch Mme. De Valdee. When Boots discovers Everett in the arms of the sculptress, she vents her indignation by gathering up all her romantic books and attempts to bury them in the cellar. While there, she discovers an underground tunnel connected to the place where President Wilson and King George meet. Boots overhears the planned assassination conspiracy, and reveals the secret tunnel to Everett. Scotland Yard captures the criminals, insuring the safety of the world, and Boots wins Everett's love.

A review in the *New York Times* wrote, "Boots, bombs, and Bolsheviki are brought together for the benefit of Dorothy Gish in a comedy at the Rialto this week. The name of the comedy is *Boots*, and it is also the heroine's name, because she is a slavey in an English inn and has to polish the footwear — when she can take her eyes from a romantic novel that ends with, 'I love you. Kiss me. And then she died.' *Boots* is delightful. Miss Gish can make a motion of hand or foot, a look, a leap, or a fall through the floor more amusing than almost any other screen actress known, and in her present film she keeps the spectators smiling or laughing all the time. She is excellently assisted by Richard Barthelmess, Fontine La Rue, Edward Peil, and Kate V. Toncray. Elmer Clifton, who directed the production, made many effective pictures."

A reviewer writing in the *Daily Kennebec Journal* said, "Dorothy Gish in *Boots* was a riot, and this lady has certainly a big following!"

THE GIRL WHO STAYED AT HOME (1919)
FAMOUS PLAYERS-LASKY-ARTCRAFT
PRODUCER: D. W. GRIFFITH
DIRECTOR: D. W. GRIFFITH
SCENARIO: Stanner E. V. Taylor and D. W. Griffith
CAST: Carol Dempster, Robert Harron, Richard Barthelmess, Adolph Lestina, Frances Parks, George Fawcett, Kate Bruce, Edward Peil, Sr., Clarine Seymour, Tully Marshall, David Butler, Joseph Scott, Syn De Conde, E. H. Crowder, General March

Boots newspaper advertisement as it appeared in the Sandusky Star Journal.

Dorothy Gish and Richard Barthelmess in Elmer Clifton's Boots (1919).

SYNOPSIS: Richard Barthelmess plays Ralph Grey, a young man who visits his father, a shipbuilder, in France. Ralph meets Blossom, the granddaughter of his father's friend, and falls in love with her, but finds Blossom is engaged to a French nobleman, Monsieur Le France.

When hostilities break out in the World War, Ralph enlists, while his brother, Jim, is drafted. After trying to get out of serving, Jim gets a promise of faithfulness from his sweetheart, a cabaret dancer known as Cutie Beautiful, and goes to a training camp where he quickly matures and accepts his responsibility to his country.

Both brothers are in the same regiment and serve admirably. Blossom's chateau is attacked and her fiancé is killed. Caught in war's grip, she saves a German officer, kills another one about to rape her, and then dies.

At the war's end, heroism honors are bestowed on Ralph. Blossom's grandfather rallies behind his former country, and flies the American flag to welcome the Americans to France, while both brothers find happiness and marriage with the women they left behind.

A reviewer for the *New York Times* wrote:

"D. W. Griffith never produces what, judged against the field of photoplays, could be called a poor work. His power of making pictures is too great and by now too instinctively self-assertive to permit his falling below the average of others . . . It is a pleasure, therefore, to record that his latest work, *The Girl Who Stayed at Home*, at the Strand this week, satisfies every expectation. Judged by the Griffith standard, it is good. In some ways it even adds to its producer's long list of achievements."

"For one thing, Mr. Griffith does in it what he usually requires a longer photoplay for. He weaves several stories together in the same plot and preserves unity, at the same time using one story to heighten the suspense of another or ease its tension, and finally bringing all of his narrative threads to an even end. Mr. Griffith has been noted for his ability to handle plots of varied and extensive range, but he has never done it so well before in a photoplay designed for routine exhibition."

"And, of course, Mr. Griffith's subtlety and strength in making pictures, scenes of pure beauty and scenes of dramatic meaning, has not failed him. He is not only an artist in pictorial composition, but, by technical skill, often along original lines, he produces effects that others in time learn to imitate. No pictures seem to have the perspective of his. Some of them are practically stereoscopic. Also, in some way that has not yet become general, he dramatically emphasizes the central figures of a scene by throwing all its other objects so out of focus that they remain to provide suitable background and environment for the action without competing with it for the interest of the spectators. This is an artistic development of the close-up. In certain scenes it has all of the psychological effect of the close-up and something else. It makes the action more eloquent by keeping it in its environment, it preserves the continuity of the story, and it adds smoothness and beauty to the picture as a whole. And when Griffith does make a close-up, it is a soft, delicately shaded portrait."

The review concluded, "The cast of *The Girl Who Stayed At Home* is excellent without exception. Lillian Gish is missed, but Clarine Seymour, who takes the part she probably would have had, is never deficient, and Robert Harron, Richard Barthelmess, George Fawcett, Tully Marshall, Adolphe Lestina, Carol Dempster, Syn De Conde, Kate Bruce, and all of the others do everything that could be required of them."

The Girl Who Stayed at Home was one of several films Griffith made as a contribution to the war effort in 1918. As an official government war picture, its purpose was to popularize the selective draft amendment. Government dignitaries appeared as themselves in the film, and some scenes were shot in the House of Representatives, in training camps, and at local California draft boards.

A reviewer for the *Coshocton Tribune* wrote, "D. W. Griffith's great story of the home-coming tells it all. It takes you through trenches defended by women's souls and answers the question of the moment, "Did they win the great fight against temptation while HE was gone?"

The Girl Who Stayed at Home newspaper advertisement as it appeared in the *Elvira Chronicle*.

D. W. Griffith's *The Girl Who Stayed at Home* (1919) featured (LEFT) **Clarine Seymour and Robert Harron,** (TOP RIGHT) **Richard Barthelmess,** (BOTTOM RIGHT) **Robert Harron as the brother learning he has been drafted.**

THREE MEN AND A GIRL (1919)
FAMOUS PLAYERS-LASKY-PARAMOUNT
PRODUCER: ADOLPH ZUKOR
DIRECTOR: MARSHALL NEILAN
SCENARIO: Eve Unsell, from a play, *Three Bears*, by Edward Childs Carpenter

Cast: Marguerite Clark, Richard Barthelmess, Jerome Patrick, Percy Marmont, Ida Darling, Charles Craig, Sydney D'Albrook, Betty Bouton, Maggie H. Fisher

SYNOPSIS: Sylvia Weston , an attractive girl of marrying age, suffers the loss of her dear father. Well-meaning relatives take her future into their own hands and select for her a man to marry. Unfortunately, their choice of a groom is an animated rich man not to Sylvia's liking. On the day of her wedding, she panics at the altar. When the officiating ministers asks her to say, "I do," she hesitates a moment, and then blurts out truthfully, "I don't!" With that, the wedding is off, and comic situations are on.

Sylvia flees to Loon Lake where her father owned a country home. On arrival, she is surprised to find three plates of supper prepared and waiting, but no one home. She nibbles on some of the food, then falls asleep, exhausted from the ordeals of the day. A little while later, she is awakened by three men surprised to find her in the house. Sylvia learns the three men are hiding out from women in general, and each one tells her of their unfortunate romantic experiences. Sylvia's elderly nurse arrives, and the two women take up quarters in the caretaker's house behind the country home.

Richard Barthelmess plays Christopher Kent, the youngest of the three men. While at the country home, he is visited by a married woman who deceived him in earlier weeks. Sylvia has grown fond of Kent, and she jealously scares the woman away by claiming to be his fiancé. In time, the other two men grow fond of her, Kent and Sylvia find true love with each other, and are serenaded by the others.

A reviewer for the *New York Times* wrote, "Even with a restricted meaning, the word comedy may be applied to *Three Men and a Girl*, in which Richard Barthelmess, Percy Marmont, and Jerome Patrick are the three men, and Marguerite Clark is the girl . . . Situation! Several situations, a whole succession of them in fact — and all most excellently carried off by the three men and the girl in the cast. Marshall Neilan directed the production and Eve Unsell made the scenario from Edward Childs Carpenter's *Three Bears*. These two, with the four principal players and others who contributed anonymously to the composition of the comedy, have provided material to fill an enjoyable hour for anyone who likes wit and skill in pictures, acting, and lines. And there is beauty, too, in a number of the scenes."

A reviewer in the *Humeston New Era* wrote, " . . . a fine story and a wonderful little actress. You will enjoy this fine picture through every reel."

Three Men and a Girl **(1919) featured Richard Barthelmess with** (TOP) **Jerome Patrick and Marguerite Clark,** (CENTER LEFT) **Ida Darling, Percy Marmont, Marguerite Clark, Jerome Patrick,** (CENTER RIGHT) **Percy Marmont, Marguerite Clark, Jerome Patrick, and** (BOTTOM) **Marguerite Clark.**

Peppy Polly (1919)
Famous Players-Lasky-Paramount- New Art Film Company
Producer: Adolph Zukor
Director: Elmer Clifton
Scenario: M. M. Stearns, from a story by Marjorie Raynale.
Cast: Dorothy Gish, Richard Barthelmess, Edward Peil, Sr., Emily Chichester, Kate Toncray, Josephine Crowell
Synopsis: Dorothy Gish is Polly, a vibrant young woman with the comeback qualities of a rubber ball. While working as a stenographer for a reformer, she accompanies her employer to visit a reformatory. While there, Polly sees flagrant abuses of the prisoners, and gets fired up with the idea of exposing the institution and its shameful system.

She takes her concern to Judge Monroe, who points out that she'll need hard evidence to affect any change, and suggests that she infiltrate the institution as an inmate. Polly manages to get arrested by throwing a brick through a jeweler's window. She is sentenced to three years in the reformatory by a different judge who knows nothing of the circumstances. Steeling herself to the opportunity, she begins investigating conditions with a vengeance.

In no time, Polly gets in trouble with the prison matron who is trying to frame a case against the house physician, Dr. James Merritt, played by Richard Barthelmess. Along comes the reformatory doctor, played by Richard, to whom she loses her heart. The two of them join forces to expose the conditions of the institution.

When the matron has the good doctor arrested on a morals charge, Polly escapes and elicits the intervention of the governor. She learns that Judge Monroe has died, and left behind a diary. An examination of the pages of his notes reveals his arrangement with Polly to investigate the reformatory. The abuses of the institution are exposed, and in the end, Polly and Dr. Merritt are happy together.

The *New York Times* reviewer wrote, "*Peppy Polly* at the Rialto this week, is not exactly original in its plot, but its leading character is Dorothy Gish, the original and only, and the treatment of the story is original in its excellence . . . The reformatory in which much of the action occurs looks like a reformatory. The people in it look and act as one surmises the inmates of such a place to look and act. And there are many scenes; it's all action, and full of touches here and there that are the essence of a real photoplay. They do not need explanatory text, and most of them are not spoiled by its superfluous interposition . . . In the character of Polly, Miss Gish has one of her best parts. She does not fall into the clownishness that has marred some of her performances and she has opportunities for serious as well as comic pantomime, which do not escape her. She is usually amusing and diverting, sometimes sad and appealing, always intelligible and convincing. Richard Barthelmess and Kate V. Toncray are especially good in her support."

A reviewer for the *Clearfield Progress* wrote, "Who can conceive a more inimitable comedienne than this clever little lady? Here is a typical, zippical Dot Gish comedy with thrills and humor in every scene. Take an evening off, see *Peppy Polly*, and treat your face to an honest laugh you won't regret."

BROKEN BLOSSOMS (1919)
D. W. GRIFFITH-UNITED ARTIST CORP.
PRODUCER: D. W. GRIFFITH
DIRECTOR: D. W. GRIFFITH
SCENARIO: D. W. Griffith, based on a story in Thomas Burke's *Limehouse Nights*
CAST: Lillian Gish, Richard Barthelmess, Donald Crisp, Arthur Howard, Edward Peil, Sr., Norman Selby, George Beranger, Ernest Butterworth, Fred Hamer, Wilbur Higby, Moon Kwan, George Nichols, Karla Schramm
SYNOPSIS: A young Chinese man leaves his homeland in China to journey to America where he hopes to change Westerner's violent behavior through his gentle Buddhist teachings. Once in the new land, he finds himself relegated to the squalor of an ugly existence in the limehouse waterfront area of Chinatown.

Lucy Burrows, the frail, abused child of a brutish boxer, "Battling Burrows," wanders the same waterfront. One day, a lustful Chinaman victimizes Lucy, and the Yellow Man protects her. She returns home to prepare dinner for her father, and accidentally spills soup on his hand. In a fit of rage, he whips her mercilessly, and leaves their tiny flat. Lucy stumbles half unconscious into the

Peppy Polly newspaper ad as it appeared in the *Fort Wayne Journal*.

Three scenes from Elmer Clifton's *Peppy Polly* (1919), with Richard Barthelmess and Dorothy Gish.

streets and faints in the Yellow Man's shop. He again rescues her, cleanses her wounds, dresses her as a princess, and respectfully watches as she recovers. With him, Lucy experiences the first blush of love and affection she has ever known.

A friend of Battling Burrows discovers Lucy, and waits until the pugilist wins a big fight before he tells him the little girl is in the Yellow Man's home. Burrows drags the girl back to their flat, and then vents his still-hot temper on her with his prize-winning fists. In a panic, Lucy hides in a closet, but Burrows rips the door off its hinges and beats her to death. The Yellow man returns home to find her gone, rushes to their flat, and when he sees her dead, he shoots Burrows, carries Lucy back to his shop, and stabs himself to death.

In the *New York Times*, a reviewer wrote, "A screen tragedy — not a movie melodrama with an unhappy ending — but a sincere, human tragedy — that what D. W. Griffith has had the courage and the capacity to produce in *Broken Blossoms*, which opened his repertory season at the George M. Cohan Theater last night. Mr. Griffith chose a tragic story of impossible love, love impossible in this world of passions and prejudices and brutal forces; he absorbed it in its full meaning, recast it in his mind pictorially, translated it from the written words of the author into the scenes and action of a photoplay, added what was needed to make it live in pictures, left out what pictures could not have adequately expressed — and *Broken Blossoms* came to the screen, a masterpiece in moving pictures."

The review went on to comment, "This bare narration of the story cannot hope even to suggest the power and truth of the tragedy that Mr. Griffith has pictured. All of his mastery of picture-making, the technique that is preeminently his by invention and control, the skill and subtlety with which he can unfold a story — all the Griffith ability has gone into the making of *Broken Blossoms*. Many of the pictures surpass anything hitherto seen on the screen in beauty and dramatic force. The whole is a photoplay that cannot fail to impress anyone who looks at it in any mood short of the most resolute hostility."

"But though the photoplay is distinctly Mr. Griffith's achievement, it is not his alone. A number of unnamed persons must have contributed to it, in addition to the cast — and the cast was triumphantly equal to everything Mr. Griffith could expect. Leading all is Lillian Gish. Miss Gish has repeatedly, in varying roles, proved hers superior talent as a screen actress, but she has never been as human and at the same time as accomplished as in the character of the child."

"The role is so difficult as to be beyond the reach of almost any actress whose name comes to mind, but it was within Miss Gish's grasp. She was such a child as the poor little delicate blossom must have been. Donald Crisp was violently realistic as the pugilist, Richard Barthelmess was a sensitive, convincing yellow man, and Edward Peil, as a Chinese of another character, made an impressive contras."

"Mr. Barthelmess, as the Chinaman, is lofty, exalted immeasurably removed from a sordid world and its sordid passions, and a calm, implacable dispenser of fate in the last phase."

A reviewer for the *Coshocton Tribune* wrote, "Of extraordinary interest, not only to lovers of the motion picture, but likewise to all who appreciate the highest of art in all of its manifestations ... and of acting, let a word be added: Lillian Gish as 'The Girl' has reached a height of dramatic interpretation, the likes of which has never been seen on the screen

The front cover of the sheet music circulated during the release of D. W. Griffith's *Broken Blossoms* (1919).

Popular sheet music capitalizing on the film, *Broken Blossoms* (1919), became a staple in many homes with a piano.

Richard Barthelmess as the gentle Yellow Man in D. W. Griffith's *Broken Blossoms* (1919).

Two portraits of Richard Barthelmess in *Broken Blossoms* (1919).

before. This little artist has labored faithfully, steadily, with an understanding marvelous in one so young, and now she comes into her full glory in *Broken Blossoms*. 'The Chink' is played by Richard Barthelmess, and to his work the critics have paid high tribute likewise. To the telling of the love story in *Broken Blossoms*, it is said that both Miss Gish and Mr. Barthelmess have brought a never-to-be-forgotten artistry . . . *Broken Blossoms* should prove the crowning achievement in the splendid gallery of film presentations . . . ."

I'll Get Him Yet (1919)
Famous Players-Lasky-Paramount-New Art Film Company-Artcraft
Director: Elmer Clifton
Scenario: Harry Carr
Length: 5 reels
Cast: Dorothy Gish, Richard Barthelmess, George Fawcett, Ralph Graves, Edward Peil, Sr., Porter Strong, Wilbur Higby
Synopsis: Bradford Warrington Jones has a vivacious daughter, Susy, who is bored with men and more interested in being a businesswoman. When Jones faces high income taxes for his interurban line, he transfers ownership to Susy. To his surprise, she insists on running the business herself. Susy meets a reporter, Scoop McCreedy, and takes him to meet her father. Jones dislikes all men of the press, and throws him out. Scoop swears never to marry a rich girl, but Susy determines to persuade him to marry her. She proposes a novel scheme: they will live only on his earnings as a reporter.

One of Susy's suitors, the editor of the newspaper, is jealous of her newfound interest in Scoop, and fires the young man. In anger, Susy joins a citizen's group protesting the trolley's decision not to stop in the suburb where they live. Susy keeps secret the fact that she is the official owner of the line, and when her old suitor visits on business, she makes up explanations to allay Scoop's suspicions. Later, he catches up with the truth of her involvement, and Susy confesses. All ends well when Scoop becomes the general manager of the trolley line and comes to terms with his wife's wealth.

The *New York Times* reviewed the film with these comments, "The photoplay has the frankness to announce itself as a farce, but it fails to maintain farce speed. However, now and then, Miss Gish's irrepressible pantomime asserts itself and is amusing. Also George Fawcett and Richard Barthelmess seem incapable of dull acting. *I'll Get Him Yet* gave them a good chance for it, but they did not take it."

A reviewer for the *Lima News* wrote, "Hat's off, folks, and make way for the Queen of the Celluloid Comedy! That Dorothy Gish gal is some champ when it comes to putting over mannerisms on the screen and getting all the laughs in the world for the cute little

I'll Get Him Yet newspaper advertisement as it appeared in the *Lima News*.

I'll Get Him Yet (1919) was appropriately titled. Dorothy Gish had to wait until Marguerite Clark had featured Richard in six films before she could co-star with him.

touches and tricks she possesses. In her current release, *I'll Get Him Yet*, which opened at the Faurot this afternoon, she pulls everything in comedy, even to a little bit of the Chaplin walk, and each time that she delivers one of these little tricks there is a howl of laughter. *I'll Get Him Yet* is a corking story by Harry Carr, built to order for the star. It is of a rather farcical nature, handled with an eye toward speed in the action . . . ."

SCARLET DAYS (1919)
FAMOUS PLAYERS-PARAMOUNT-LASKY-ARTCRAFT
PRODUCER: D. W. GRIFFITH
DIRECTOR: D. W. GRIFFITH
SCENARIO: STANNER E. V. TAYLOR
CAST: Richard Barthelmess, Carol Dempster, Clarine Seymour, George Macquarrie, Creighton Hale, Ralph Graves, Eugenie Besserer, George Fawcett, Walter Long, Kate Bruce, Rhea Haines, Adolph Lestina, Herbert Sutch, J. Wesley Warner
SYNOPSIS: In California in 1849, a dance hall girl is saved from

Dorothy Gish with Richard Barthelmess in a scene from Elmer Clifton's *I'll Get Him Yet* (1919).

Dorothy Gish with Richard Barthelmess in a scene from Elmer Clifton's *I'll Get Him Yet* (1919).

hanging by the arrival of her daughter from Boston. Rosie Nell, the popular girl from the saloon, has spent years carefully saving gold from her customers to pay for her daughter's upbringing away from the wild West. When her daughter, Lady Fair, arrives, she attracts the attention of Alvarez, a Mexican bandit.

Alvarez is not alone in his desire for sweet little Lady Fair. A Virginia miner, John Randolph, vies for the girl's attention, and persuades the sheriff to allow her mother three days to visit with her daughter. Nell revels in the holiday with her daughter, but unfortunately, cannot keep the truth of her livelihood from her innocent daughter.

King Bagley, the proprietor of the saloon, decides to make hay from the attention Lady Fair draws, and attempts to force her to perform before the drunken miners. Alvarez and Randolph protect the women by hiding them in a cabin. A posse soon catches up with the bandit, and he gives himself up and his gang is disbanded. Tragedy strikes when Nell suddenly dies, but Alvarez returns to his first love, Chiquita, a Mexican dance hall girl. All ends well when Lady Fair gives her hand in marriage to Randolph.

A review in the *New York Times* expressed, "In *Scarlet Days* Mr. Griffith shows the Forty-niners and their life as many have tried with little or no success to imagine them. The characters come to life from stories once read and dimly remembered. They ride and should, laugh and fight, as they must do to preserve the glow of the year 1849 in American history. Sometimes they come rather harshly to life in Mr. Griffith's work and are not pretty and pleasant — as though they feel it a duty to remind the people of 1919 that they were not Sunday school children on a picnic. But for the most part the bold lines and strong colors with which they are stamped bring out the elemental virtues and vices popularly attributed to primitive people. The hand of Mr. Griffith is clearly seen throughout their adventurous lives. They seem to live largely by his animation and the scenes and surroundings in which they fit so naturally are of his building. There are many eloquent moving pictures in *Scarlet Days*, and several novel out-of-focus effects. But why does Mr. Griffith, who can make moving pictures so lucid, label them with words that are needless, and to some at least, irritating?"

"Clearest and most compelling among the characters is Alvarez, a Spanish bandit and adventurer, impersonated by Richard Barthelmess. Mr. Barthelmess is rising rapidly. As the Chinese hero of *Broken Blossoms,* he set a new standard for himself, and in *Scarlet Days* he shows that he did not just once go beyond his reach. He makes Alvarez the bright center of the story. At all times he is the romantic Spaniard, and never more exactly and completely than when, defending himself against attack, he dodges and darts about, shoots this way and that, in an evident ecstasy of joy, a throbbing delight that comes from pure love of excitement. It is anti-climatic when he recovers from his wound and goes away with the girl who loves him."

About Richard's work, James Smith, a reviewer for *Motion Picture Classic,* wrote, "Richard Barthelmess' portrayal of Alvarez, a sensitive, finely attuned romantic performance."

Scarlet Days was long considered a lost film until it was recovered by the Museum of Modern Art from the Soviet film archive, Gosfilmofond, in the early 1970s. In 2006, a restored print of the film was screened at the 25th Pordenone Silent Film Festival in Sacile. From the D. W. Griffith Collection at the Museum of Modern Art, title sheets marked "corrected" and dated 19 September, 1919, were used to reconstruct new English titles, but as of 2008, the full restoration of *Scarlet Days* remains incomplete.

Scarlet Days advertising poster from the Paramount-Artcraft Studios.

Two scenes from D. W. Griffith's *Scarlet Days* (1920): (TOP) **Ralph Graves, Richard Barthelmess, and Carol Dempster;** (BOTTOM) **Richard Barthelmess and Carol Dempster.**

Two scenes from D. W. Griffith's *Scarlet Days* (1920): (TOP) **Richard Barthelmess with Clarine Seymour and,** (BOTTOM) **Richard robbing George Fawcett by surprise.**

THE IDOL DANCER (1920)
FIRST NATIONAL
PRODUCER: D. W. GRIFFITH
DIRECTOR: D. W. GRIFFITH
SCENARIO: Stanner E. V. Taylor, from a story by Gordon Ray Young
LENGTH: 7 REELS
CAST: Richard Barthelmess, Clarine Seymour, George MacQuarrie, Creighton Hale, Kate Bruce, Porter Strong, Florence Short, Anders Randolf, Walter James, Thomas Carr, Herbert Sutch, Adolph Lestina, Ben Grauer, Walter Kolomoku
SYNOPSIS: Dan McGuire, a South Sea beachcomber, lands his boat on an island where he meets Mary, a beautiful, half-caste girl raised with the natives. Walter Kincaid, the consumptive nephew of the island's missionary, comes in search of the healing environment of the tropics. Walter is attracted to Mary, and uses his infatuation to inflame Dan's jealousy. His health takes a turn for the worst, and when he collapses, both Mary and Dan rush to his bedside. They are deeply moved by his Christian spirit, and Mary throws her wooden idol into the sea. Dan renounces alcohol, decides to live a better life.

One day, while the male inhabitants of the island are on a fishing trip, the island is invaded by a band of slave traders. Walter rallies to beat war drums to alert the islanders, but the slavers engage him in a hand-to-hand battle. The men rush back to the village, rescue the women, and find Walter dying from the beating. His death sanctifies Dan and Mary's love, and they unite in a Christian marriage.

In the *New York Times*, a reviewer wrote, "D. W. Griffith's latest work, *The Idol Dancer*, with Clarine Seymour, Richard Barthelmess and Creighton Hale in the leading roles, is at the Strand this week. Apparently it seems to set forth a story of savage, semi-savage and civilized human beings thrown together on an island of the South Seas and transformed into better beings by the actions on their common humanity of eternal truths, true in the tropics as well as in New England."

"As movies go, it is moderately good, and Mr. Griffith may be commended for another effort to keep out of the run worn deep by others; but Mr. Griffith certainly meant his pictures to be something more than just a movie, and isn't it possible that he is in danger of getting into a run of his own?"

"Mr. Barthelmess, as the beachcomber, more nearly approaches the genuine, but he, too, for the most part, seems to be merely acting a part. And so do the others."

About Richard's performance, Burns Mantle wrote in *Photoplay*, "Richard Barthelmess is the heavy-eyed beach-comber, a youngish youth to carry his philosophy of life, but handsome and a good screen actor, with personal appeal plus."

Richard Barthelmess as Dan McGuire, the beachcomber, in D. W. Griffith's *The Idol Dancer* (1920), a tale of love in the South Seas.

Two scenes from D. W. Griffith's *The Idol Dancer* (1920): (TOP) Kate Bruce, Herbert Sutch, Clarine Seymour, George McQuarrie, and Richard Barthelmess; (BOTTOM) Richard Barthelmess with Clarine Seymour.

THE LOVE FLOWER (1920)
D. W. GRIFFITH — UNITED ARTISTS
PRODUCER: D. W. GRIFFITH
DIRECTOR: D. W. GRIFFITH
SCENARIO: D. W. Griffith, from a story, *The Black Beach*, by Ralph Stock.
CAST: Richard Barthelmess, Carole Dempster, George MacQuarrie, Anders Randolf, Florence Short, Crauford Kent, Adolphe Lestina, William James, Jack Manning
SYNOPSIS: In this South Seas story of detectives and false accusations, Stella Bevan sees her father come home from an unjust imprisonment. Stella's stepmother, Crane, is involved with another man, and when her father finds the two of them together, he unwittingly becomes implicated in the man's death by the same detective responsible for his first conviction. This time, he flees to a South Seas island with his daughter.

Richard Barthelmess plays Bruce Sanders, a sailor wandering the seas, who comes to beach on the same island where Stella and her father are living as fugitives from the law. He falls in love with the girl, and without realizing his error, ferries Crane to the island. Their idyllic romance abruptly ends when Stella thinks he deliberately brought the detective to confront her father. Bruce goes to great lengths to convince Crane that Stella's father has died in a fall from a cliff, and sails away from the island with the detective. Later, they return, free from the pursuing detective, and as man and wife, rejoin her father for a life together.

According to a review in the *New York Times*, "In *The Love Flower* is a man who is hunted all over the world as a murderer. The part is played by George MacQuarrie, and though some of his scenes are well, even excellently, acted, others are very much overdone. The murderer is accompanied by his daughter, who is represented as being devoted to her father and, at the same time, a free-spirited young person with a keen zest for life. Carol Dempster has the role, and she, too, is convincing in some scenes, but in others is merely sugary and kittenish."

"Richard Barthelmess, the 'hero' of the story, likewise has his scenes of genuineness and obvious acting. The most consistently human person in the story is the leader of the man-hunt, played by Anders Randolf."

"It must be added that Mr. Griffith has not lost his ability as a maker of moving pictures. The photoplay, presumably, was made in the Bahamas, which pass as South Sea Islands, and there are seascapes, under-water shots, and views of native life and rugged land. Some of the scenes are tinted to the enhancement of their dramatic value."

James Frederick Smith reviewed the film in *Motion Picture Classic*, writing, "D. W. Griffith's story of a man-hunt in the South Pacific. Griffith lost his theme in prettying a romance between the pursued man's daughter and a young adventuress. Does not seem real anywhere but it establishes Carol Dempster as a cinema personality. Here is a young girl with charm, distinction and vividness. Dick Barthelmess is not at his best."

The Colonial Theater in Reading, Pennsylvania, circulated this typical program for the D. W. Griffith film, *The Love Flower* (1920).

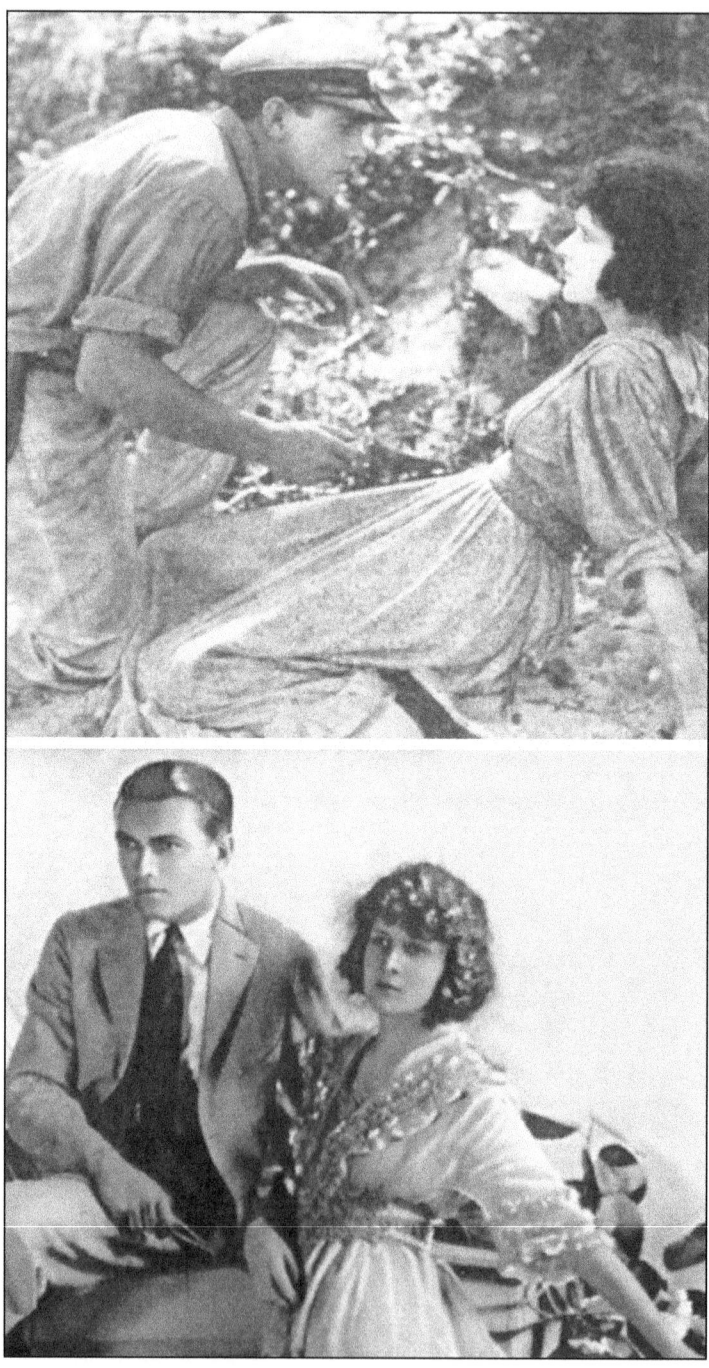

Two scenes from D. W. Griffith's *The Love Flower* (1920), with Richard Barthelmess and Carol Dempster.

Richard Barthelmess as Bruce Sanders, a wanderer of the sea, in D. W. Griffith's *The Love Flower* (1920).

WAY DOWN EAST (1920)
D. W. GRIFFITH-UNITED ARTIST
PRODUCER: D. W. GRIFFITH
DIRECTOR: D. W. GRIFFITH
SCENARIO: Anthony Paul Kelly, based on three stage plays by Lottie Blair Parker, William A. Brady, and Joseph R. Grismer
CAST: Lillian Gish, Richard Barthelmess, Lowell Sherman, Burr McIntosh, Mary Hay, Creighton Hale, Kate Bruce, Edgar Nelson, Porter Strong, George Neville, Edgar Nelson, Emily Fitzroy. People playing unaccredited extra roles include Mrs. Morgan Belmont, Josephine Bernard, Carol Dempster, Patricia Fruen, Mrs. David Landau, Una Merkel, Vivia Ogden, Athole Shearer, Edith Shearer, Norma Shearer, Florence Short, Frank Walsh

SYNOPSIS: Anna Moore, an innocent country girl, faces financial difficulties with her mother. They decide she should go and live with her rich relatives in Boston, the Tremonts, and ask for their help. In a short time, Lennox Sanderson, a wealthy playboy, seduces Anna, and tricks her into a phony marriage. After she becomes pregnant, Lennox leaves her, and Anna faces the birth of her child alone in a rooming house in Belden. Her baby is born sickly, and Anna baptizes the dying child alone with her faith in God. After the baby dies, Anna is expelled from the rooming house by an unsympathetic landlady. She wanders penniless and alone to the country ranch of the Bartlett family. They take her in, and give her work as a servant.

David Bartlett, the young son of the family, falls in love with Anna. In a short time, gossips arrive who see Anna and start spreading rumors of her past. When Squire Bartlett learns of her indiscretion, he turns Anna out of their home on the day of a bitter, winter storm. Anna wanders awash in her tears through the snowdrifts and faints on an ice floe as it slowly courses down the river. David comes to the rescue, but finds Anna already nearing the waterfall on the slab of ice. In a race against time, David leaps from floe to floe in the blinding snowstorm, reaches Anna at the moment the floe on which he stands begins to teeter over the falls, and gathers her in his arms. Against all odds, he steps off the crumbling ice to the safety of a following slab of ice, and from there, makes his way to shore with Anna secure in his arms.

In a final denouement, Anna confronts Lennox and accuses him of framing her in the false wedding ceremony in front of the whole family. The Bartletts forgive, and everyone lives happily after with a multiple wedding uniting David and Anna in marriage.

The *New York Times* reviewer said, "Anna Moore, the wronged heroine of *Way Down East*, was turned out into the snowstorm again last evening, but it was such a blizzard as she had never been turned out into in all the days since Lottie Blair Parker first told her woes nearly twenty-five years ago. For this was the screen version of that prime old New England romance and the audience that sat in rapture at the Forty-fourth Street Theater to watch its first unfolding here realized finally why it was that D. W. Griffith has selected it for a picture. It was not for its fame. Nor for its heroine. Not for the wrong done her. It was for the snowstorm . . . There are two kinds of super-feature productions — the Griffith kind and the others . . . Richard Barthelmess is a good choice for the honest farm boy . . . ."

Film Daily wrote rhapsodies about the film, explaining, ". . . This is a splendidly treated melodrama rising to the greatest climax ever screened; the comedy strikes a false note. It is the biggest box office attraction of the times; it is artistic, lasting, and powerful. D. W. Griffith's name and that of Lillian Gish will help to put it over too."

When the film was reissued in a retrospective at the Museum of Modern Art in 1940, Iris Barry said, "The extremely improbable plot creaks loudly . . . yet if most of the characterizations are two-dimensional, they are handled with vigor and skill, and the study of Anna is entire and convincing."

Two pictures of Richard Barthelmess at the time of the making of *Way Down East* (1920).

Richard Barthelmess as David Bartlet in D. W. Griffith's *Way Down East* (1920).

Three scenes from D. W. Griffith's *Way Down East* (1920) featuring Richard Barthelmess, Kate Bruce, and Burr McIntosh.

After the releases of *Broken Blossoms* and *Way Down East*, Richard began appearing on the cover of movie magazines.

Tol'able David (1921)
Inspiration Pictures–First National
Producer: Charles H. Duell
Director: Henry King
Scenario: Edmund Goulding and Henry King, based on a novel by Joseph Hergesheimer
Length: 8 reels
Cast: Richard Barthelmess, Gladys Hulette, Ernest Torrence, Warner P. Richmond, Edmund Gurney, Laurence Eddinger, Forrest Robinson, Walter P. Lewis, Ralph Yearsley, Marion Abbott, Laurence Eddinger, Henry Hallam, Patterson Dial, Lassie
Synopsis: A parable of the David and Goliath story, told in the mountains of Appalachia. Young David Kinemon, an adolescent living in rural Virginia, is desperate to show both his love interest and his family that he is worthy of being regarded as a man. He wants nothing more from life than to drive the mail wagon, as does his older brother, Allen. The bucolic community of Greenstream suddenly darkens with the arrival of three thoroughly evil mountain men, Luke, Iska, and Buzzard Hatburn, fugitives from justice who are bent on mischief and impose themselves upon the unwilling hospitality of Esther Hatburn's grandfather. They kill David's dog, cripple Allen for life, and indirectly cause the death of David's father. When the mountain men attempt mail robbery, David is forced to make a stand and declare himself a man, resulting in a climactic sequence in which David takes on the brothers and settles the score in a rip-roaring fight with Torrence in which he is nearly killed. Victorious, but badly hurt, he takes his brother's place and gets the mail delivered.

The *New York Times* noted the over-used, stock ingredients of the basic story and how these elements had been used in countless homespun melodramas. However, this film was seen to soar above all other attempts with its realistic cast, exciting photography, and realism. "In all things, except, possibly, the fight between David and the three hyenish mountaineers, it is restrained, imaginatively suggestive when not briefly literal. For this reason it is stimulating."

"Mr. King has accomplished this result in the only way in which it can be accomplished on the screen . . . they applied principles of pictorial composition and cinematography to make their scenes expressive and pleasing to the eye. *Tol'able David* has vitality, therefore. It lives as a motion picture."

"Largely, of course, because of the acting. Mr. Barthelmess, for instance, does the best work of his screen life. In a role somewhat similar to the one he had in *Way Down East*, he has dropped most of the mannerisms and exaggerated poses that marred his performance in that picture. He doesn't grin foolishly any more, and he seems to be under better control in his more intense moments. His work, on the whole, is more finished and promising. He ought to go on to still better things."

The anonymous reviewer from *Variety* said, "Richard Barthelmess, in his initial release through First National, has turned out a program feature worthy of presentation in any of the more pretentious film theaters . . . the photography is excellent, though no one either on the program or in the first few feet of film is given credit for it. *Tol'able David* is a sweet vehicle for Barthelmess in which to inaugurate his campaign as a name in pictures, and should prove a means of strengthening his present following, which past efforts have gained him, besides opening the way for many other film productions of his."

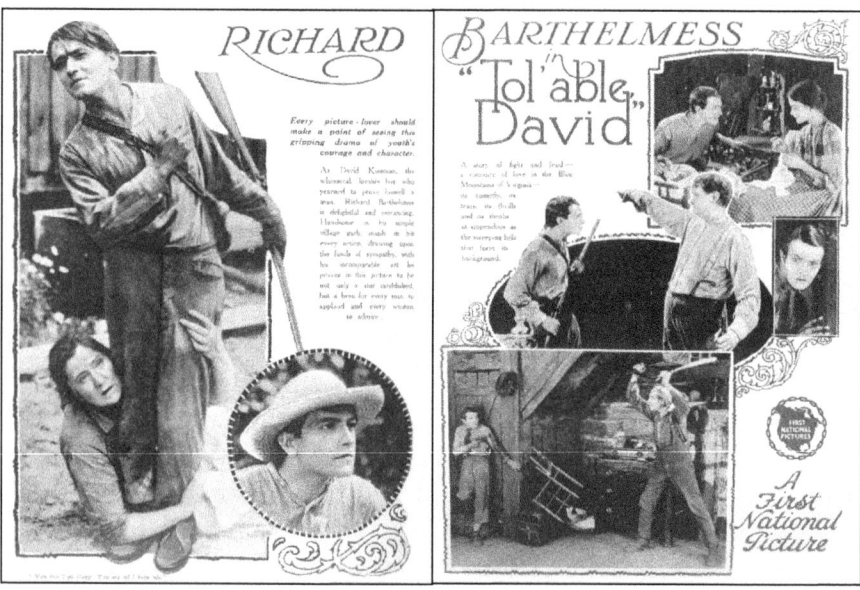

Tol'able David **print advertisement as it appeared in many magazines around the country.**

Richard Barthelmess as the title character in Henry King's *Tol'able David* (1921).

Edward Weitzel wrote in *Moving Picture World*, "Easily the most romantic figure on the screen today among the male stars, Richard Barthelmess scores a great personal hit in his first starring vehicle . . . As David, the earnest and finely molded young boy whose great ambition is to drive the United States Mail Coach, Richard Barthelmess fulfills every promise made by him in the past in characters that called for fine qualities of heart and mind. It is difficult to find one flaw in his impersonation."

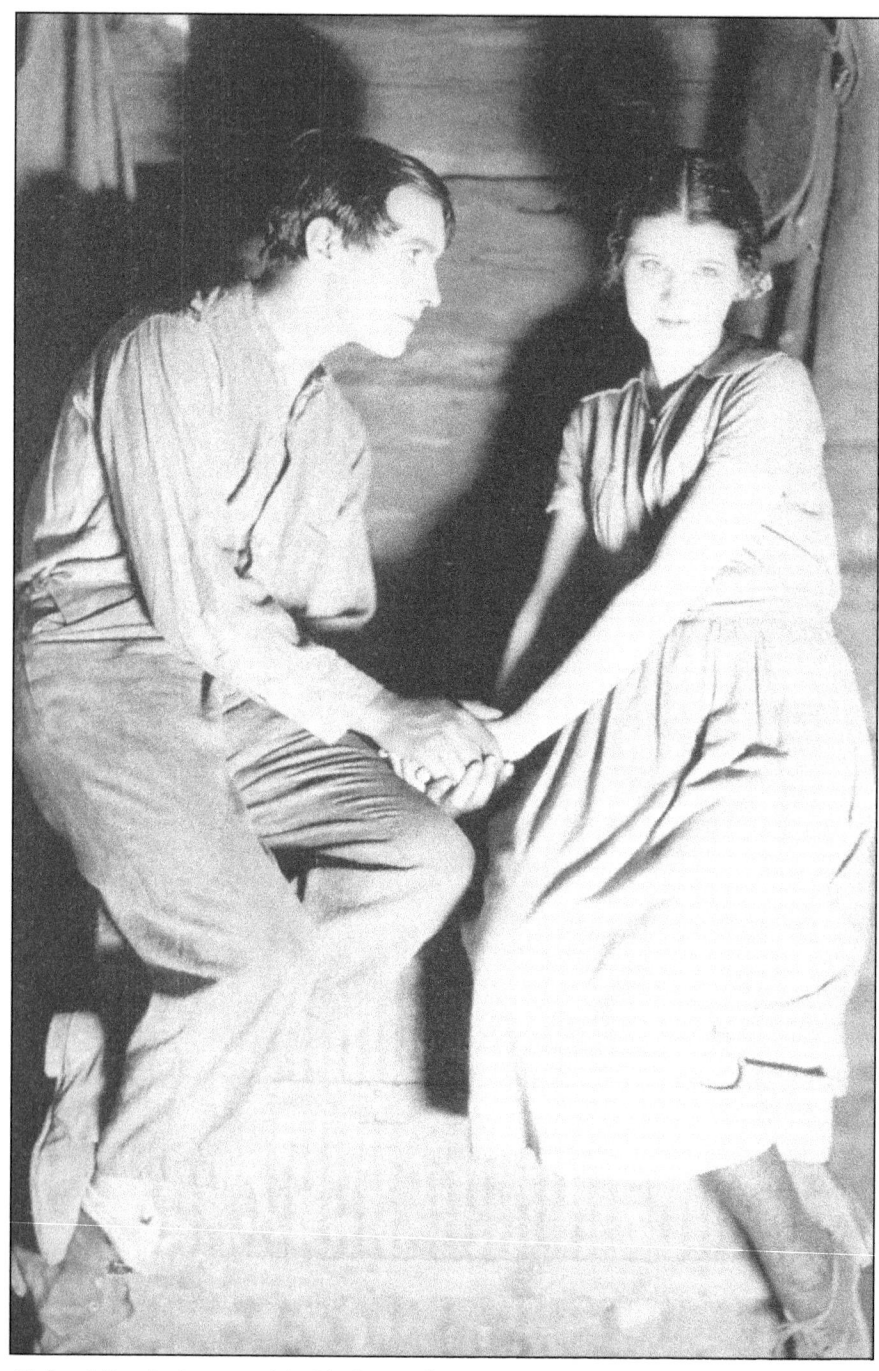

Richard Barthelmess with Gladys Hulette in Henry King's *Tol'able David* (1921).

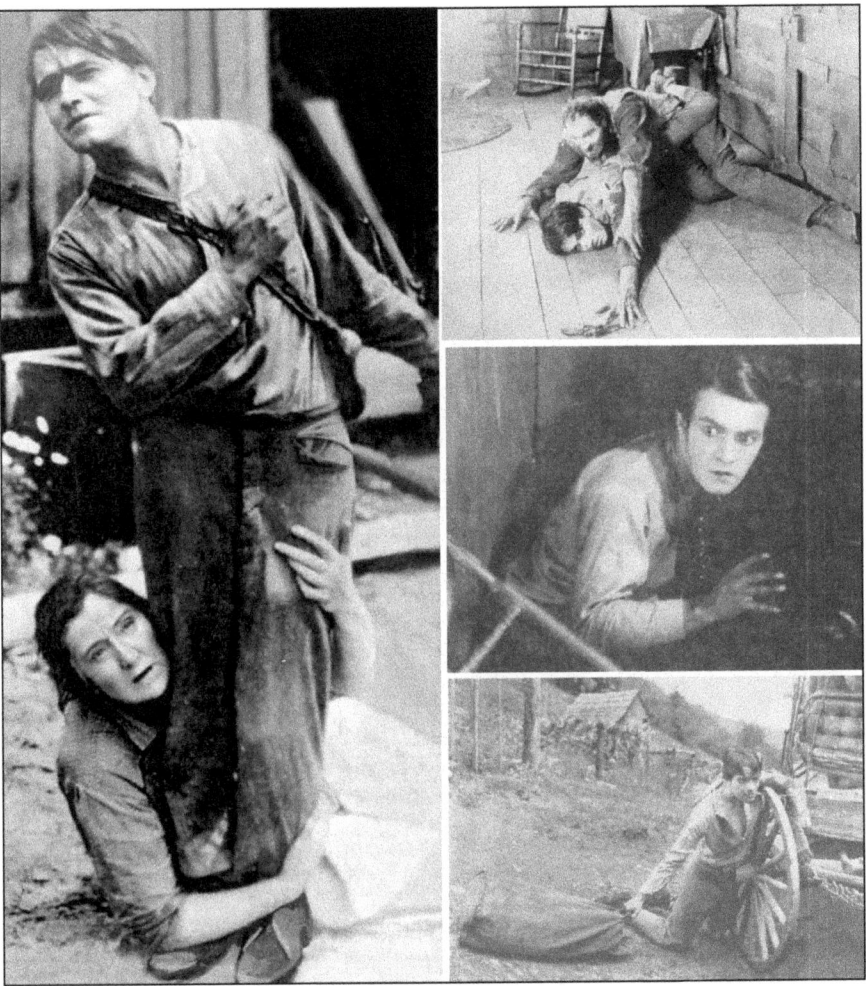

Four scenes from the climax of *Tol'able David* (1921), the dramatic story of a backwoods feud and a boy's determination to deliver the mail.

EXPERIENCE (1921)
FAMOUS PLAYERS-LASKY-PARAMOUNT
PRODUCER: ADOLPH ZUKOR
DIRECTOR: GEORGE FITZMAURICE
SCENARIO: Waldemar Young, based on a play by George V. Hobart
CAST: Richard Barthelmess, Reginald Denny, Marjorie Daw, Lilyan Tashman, Nita Naldi, John Miltern, Kate Bruce, Helen Kelly, Edna Wheaton, E. J. Radcliffe, Betty Carpenter, R. Senior, Joseph W. Smiley, Fred Hadley, Harry J. Lane, Helen Ray, Jed Prouty, Barney Furey, Leslie King, Charles A. Stevenson, Yvonne Routon,

Ned Hay, Sibyl Carmen, Robert Schable, Frankie Evans, Frank McCormack, Louis Wolheim, Agnes Marc, Mrs. Gallagher, Florence Flinn, Mac Barnes, Leslie Banks

SYNOPSIS: The story is an allegorical tale full of romantic idealism and a haunting touch of sadness. It follows Youth, played by Richard Barthelmess, as he leaves his mother and follows the call of Ambition. Love and Hope accompany him on his journey to the city. Once there, Youth faces the allure of Pleasure. His friend, Opportunity, is asked to wait, but the tempestuous woman refuses and leaves him.

At a Cabaret known as the Primrose Path, Pleasure introduces him to Beauty, Wealth, Fashion and Temptation When Youth's mother dies, Love sends him a telegram. Temptation intercepts the communication, and foils her outreach. When Love comes to the city, she is turned from the Primrose Path. By Chance, Youth enters a gambling house where he loses everything except the ring given to him by love.

Alone and lonely, Youth is haunted by the specters of Poverty and Delusion. Habit and Vice enter his path and lead him to go with Crime to robe the home of Wealth. On the way, he hears the sound of a church choir and decides to go home to Love and Hope, taking with him Experience.

An anonymous reviewer in the *New York Times* wrote, "The screen version of George V. Hobart's play of the same name. *Experience* was a morality play. The leading character is Youth. He had Mother and Love in the beginning, but after Ambition called him to Opportunity, Pleasure, Intoxication, Excitement and Temptation in the big city, he was reduced to Poverty."

The *New York Times* reviewer also wrote, "If you examine this simple story at all closely, it shows itself to be a meaningless jumble, and, as you look it over, you may notice that nowhere does Truth appear in it. Consistency, Logic and Sincerity are also absent. Tediousness and Triteness are present from the beginning, however." The review went on to describe the production: "Mr. Fitzmaurice, who directed the production, has shown himself a skillful maker of pictures in previous works, but there are only a few shots in *Experience* to sustain his reputation, and almost no sample of cinematography. The settings are elaborate. The large cast overacts, for the most part, though there are bits by Mr. Barthelmess, Kate Bruce and a few others which would be worth while in a more persuasive setting."

The reviewer from *Variety* wrote, "As Youth, Mr. Barthelmess gave a performance pleasing and studied. Marjorie Daw, playing opposite as Love, was a delight in the simplicity with which she endowed the characterization. But the wallop of the entire performance was that put over by Nita Naldi. This beautiful creation of God's handicraft caused everyone to catch their breath when she appeared on the scene and then the vamping bit that she did stamped her as an actress as well as a looker . . . *Experience* is a big picture that admits of endless exploitation on the part of the exhibitor and he should not be afraid to go strong on this end for it will draw and satisfy any picture audience."

Richard Barthelmess and Marjorie Daw in a scene from George Fitzmaurice's *Experience* (1921).

Richard Barthelmess in scenes from George Fitzmaurice's *Experience* (1921): (TOP AND CENTER) **with Nita Naldi, and** (BOTTOM) **with Mildred Reardon, Helen Kelly, Lilyan Tashman, and Charles Stevenson.**

THE SEVENTH DAY (1922)
INSPIRATION PICTURES-FIRST NATIONAL
DIRECTOR: HENRY KING
SCENARIO: Edmund Goulding, from a story by Porter Emerson Browne
LENGTH: 6 REELS
CAST: Richard Barthelmess, Louise Huff, Frank Losee, Leslie Stowe, Tammany Young, George Stewart, Alfred Schmid, Grace Barton, Anne Cornwall, Patterson Dial, Teddy Gerard
SYNOPSIS: The story of idle gamblers in New England begins when a yacht filled with disillusioned cynics from New York runs into trouble and must put to port in a small coastal village. Patricia Vane, a sophisticated flapper, and her fiancé, Reggie Van Zandt, run ashore, eager for diversion while the yacht goes in for repairs. They find amusement when they meet some attractive locals, John Alden and his sister, Betty. During the four-day hiatus, Patricia lets John escort her around the town, while Reggie amuses himself with Betty.

John invites Patricia to attend church services on Sunday, and while there, she is conscience-stricken. Later, she confesses that she is actually engaged to Reggie and has been flirting with him as a lark. John is heartbroken, and prepares to leave his home and go to sea to forget her. Then, he learns that a similar unscrupulous fate has fallen to his sister and her involvement with Reggie.

In a final confrontation between the good people of the village and the idle society wastrels, John attacks them while they play on board the yacht and denounces the entire party. Because of his show of sincerity, Reggie and Patricia awaken to their error, and realize their respective love for the New England youths is genuine.

In March of 1922, the *New York Times* had this to say about *The Seventh Day*: "So far as the direction of Henry King goes, and the acting of Richard Barthelmess and the others in the cast, *The Seventh Day*, which is at the Strand this week, is a satisfactory successor to *Tol'able David*, the first production resulting from the King-Barthelmess combination. With a New England fishing village as his background this time, instead of the Southern mountains, Mr. King has again brought his settings expressively into his story, and, Mr. Barthelmess, cast now in the role of a young fisherman, is once more simple, genuine and equal to the dramatic demands of his part."

"There are also a number of others who help to give something of life to the picture. There's Louise Huff in the role of a New York society girl who comes to mock and remains to marry the young fisherman. She's as convincing as the story will let her be. George Stewart and Alfred Schmid, as two gilded youths designed to suggest the environment from which the heroine emerges, do their work smoothly, as they should, and, as contrasting types, furnishing an environment for the hero, Frank Losee and Leslie Stowe are as picturesque a pair of retired skippers as you'd be likely to find anywhere along the coast. Others who add to the general effect are Anne Cornwall, Patterson Dial and Tammany Young. But, despite all this, *The Seventh Day* is by no means the equal of *Tol'able David*, as a photoplay. Both productions are what are called 'homespun' or 'rural' stuff in the trade, but *Tol'able David* was sincere, and *The Seventh Day* is not. *Tol'able David* dealt, in the main, with people as they are. It indulged only occasionally in heroics and hokum. *The Seventh Day* seems obviously fabricated out of old theatrical fictions . . . There's one thing to be said for the scenes in the photoplay, however. They are not nearly as smug and self-righteous as the subtitles. With another set of captions, in fact, *The Seventh Day* might approach genuineness. But with the affected Puritanism of its present text, it paints the traditional picture of Salem against Sodom, and would have you believe that there is nothing else in the world."

Photoplay reviewed the film, reporting, "This picture comes from the same source as *Tol'able David*; that is to say, it was directed by Henry King, and Richard Barthelmess is its star. It lacks the rugged vigor of the Hergesheimer story and it is marred by some crude attempts at comedy relief, but for all that it is a thoroughly worthwhile picture, and proves that the talent displayed by King and Barthelmess in *Tol'able David* was something more than a momentary flash . . . As in *Tol'able David*, the direction of Henry King stands out. There is the same quality of genuineness that was so much in evidence in his previous picture."

Variety had this to say about the film: "It's a very old story, that's the best thing about it" reads one of the subtitles, and it states, approximately, all there is to be said concerning Richard Barthelmess' second starring vehicle. Inspiration Pictures, Inc., is presenting, releasing through First National, from the story by Porter Emerson Browne, under the direction of Henry King."

"Barthelmess predominates and is in no danger of being overshadowed by any other member of the cast. Louise Huff proves a satisfactory society miss. George Stewart as Reggie has turned in a capable piece of work, also causing some favorable comment amongst the feminine onlookers for secondary honors. The remaining members flash nothing above the average."

"*The Seventh Day* is somewhat indistinct in its sub-titling. It will suffer if compared to *Tol'able David*."

The Seventh Day print advertisement as it appeared in many magazines around the country.

Two scenes from Henry King's *The Seventh Day* (1922): (TOP) **Louise Huff, Richard Barthelmess, and Anne Cornwall;** (BOTTOM) **Frank Losee, Louise Huff, Richard Barthelmess, and Anne Cornwall.**

Louise Huff and Richard Barthelmess in Henry King's *The Seventh Day* (1922).

SONNY (1922)
INSPIRATION-FIRST NATIONAL
PRODUCER: CHARLES H. DUELL
DIRECTOR: HENRY KING
SCENARIO: Francis Marion and Henry King, based on a play by George V. Hobart
LENGTH: 7 REELS
CAST: Richard Barthelmess, Pauline Garon, Margaret Seddon, Lucy Fox, Herbert Grimwood, Patterson Dial, Fred Nicholls, Margaret Elizabeth Falconer, Virginia Magee

SYNOPSIS: Richard Barthelmess portrays two men who look alike: Charles "Sonny" Crosby, a well-to-do youth with a blind mother, and Joe Marden, a poolroom owner. The two men join World War One at the same time. While in the service, their friendship grows, and many people mistake one for the other.

Sonny is mortally wounded in battle, and begs his friend to promise to assume his identity, visit his mother, and spare her the grief of his death. Joe agrees to the deception just before Sonny dies, and after the war, returns to Sonny's family home. There, he meets and falls in love with Sonny's sister. One night, Sonny's mother has a dream in which her dead son reveals himself. The next day, she reveals her vision to Joe, and in a moment of motherly tenderness, shows him the true warmth he deserves, and accepts him as part of their family.

In Sonny, Barthelmess tackled the difficult assignment of playing two characters in the same film. The *New York Times* reviewer noticed the ease with which any film made by Henry King with Barthelmess would submit to comparison with *Tol'able David*, however their new film compared favorably to the others in their series.

"Considered by itself, without reference to its family, it is, on the whole, worth while," wrote the reviewer from the *New York Times*. "A majority of its scenes have been efficiently directed; its settings and photography, which really come under the direction of the film, are usually, though not always, excellent; Mr. Barthelmess does some of his best work in it, and several others in the cast succeed in giving meaning to their parts. Its story is unoriginal and, in its later stages, rather obviously set and stretched, but it provides Mr. Barthelmess and the others with opportunities for several appealing characterizations. Also, except where its sentimentality becomes too sticky, it is emotionally sound, and pleasantly touched with humor, too . . . In portraying the two characters, and in differentiating between them, Mr. Barthelmess points his performance skillfully."

Variety wrote in its review, "It is going to be a question whether or not the public at large is willing to look at war stuff of this sort at this time and accept it as entertainment. They certainly did not seem ready in New York a few months ago . . . As a picture, *Sonny* is a corking feature, but the question the exhibitor will have to find out for himself is whether or not his audiences are willing to sit through a story where the son of a blind mother is killed at the front and a double in the same company consents to go back to his home and impersonate him for the mother's sake . . . the picture is a corking one for Barthelmess, and he enacts the dual role with cleverness. The double exposure scenes in the early part as well as the vision bits later are masterly bits of photography, working out very well to the advantage of the star."

Richard Barthelmess in Henry King's *Sonny* (1922), as the worthless soldier who returns from World War I to take another man's place.

Four scenes from Henry King's *Sonny* (1922). Richard played a difficult dual role as two doughboys, one rich, one poor.

THE BONDBOY (1922)
INSPIRATION-FIRST NATIONAL
PRODUCER: CHARLES H. DUELL
DIRECTOR: HENRY KING
SCENARIO: Charles E. Whittaker, based on a story by George Washington Ogden
LENGTH: 7 REELS
CAST: Richard Barthelmess, Ned Sparks, Mary Alden, Charles Hill Mailes, Lawrence D'Orsay, Robert Williamson, Leslie King, Jerry Sinclair, Thomas Maguire, Lucia Backus Segar, Virginia Magee, Mary Thurman
SYNOPSIS: Richard Barthelmess portrays Joe Newbolt, a youth who indentures himself to a bitter, old skinflint, Isom Chase. His wife, Ollie, is weary of the impoverished life she is forced to live with Isom, and secretly plans to elope with another man, Cyrus Morgan.

Joe comes between the misguided couple, and persuades Ollie to stay with her husband. When Isom discovers the two of them together, he responds with rage and threatens to kill Joe. His gun is fired in the struggle, and he accidentally kills himself. When the authorities arrive, Joe protects Ollie's secret plans for elopement and takes the blame for the accident. He is tried, convicted, and sentenced to hang for the killing. In a moment of passion, Joe escapes prison, returns to Ollie, and convinces her to tell the truth to the authorities. In a surprising turn of events, Joe discovers that he is the rightful owner of the Chase farm, and happily begins a new life with his old sweetheart.

In a review appearing in the *New York Times*, *The Bondboy* was praised: "Richard Barthelmess, as the poor country boy who is bound out to an old skinflint and later accused of his murder, is true to his part and often arouses a responsive sympathy in the spectator. Mr. King, Mar. Barthelemess and most of the others in the cast do, in fact, everything they can to give their story vitality, and here and there they succeed. The trouble is that their efforts are spent on a work that is obviously mechanical. There is little or no pretense of logical development in the plot. It never gives an impression of inevitability or even of probability. Everything hangs on coincidence and arbitrary regulation by the author . . . so you will probably have the feeling that the story, as it goes along, is unreal, that it is merely another made-to-order movie, but, unless you are too impatient, this will not prevent your enjoying the performance of Mr. Barthelmess, the enhancing photography of many of the scenes, and the numerous little natural and human touches with which Mr. King has made his pictures mean something."

A reviewer for the *Mexia Evening News* wrote, "How would you like to watch from the window of a prison cell the construction of a gallows upon which you were to be hung for a crime you did not commit? This is the unnerving experience of Joe Newbolt, the young farmhand, played by Richard Barthelmess . . . one thing alone keeps up the spirit of the prisoner. That is the loyalty of the girl of his dreams, who, believing in his innocence, visits him daily in his cell. With the strength of a mad man, Joe forces his way out of the old jail and a dramatic chase with bloodhounds follows, bringing a solution to the mystery and a happy conclusion of the plot. An excellent cast supports Barthelmess...."

The Bondboy print advertisement as it appeared in many magazines around the country.

Richard Barthelmess in Henry King's *The Bondboy* (1922).

FURY (1923)

INSPIRATION-FIRST NATIONAL
PRODUCER: HENRY KING
DIRECTOR: HENRY KING
SCENARIO: Edmund Goulding, based on a story by Edmund Goulding
LENGTH: 9 REELS
CAST: Richard Barthelmess, Dorothy Gish, Tyrone Power, Sr., Pat Hartigan, Barry Macollum, Jessie Arnold, Harry Blakemore, Adolph Milar, Ivan Linow, Emily Fitzroy, Lucia Backus Seger, Patterson Dial
SYNOPSIS: In this tale of courage and revenge among sailors docking in the Limehouse district of old London, the story follows stern Captain Leyton and his son, Boy. When his vivacious sweetheart, Minnie, is wronged, Boy courageously comes to her defense. His father, who had been a harsh disciplinarian until that time, is so overjoyed at seeing his son come to his girl's defense, he has a heart attack. Leyton has long held deep resentment for the man who lured his wife away from him. His dying wish is that his son should seek revenge on the man. True to his promise to his dying father, Boy finds his mother, and discovers the man is Morgan, a former first mate on his father's ship. In a rousing, action-packed climax, Boy hurls Morgan overboard, and returns to the arms of his sweetheart, secure that his father's dying wish has been avenged.

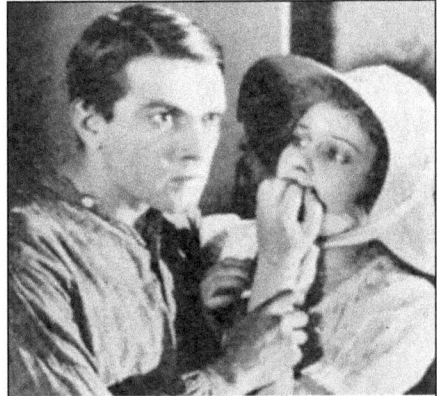

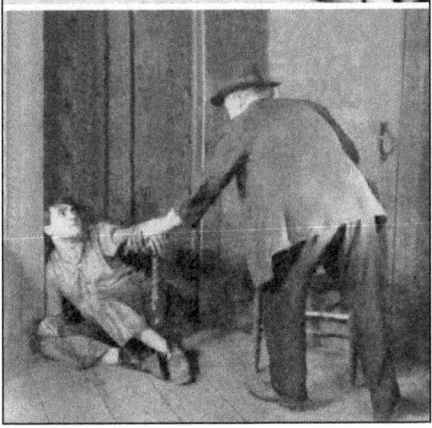

Three scenes from Henry King's *The Bondboy* (1922).

An anonymous reviewer in *Variety* wrote, "Here is the best picture that Richard Barthelmess has appeared in since *Tol'able David*. It isn't as great a wallop as *David* was, but it is a picture that is going to do a whale of a business. It is the first picture that Edmund Goulding has done for this star since he adapted the *David* tale and that may account somewhat for the punches that there are in it. Goulding seems to know how to fit Barthelmess, and seemingly this current attraction and the previous one that this writer did for him are the proof of the pudding. The coupling of Miss Gish with the star is also bound to develop a certain pull at the box office. In addition, *Fury* is a great story as screened . . . through it all, Barthelmess as the boy carries with him a certain wistfulness bound to appeal, especially with Miss Gish acting as an excellent foil for his work. Miss Gish gets the laughs in the picture, she again easily qualifying as being absolutely alone in her particular style of work on the screen. In direction, the picture holds the interest all the way."

Fury print advertisement as it appeared in many magazines around the country.

Two scenes featuring Dorothy Gish with Richard Barthelmess in Edmund Goulding's *Fury* (1922).

Dorothy Gish with Richard Barthelmess in Edmund Goulding's *Fury* (1922).

THE BRIGHT SHAWL (1923)
INSPIRATION-FIRST NATIONAL
PRODUCER: CHARLES H. DUELL
DIRECTOR: JOHN S. ROBERTSON
SCENARIO: Edmund Goulding, based on a story by Joseph Hergesheimer
CAST: Richard Barthelmess, Mary Astor, Dorothy Gish, Jetta Goudal, William Powell, Edward G. Robinson, Andre de Beranger, Luis Alberni, Anders Randolf, Margaret Seddon, George Humbert
LENGTH: 8 REELS
SYNOPSIS: In this historic tale of revolutions and duels, Richard Barthelmess plays Charles Abbott, a wealthy, idealistic, and imaginative youth who travels to Cuba to contribute support for the Cuban independence cause. His companion, Andres Escobar,

introduces him to his sister, Narcissa, with whom he is soon entranced. However, a Cuban dancer, La Clavel, played by Dorothy Gish, also fascinates him. She is passionately in love with the young man, and in an attempt to help, gives him information she has gained from various Spanish officers.

La Pilar, a spy for the Spanish government, discovers their plan and sets a trap. When La Clavel learns of this, she intervenes, and loses her life in the attempt. A government official steps into the intrigue and enables the American's to escape to the safety of their homeland.

According to a review in the *New York Times*, "There is no denying Barthelmess's ability as an actor. With whiskers, long hair and garbed in an old-fashioned coat and hat of the period, tight trousers and stock, he is a sympathetic and interesting personality."

"Dorothy Gish's eyes may not be Cubanesque, but nevertheless she makes such a charming dancer that one does not wonder that Havanna raves about her. She is especially appealing when flirting with Abbot."

"There is plenty of interesting local color in the production, as the exterior scenes were all made in Havana. The picture is an elaborate one, with fascinating costumes. There is good acting by the members of the well-chosen cast, but the story is rather aimless."

In *Variety*, a reviewer wrote, "Here is an all-round fine contribution to the screen, especially fine in its production rather than in the subject matter of the story. It is an atmosphere and costume play done in a splendid, artistic style. It gives Richard Barthelmess the best romantic role probably he has ever had, and it furnishes a picturesque character type for Dorothy Gish which displays that charming young woman in an entirely new aspect, as a dark-eyed Cuban dancing girl."

Frederick James Smith wrote in *Photoplay*, ". . . marks a milestone in the career of Richard Barthelmess. It is his first stellar venture into the field of the costume drama. The result, under the careful guidance of John Robertson, is a pretty play of distinct atmospheric charm . . . Barthelmess does surprisingly well with his character of Charles Abbott. Into it he puts all his technique and intelligence and no young actor has more of either. But he never can quite overcome the negative quality of the role."

Mary Astor wrote about *The Bright Shawl* in her book, *A Life on Film*: "We made tepid love in front of the camera and we rode a cushioned, flowered gondola in a reproduction on the back lot of the canals of Xochimilco . . . ."

The Bright Shawl print advertisement as it appeared in many magazines around the country.

Richard Barthelmess as Charles Abbott in John S. Robertson's *The Bright Shawl* (1923).

Dorothy Gish as La Clavel, a Spanish Dancer, in John S. Robertson's *The Bright Shawl* (1923).

Dorothy Gish and Richard Barthelmess in John S. Robertson's *The Bright Shawl* (1923), a tale of revolutionists in old-time Cuba.

"All eyes turned on the dancer . . ." read the subtitle, as Dorothy Gish performed while Richard Barthelmess watched, in John S. Robertson's *The Bright Shawl* (1923).

"That's what happens to spies!" read the subtitle, in John S. Robertson's *The Bright Shawl* (1923).

THE FIGHTING BLADE (1923)
INSPIRATION-FIRST NATIONAL
PRODUCER: CHARLES H. DUELL AND JOHN S. ROBERTSON
DIRECTOR: JOHN S. ROBERTSON
SCENARIO: Josephine Lovett, based on a novel by Beulah Marie Dix
LENGTH: 9 REELS
CAST: Richard Barthelmess, Dorothy Mackaill, Lee Baker, Morgan Wallace, Bradley Barker, Frederick Burton, Stuart Sage, Phillip Tead, Walter Horton, Allyn King, Marcia Harris
SYNOPSIS: The story of soldiers of fortune in the days of King Charles II of England follows Richard Barthelmess as Karl Van Kerstenbroock while on the trail of Basil Dorner, a man he believes responsible for the death of his sister. In England, he finds Dorner, and avenges his sister's death.

When Watt Musgrove, a Royalist, hears of the death of his friend, he challenges Karl to a duel. His sister, Thomsine, disguises herself as a boy and beseeches Watt to cancel the duel. She succeeds, saving Karl's life, and enables him to escape.

Karl joins forces with Cromwell and leads them against Charles II, while also acting as a spy. Once again, Thomsine saves his life by hiding him from pursuing Royalists, helping him to escape and ultimately, lead a battalion to conquer and dethrone Charles II. In a last minute rescue, Karl saves Thomsine.

A reviewer in the *New York Times* wrote, ". . . a better class production pictured with sincerity and unusual care, and taking into consideration the sympathetic and sometimes capable, although solemn, acting of Richard Barthelmess, one must admit that it is an entertainment of certain merit. At the same time one leaves this photoplay with the impression that it fails in subtlety and suspense, and that the narrative has not been made as effective as was possible . . . it lacks life and sparkle, which may be due to the fact that a young Dutch swordsman, played by Mr. Barthelmess, has been selected as the central figure . . . it is moreover dubious whether such roles suit Mr. Barthelmess, which is no reflection upon his acting, except that he would be a great deal more appealing in modern parts. As one sees Barthelmess smiling only once in the course of this lengthy picture, it seems that it might have been worth while for John S. Robertson, the director of this effort, to visit Barthelmess in his own home, note the expressions his face undergoes with his wife and child, and then tell him to look a little like that in at least some of the scenes of the photoplay. Also, in these times, one does not expect the hero to conquer his adversaries with such ease as that which occurs in several scenes of *The Fighting Blade*."

The *New York Times* went on to compliment the well-done costumes. The many posed close-ups were thought to be an unneeded star turn for Barthelmess. "If he is going upstairs, he halts, looks around, starts again, pauses, gazes at the camera, and then, with suspicion, goes forward, all of which occurs at a time when one knows he could have gone straight ahead with but one glance. There is too much of this sort of thing, and Barthelmess appears to be overburdened with the great solemnity of the occasion."

A reviewer for the *Coshocton Tribune* wrote, "It is not amiss to call to mind the never-to-be-forgotten performances of Richard

Barthelmess in *Tol'able David*, in *Sonny*, in *The Bright Shawl*. Never has a star reached the hearts of his audiences as sincerely or as consistently as this versatile star. And now, a romance role; a drama of the days of chivalry; a special among special productions — with the star in a role more vigorous, more dashing, more lovable. The picture of all of his pictures you will find most glorious . . . ."

The Fighting Blade newspaper advertisement as it appeared in the *Lima News*.

Richard Barthelmess as a gallant swordsman who joins the forces of Parliament for the sake of a woman, in John S. Robertson's *The Fighting Blade* (1923).

Four scenes from John S. Robertson's *The Fighting Blade* (1923), with Richard Barthelmess and Dorothy Mackaill.

TWENTY-ONE (AKA 21) (1923)
INSPIRATION-FIRST NATIONAL
PRODUCER: JOHN S. ROBERTSON AND CHARLES H. DUELL
DIRECTOR: JOHN S. ROBERTSON
SCENARIO: JOSEPHINE LOVETT
LENGTH: 7 REELS
CAST: Richard Barthelmess, Dorothy Mackaill, Jo King, Dorothy Cumming, Elsie Lawson, Bradley Barker, Ivan Simpson, Betty Bronson, Nellie Parker Spaulding, Helen Tracy
SYNOPSIS: In this tale of family life torn by divorce, the story follows the struggles of a youth whose parents have permitted him to grow up according to their whim and not according to their wishes. Julian MacCullough, played by Richard Barthelmess, is the spoiled

darling of his society-loving mother. When he meets the factory girl with whom he falls in love, he rebels against the circumstance of his family and drops his mother's fast crowd for her company. He gets into a scrap on her account, and is and is shocked when his father threatens to have him arrested.

In an exciting twist, he turns the tables on his parents by running away from home and getting work as a taxi driver. Later, he blunders into a nest of taxi bandits, and in saving his father from their blackmailing schemes, he proves his manhood. In the end, Julian marries the girl of his choice and reconciles with his frivolous parents.

The *New York Times* reviewer hoped that there would be something in the new film to remind viewers of the remarkable production, *Tol'able David*, but found that the film did not begin to compare. The reviewer lamented the opening scenes showing "the virile but unsmiling young actor prancing about as Pan, and being flattered by girls and women who likened him to al Greek god." Strong objections were pointedly mentioned involving a scene when the youth buys undergarments as a gift for a factory girl, with the reviewer calling it "singularly absurd and not quite nice." Barthelmess, in some scenes, exhibited acting skill recalling his great work in *Tol'able David*, but the reviewer warned readers that the story would disappoint them, "now matter how much they liked looking at pictures of the popular star."

Variety's reviewer differed in opinion with the *New York Times*. The film was schedule to open in New York at the Strand, but the theater passed on the opportunity, leaving the Rialto, controlled by Famous Players, to second choice. The anonymous reviewer in *Variety* said, "Ad it looks as if the Strand pulled a boner and the Rialto got a break, thereby, for *Twenty-One* is a good picture. It kept 'em waiting in line at the Rialto Sunday . . . The production has been lavishly staged scenically and the director has turned out a compact story with continuity that holds consistently from leader to fade-out. Barthelmess plays the rich youth with a complete understanding, and it's a decidedly difficult role that calls for the most intelligent shading and high-lighting."

21 **print advertisement as it appeared in many magazines around the country.**

Dorothy Mackaill and Richard Barthelmess as the romantic lovers in John S. Robertson's film, *21* (1923).

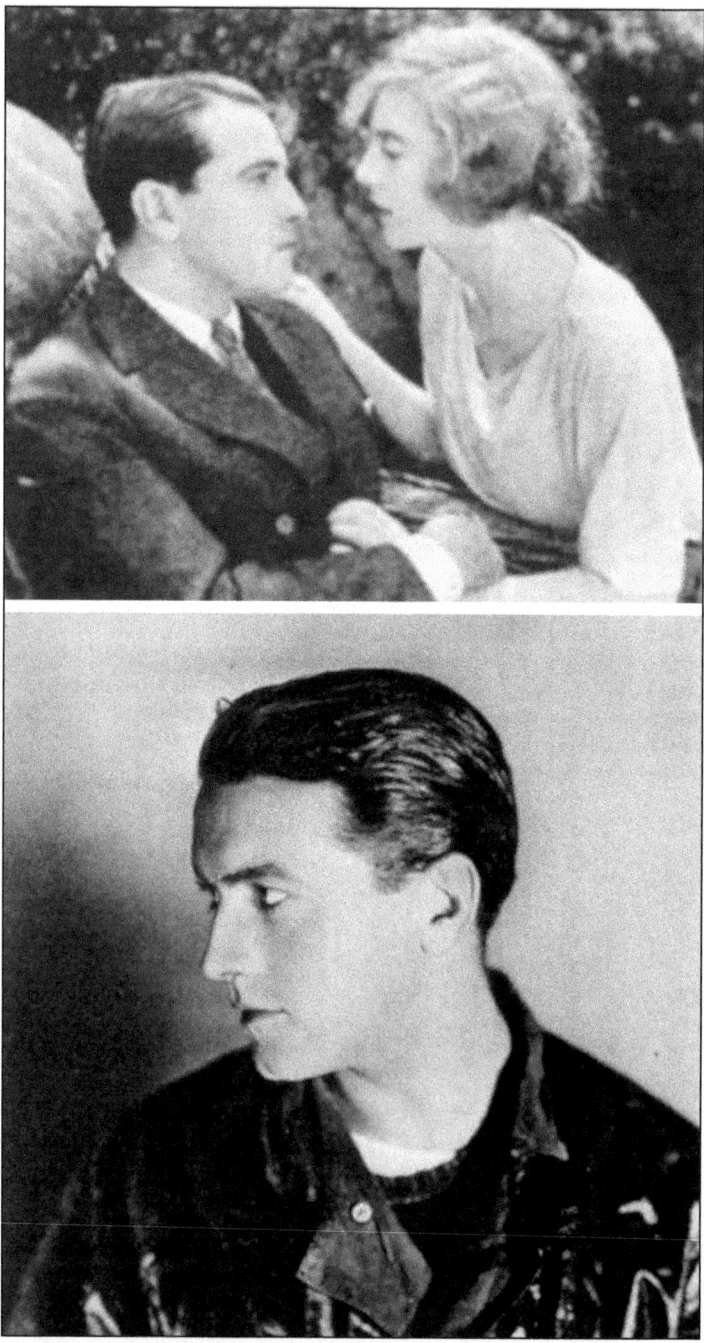

(TOP) **Dorothy Mackaill and Richard Barthelmess, and** (BOTTOM) **Richard as the 1923 model of a misunderstood rich boy in John S. Robertson's film,** *21* **(1923).**

THE ENCHANTED COTTAGE (1924)
INSPIRATION-FIRST NATIONAL
PRODUCER: JOHN S. ROBERTSON
DIRECTOR: JOHN S. ROBERTSON
SCENARIO: Josephine Lovett, based on a play by Sir Arthur Wing Pinero
LENGTH: 7 REELS
CAST: Richard Barthelmess, May McAvoy, Ida Waterman, Alfred Hickman, Holmes Herbert, Florence Short, Marion Coakley, Ethel Wright, Harry Allen
SYNOPSIS: The story follows Richard Barthelmess as Oliver Bashforth, physically wrecked by the war, who searches for seclusion and solitude by leaving his family to move into a lonely cottage.

There, he meets Laura Pennington, an ugly girl with protruding teeth, tired eyes circled with wrinkles, and a prominent nose, a plain and unattractive English governess who is escaping the attentions of her family.

He marries her, not because he loves her, but to deter his energetic sister from visiting him and imposing her own choice of a wife on him. Soon after the marriage, the couple discovers the names of other honeymooning couples from centuries past written with diamonds on the windowpanes of the enchanted cottage. When they carve their names into the panes, a beautiful love dawns over them. As if by magic, they see each other utterly transformed. Bashforth straightens his body and a smile crosses his handsome face. The striking change in Laura causes her teeth to even, her lips pretty and her nose straightens. Although initially united out of pity for each other, their love causes each to see the other's inner beauty. This realization transforms before each other's eyes into the physical perfection denied them by reality. The man is made whole and the woman becomes beautiful.

Mordaunt Hall of the *New York Times* thought the story "admirably suited to Mr. Barthelmess' youth, ability and good looks . . . Just suppose the Prince of Wales came to the United States and fell in love with an American girl, and you would have the plot of this film fashioned form A. E. Thomas's play of the same name . . . He pulls his hat brim down, like the Prince of Wales did. He smokes a pipe and he falls off his horse. It is through a golf ball striking Linda Lee

Stafford that he meets the girl who captures his young heart. She is portrayed by little Lois Moran, the young actress, who won film fame through her brilliant performance in *Stella Dallas*."

"Due to the modern magic of the camera, resourceful direction and thoroughly competent acting, Sir Arthur Wing Pinero's fantasy is much more satisfying on the screen than it was on the stage . . . in this weird effort, which is being unfurled at the Strand this week, Richard Barthelmess gives a good performance in the difficult, gloomy role of a maimed, shell-shocked officer, perpetually conscious of his wrecked form and distorted face . . . It is a production infinitely superior to anything in which Barthelmess has appeared since *Tol'able David*."

A reviewer in *Variety* wrote, "This picture is too far advanced and too artistic for the screen. It is one of those things certain to be above the heads of all but a few of the regulars at picture theaters . . . Richard Barthelmess plays the war cripple whose life has been ruined, and the performance he gives is decidedly clever; but despite this, the picture in reality belongs to Miss McAvoy, who practically walks away with the production as the ugly duckling."

May McAvoy and Richard Barthelmess as the idealized lovers in John S. Robertson's *The Enchanted Cottage* (1924).

In John S. Robertson's *The Enchanted Cottage* (1924), (TOP) May McAvoy and Richard Barthelmess as the disfigured lovers in reality, and (BOTTOM) as they saw each other beautified by love.

Two scenes from John S. Robertson's *The Enchanted Cottage* (1924): (TOP) the vision of a bygone couple who spent their honeymoon in the cottage, and (BOTTOM) the couple confront parents who cannot see them through eyes of love as they see each other.

CLASSMATES (1924)
INSPIRATION-FIRST NATIONAL
PRODUCER: John S. Robertson, with West Point scenes by authority of the United States Military Academy
DIRECTOR: JOHN S. ROBERTSON
SCENARIO: JOSEPHINE LOVETT
LENGTH: 7 REELS
CAST: Richard Barthelmess, Madge Evans, Charlotte Walker, Claude Brooke, Reginald Sheffield, Beach Cooke, James Bradbury, Jr., Antrim Short, Henry B. Lewis, Herbert Corthell, Richard Harlan
SYNOPSIS: Richard Barthelmess portrays Duncan Irving, Jr., a poor southern boy from a small town. Excitement comes to him when he receives an appointment to West Point, and the young man enters the United States Military Academy with great enthusiasm, a joy shared by his aristocratic sweetheart, Sylvia Randolph. In his final year, Bert Stafford, Sylvia's cousin, joins him at the Academy. He no sooner arrives than he exhibits visible resentment toward Duncan, an upper classman who is entitled to give him orders. Bert considers Duncan his social inferior, and sneers many an insult toward Duncan. One day, in retaliation for Bert's constant hazing, Duncan strikes Bert. West Point immediately expels him, and Duncan returns to civilian life. While heading up an expedition into the jungles of South America, Duncan encounters Bert lost during maneuvers, and a confrontation follows in which Bert reveals the reasons behind his previous hatred. Because Bert divulges the truth to West Point, Duncan is ultimately reinstated, and upon graduation, marries Sylvia.

The *New York Times* reviewed the West Point story, citing, "The most stirring chapters in Richard Barthelmess's latest vehicle, *Classmates*, are those that were photographed at West Point. They are sincere and informing, revealing the disciplinary mill through which the young men from all walks of life pass before they become officers of the United States Army. One gains a vivid impression of the glories and traditions of the military institution. The fact that John Robertson, the director of this film, received the hearty cooperation of the West Point officers materially adds to the interest of these sequences, without which this photoplay would be rather tame."

"Mr. Barthelmess is quite a serious stoic in his acting. He ought to relax more in his expressions and forget the camera. He exudes heroism, and appears to be afraid in some of the scenes to look as he does when away from the studio. He spoils his good looks by his frequent frown and heroic consciousness."

The reviewer from *Variety* praised the film: "It's hard to see how Richard Barthelmess can miss with this picture. There doesn't seem to be much doubt it's his best since *Tol'able David*, and that's going back a few. The West Point angle alone is sufficient to have almost put any film across. With the addition of Barthelmess and the personal performance he gives they make this release a sure thing . . . Barthelmess blends into the characterization as if it had been originally written for him. It's doubtful if any other male name in pictures could have done as well with the role, even though the picture would have carried almost anyone . . . It's a whale of a picture that has already run up sizable grosses out of town and will do as well wherever it plays unto foreign countries simply on the strength of the West Point thing, if nothing else."

An advertisement for the John S. Robertson film, *Classmates* (1924).

Richard Barthelmess in scenes from *Classmates* (1924) with Madge Evans.

NEW TOYS (1925)
INSPIRATION-FIRST NATIONAL
PRODUCER: JOHN S. ROBERTSON
DIRECTOR: JOHN S. ROBERTSON
SCENARIO: Josephine Lovett, based on a story by Agnes Smith
LENGTH: 8 REELS
CAST: Richard Barthelmess, Mary Hay, Clifton Webb, Katherine Wilson, Francis Conlon, Bijou Fernandez, Tammany Young, Pat O'Connor, Jules Jordan, Jacob Kingsbury
SYNOPSIS: This story of actors and actresses in the theater follows Richard Barthelmess as Will Webb and Mary Hay as Mary Lane. The two young thespians in amateur theatricals marry and settle into their new domestic lives together. Along comes Natalie, one of Will's old girlfriends, determined to recapture the affection of her lost love. She returns from Europe, and Mary is both surprised and jealous at the attention she throws at her husband. To spite him, she accepts a role of in a play produced by an old friend of hers, Tom Lawrence. Will is against the idea of his wife continuing in the theater, and vows to stay away from her opening night. Natalie urges him to attend, and together, they watch Mary experience one mishap after another. First, her makeup melts and a putty nose she wears comes loose. Later, she falls down a stage stairs in front of the entire audience. The play is a riot of misadventures, and closes after the one performance. Will rejects Natalie's attentions, and reconciles with Mary.

Women loved seeing Richard with his wife, Mary Hay, acting the principal roles in this film of a play by Milton Herbert Gropper and Oscar Hammerstein 2nd. The farce told a boisterous narrative about married life, comically aggravated by the appearance of the young man's old flame. The *New York Times* called it "a rather thin affair," enjoyed only by the women in the audience.

A reviewer for the *Mansfield News* wrote, "Unlike the glamorous *Classmates* and the thrilling *Way Down East*, *New Toys* confines its action strictly to problems of the present day home. It weaves a story, however, and reaches a climax, which proves as tensely dramatic and as thrilling as anything Barthelmess has done . . . the role of the husband is ideally suited to Barthelmess, affording him a wide scope of emotional acting of the type in which he shines.

Miss Hay steps into the enactment of the wife with a histrionic ability and understanding that is a delight."

A reviewer for the *Mansfield News* wrote, ". . . a delightful and entertaining picture . . . Miss Hay's unique ability as a comedienne stood out as clear-cut and distinctive in her screen work in this picture as behind the footlights. Motion picture audiences find her performance as the young wife to be a wholly delightful one. Her personality is just as piquant and vivacious on the silver-sheet as on the stage. *New Toys* is distinctly a family picture in more senses than one. It is, first of all, a domestic comedy, relating the tribulations and tragedies of the first two or three years of married life. The action revolves around a young married couple. Thus, *New Toys* is a family picture in every sense of he word. Indeed, it is this home spirit of the Barthelmess studio that makes it a thing apart in the motion picture world. There is a cheery, pleasant atmosphere about the Barthelmess studio unlike anything to be found anywhere in screendom, with the possible exception of the Mary Pickford–Douglas Fairbanks organization."

New Toys newspaper advertisement as it appeared in the *Iowa City Press Citizen.*

John Decker caricature of Mary Hay and Richard Barthelmess in John S. Robertson's *New Toys* (1925).

Four scenes with Mary Hay and Richard Barthelmess in John S. Robertson's *New Toys* (1925).

SOUL-FIRE (1925)
INSPIRATION-FIRST NATIONAL
PRODUCER: JOHN S. ROBERTSON
DIRECTOR: JOHN S. ROBERTSON
SCENARIO: Josephine Lovett, based on a play, *Great Music*, by Martin Brown
LENGTH: 9 REELS
CAST: Richard Barthelmess, Bessie Love, Carlotta Monterey, Percy Ames, Charles Esdale, Lee Baker, Helen Ware, Walter Long, Harriet Sterling, Richard Harlan, Arthur Metcalfe
SYNOPSIS: The story begins with the parents of Eric Fane as they are about to listen to a symphony composed by their son. Before the concert, a music critic in an adjacent box relates the story of Eric's struggles to become a composer. The orchestra fades to a busy jazz band in a Paris café playing one of his less ambitious compositions.

While in Paris, Eric becomes infatuated with a Russian princess. Although leading a wild nightlife, Eric tires of the artificiality and leaves the princess to take up a bohemian existence in Port Said. There, he plays piano in a dancehall, and one night, gets into a fight with a drunken sailor. The gob is accidentally killed, and Eric takes the opportunity to assume the man's identity and flees to the South Seas. While there, he meets and falls in love with Teita, a native girl played by Bessie Love, who was once a beautiful young English girl. He learns that after her parents died, Teita moved to the South Seas retreat. She and Eric fall in love and are about to be married when Eric discovers the mark of the leapers on her shoulder. A Christian doctor provides ministrations, and Eric finds the inspiration to compose a great concerto. A doctor reveals that Teita's illness is a minor ailment.

The story returns to the present where the concert is performed in London before a distinguished audience, including his parents, and is well received by both audience and critics.

A reviewer in *Variety* wrote, "Here is a corking box-office picture, screen entertainment that will get money, almost anywhere with a star name to draw 'em in and something on the celluloid to entertain after they are in their seats. It doesn't matter that the star is overshadowed by Bessie Love, who only comes into the picture after about three reels of it have passed, for the audience is getting real entertainment out of the picture. The role that Richard Barthelmess has, that, virtually, of a pander, is not one that will win any sympathy for him, albeit he plays it for its full worth . . . *Soul Fire* is a picture for the money. It is sexy, but not to the extent to arouse the censors."

"There is no little fascination about *Soul Fire*," wrote Mordaunt Hall in the *New York Times*, "the scorching title selected by the film producers for their adaptation of the Martin Brown play, *Great Music*. This vehicle profits by the elasticity of the screen, as the fading in and out of scenes helps much in the unfurling of the story, which concerns the son of a wealthy New Yorker whose consuming ambition is to be a composer of classical music. It is a distinctly novel idea to have the scenes in which the parents are listening to the son's symphony inserted at different points. It is also an excellent stroke to have the young man still in the South Sea island while the New York orchestra is playing the symphony of his life."

Newspaper advertisement for John S. Robertson's *Soul-Fire* (1925) as it appeared in many publications around the country.

Richard Barthelmess and Bessie Love in John S. Robertson's *Soul-Fire* (1925).

The happy ending from John S. Robertson's *Soul-Fire* (1925), with Bessie Love and Richard Barthelmess.

Shore Leave (1925)
Inspiration-First National
Producer: John S. Robertson
Director: John S. Robertson
Scenario: Josephine Lovett, based on a play by Hubert Osborne
Length: 7 reels
Cast: Richard Barthelmess, Dorothy MacKaill, Ted MacNamara, Nick Long, Marie Shotwell, Arthur Metcalfe, Warren Cook, Samuel Hines
Synopsis: "Bilge" Smith, a handsome, easy-going sailor, played by Richard Barthelmess, puts to anchor with his fleet at a port in a small, New England town. While on shore leave, Bilge meets the village dressmaker, Connie Martin, and true to the reputation of all sailors, he flirts with her. Unknown to him, Connie has never had a sweetheart, and she takes his show of affection seriously. The shore leave ends, and Bilge promises to return.

After he leaves town, she converts an old ship belonging to her deceased father into a tearoom. When the fleet returns, she tries to invite him to call, but is unable to reach him because she doesn't know his real full name. In an impulsive moment, Connie invites all the sailors named Smith. Sailors fill the tearoom, and among them is Bilge. At first, he fails to remember her, but when she shows the serious nature of her interest, he proposes marriage.

Bilge learns of her newfound wealth, refuses to live off a rich woman, and returns to his ship. Connie informs him that she has been reduced to poverty, and he quickly returns to her. When he discovers that she is still the proprietress of the tearoom, he feels tricked and is about to leave again. Connie stops him in his tracks, announces she has placed the ownership of the property into a trust fund for her first baby — providing that his name is Smith. Bilge changes his mind, and stays with Connie.

Mordaunt Hall wrote in his *New York Times* review: "It is the sort of production in which there is nothing much to be elated over, but at the same time, it is a film which will prove mildly diverting to those who don't care much about plausible incidents and situations . . . there are moment that are quite good in this story, and Mr. Barthelmess is a little more natural than usual in his performance. Dorothy Mackaill is quite effective as the young heroine who is enabled through the author and the director to run her ship as if she were the heroine in a fairy story."

"In so far as the average audience is concerned, this is very close to being the best picture Barthelmess has yet turned out," wrote a reviewer in *Variety*. "It has good comedy, pathos, and a plot that neither sags nor prolongs itself. Added to this is the good characterization Barthelmess gives to his role, that of 'Bilge' Smith, a sailor in the US Navy . . . Barthelmess has put over a rather uncompromising characterization of his sailor. There is no bid for sympathy made until nearly at the end of the picture, unless it can be that his code of morals forbid his marrying a woman for her money. Dorothy Mackaill, as the little dressmaker, is also very fine, ranking almost with the star for a sincere and consistent performance . . . *Shore Leave* is a cinch, and in the week stand places the bet it's business increases daily instead of slumping. It's that kind of a picture."

Richard Barthelmess and Dorothy Mackaill in John S. Robertson's *Shore Leave* (1925).

Scenes with Richard Barthelmess and Dorothy Mackaill in John S. Robertson's *Shore Leave* **(1925).**

The Beautiful City (1925)
Inspiration-First National
Director: Kenneth Webb
Scenario: Edmund Goulding, based on an adaptation by Violet E. Powell
Length: 7 reels
Cast: Richard Barthelmess, Dorothy Gish, William Powell, Frank Puglia, Florence Auer, Lassie Bronte
Synopsis: This tale of Irish-American gangsters was written especially for the screen by Edmund Goulding who wrote the screenplay of *Tol'able David*, one of the biggest hits of Richard Barthelmess' career. The story follows a Chinese theater used as a front for the illegal activities of a gangster, Nick Di Silva. A young Italian flower vendor, Tony Gillardi, played by Richard Barthelmess, works undercover for the gang, and serves as the patsy for a robbery committed by Nick and one of his cohorts. Tony is sentenced to a prison term for the crime he did not commit, and only his sweetheart, Mollie O'Connor, played by Dorothy Gish, believes in his innocence.

When he returns from serving his time, Tony learns that his brother, Carlo, is still under the influence of Nick and his gang. Tony confronts Nick, and in the ensuring fight, a gunshot accidentally wounds Tony's mother. Nick attempts to flee the scene, but falls to a sudden death.

Fortunately, Tony's mother recovers from the gunshot, and lives to see Mollie and Tony marry. The beauty of his city comes to full realization with Tony, as he and Mollie go through the Battery on their way to Coney Island.

In the *New York Times*, Mordaunt Hall wrote, "Mr. Barthelmess is engaging, but a little high strung in some of the scenes. Dorothy Gish enacts the part of Mollie, which calls for little in the way of talent. William Powell makes the villainy as impressive as possible. It takes a great admiration for Mr. Barthelmess to be blind to the weaknesses in this film."

Variety's review noted, "A fair story and release, but far below the recent standards . . . it is not of the type expected form a star who ranks so high . . . In so far as atmosphere goes it is good, and the cast is also good . . . lighting and photography just fair and direction weak. But the star gives a good performance and Miss Gish is likeable in her part, so that may save the day."

Advertisement for the Kenneth Webb film, *The Beautiful City* (1925).

Richard Barthelmess with Dorothy Gish in Kenneth Webb's *The Beautiful City* (1925).

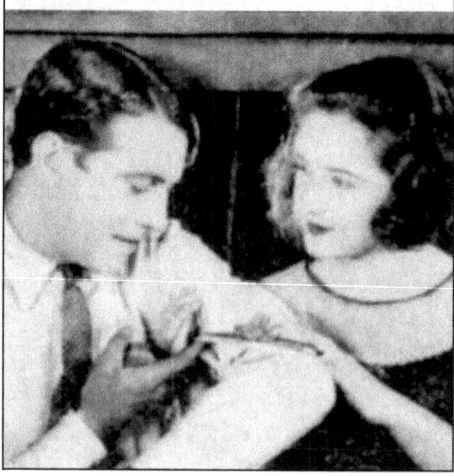

Three scenes from Kenneth Webb's *The Beautiful City* (1925), featuring Richard Barthelmess, Dorothy Gish, and William Powell.

JUST SUPPOSE (1926) ALSO KNOWN AS GOLDEN YOUTH

INSPIRATION-FIRST NATIONAL
DIRECTOR: KENNETH WEBB
SCENARIO: C. Graham Baker, from an adaptation by Violet E. Powell
LENGTH: 8 REELS
CAST: Richard Barthelmess, Lois Moran, Geoffrey Kerr, Henry Vibart, George Spelvin, Harry Short, Bijou Fernandez, Prince Rokneddine
SYNOPSIS: This story of royal courtship between twins in a mythical land follows Richard Barthelmess as Prince Rupert as he travels from Koronia to America. The Prince is bored with the trappings of his monarchy, and while in American, finds himself falling in love with Linda Lee Stafford, played by Lois Moran. The romance is interrupted when his father, the crown prince, unexpectedly dies. Rupert rushes home, and after his father's funeral, learns he is bound to assume the head of the monarchy and take place in an arranged, royal wedding.

In a surprising plot twist, the widow of the late crown prince gives birth to twins, who usurp Rupert's position as the next in line for the crown. Freed from the arranged marriage by fate, Rupert brings Linda to his home in Europe where they are married.

Just Suppose was released in Europe as *Golden Youth*. A review in the British magazine, *Picture Show*, said, "Ruritanian romance, in which Richard Barthelmess works hard as the Prince. Lois Moran is charming as the American girl with whom he falls in love. Their combined histrionic efforts and personal charm fail, however, to win the film high recommendation.

In *Variety*, a reviewer wrote, ". . . it ranks as the best thing (from the public viewpoint) he has ever done. It is a sweet proposition, filled not only with sentiment but with a gentle whimsicality, which both Mr. Barthelmess and Miss Moran express competently. The production is superb, ditto the direction, and the acting in every instance is of the best, and right here it is predicted that the week's receipts at the Strand, where a big revue is also on the bill, will reflect the merit of the show . . . Barthelmess is great in every foot of film."

Just Suppose newspaper advertisement as it appeared in the *Decatur Review*.

Three scenes from Kenneth Webb's *Just Suppose* (1926), featuring Richard Barthelmess and Lois Moran.

RANSON'S FOLLY (1926)
INSPIRATION-FIRST NATIONAL
PRODUCER: SIDNEY OLCOTT
DIRECTOR: SIDNEY OLCOTT
SCENARIO: Lillie Hayward, based on a story by Richard Harding Davis
LENGTH: 8 REELS
CAST: Richard Barthelmess, Dorothy Mackaill, Andes Randolph, Pat Hartigan
SYNOPSIS: This story of stagecoach robberies on the early American frontier had been made into films twice before: an early 1910 Edison version starring William J. Sorelle, and a 1915 version starring Marc MacDermott.

This new version follows Richard Barthelmess as Lieutenant Ranson, a United States Army officer stationed at a dreamy outpost on the Western frontier. Adventure escapes his post, though the lovely Mary Cahill, played by Dorothy Mackaill, brightens his life. As a harmless prank, Ranson holds up a stagecoach while disguising himself as a mysterious bandit, calling himself the "Red Rider." Two passengers, Miss Post and her aunt, witness the robbery and watch the Red Rider disappear into the dust of the prairie. The stage leaves the scene of the hold-up and returns safely to the outpost where the two traveling companions visit Colonel Bolland.

Unknown to them, Ranson has doubled back to the post, quickly returned to his Army uniform, and suddenly reappears to innocently dance with Miss Post. To everyone's surprise, word arrives that the real Red Rider has shot the paymaster on the stage, and Ranson is arrested by the military police for the crime. Mary Cahill is the only person who believes in his innocence. Ranson is court-martialed and found guilty, partly by the testimony of Mary's father. Ranson believes that Mary will suffer if he is freed, so he pleads guilty. Mary's father realized the girl is in love with Ranson, and at the same time, the real Red Rider is caught. Mary's father changes his testimony, saving Ranson and clearing the way for the two young lovers.

Mordaunt Hall wrote in the *New York Times*, "That popular cinema actor, Richard Barthelmess, portrays the part of Lieutenant Ranson, and as there must be a romance in almost every picture, Dorothy Mackaill officiates as the fuzzy-haired Mary Cahill, the girl who never doubts her hero. Sidney Olcott, who has a number of sterling pictures to his credit, directed *Ranson's Folly*, and he permits Mr. Barthelmess to play the giddy garden goat during a fire episode. Ranson is supposed to be inspiring the soldiers in their attempt to extinguish the blaze, but the goes a little too far when his spirits soar to the extent of playing leap-frog over the men's backs while they are pouring water on the flames . . . Mr. Barthelmess, except for his gymnastic exhibition, is a little more natural than he has been in some other productions."

Variety's reviewer disagreed with Mordaunt Hall, writing, "*Ranson's Folly* is not a good picture and must wholly depend upon the drawing power of Richard Barthelmess or Dorothy Mackaill or both. Where neither is a draw, this picture cannot stand up. It is silly to the point of aggravation, old fashioned in story and picturization, while its western tale is almost farcical all of the time and dreadfully farcical at the finale. Its direction is not any too brilliant, held down by the story's limitations, while the photography is often annoying through so many long shots."

A writer in *Motion Picture Classic* agreed with *Variety* in their review: "I don't find many pictorial values in *Ranson's Folly*, Richard Barthelmess' new canvas. As fiction, it had its appeal when Richard Harding Davis wrote it many years ago. But shaping itself on the screen it doesn't resemble anything but an old-fashioned romantic melodrama with the obvious always in the offing, so that any quality of suspense is destroyed. The piece carries Barthelmess and the spectators back to the last century at the time the slippery Sioux had been driven across the border. It gives the star an opportunity to portray one of those dashing lieutenants who, to overcome the boredom of the post, stages a hold-up out of pure mischief. The plot revolves around the circumstantial evidence piled up against him. And he, in a spirit of self-sacrifice, admits the guilt to spare the father of the girl who captured his heart. This parent, in the meanwhile, has also acted in the same spirit. But it is easy to anticipate that neither will be held accountable for the crime. That's how hackneyed this picture is — what with a plot that never develops any stirring action. There are some first-rate atmospheric details — the old army uniforms and the flouncing dresses worn by the officers' wives lending a picturesque note. And the backgrounds are praise-worthy, too. The trouble is the weakness of the picture — for it is not up to the Barthelmess mark. He conducts himself heroically enough, but there are no occasions for him to display any emotional fire. As for Dorothy Mackaill, she wears her hair down her back and affects an innocent appeal. It is just a part — and nothing else. So I catalog this as just an ordinary melodrama. Barthelmess doesn't need these old-fashioned stories with their old-fashioned heroics. He shines best in the unusual characterizations."

Ranson's Folly **print advertisement as it appeared in many magazines around the country.**

Richard Barthelmess in Sidney Olcott's *Ranson's Folly* (1926).

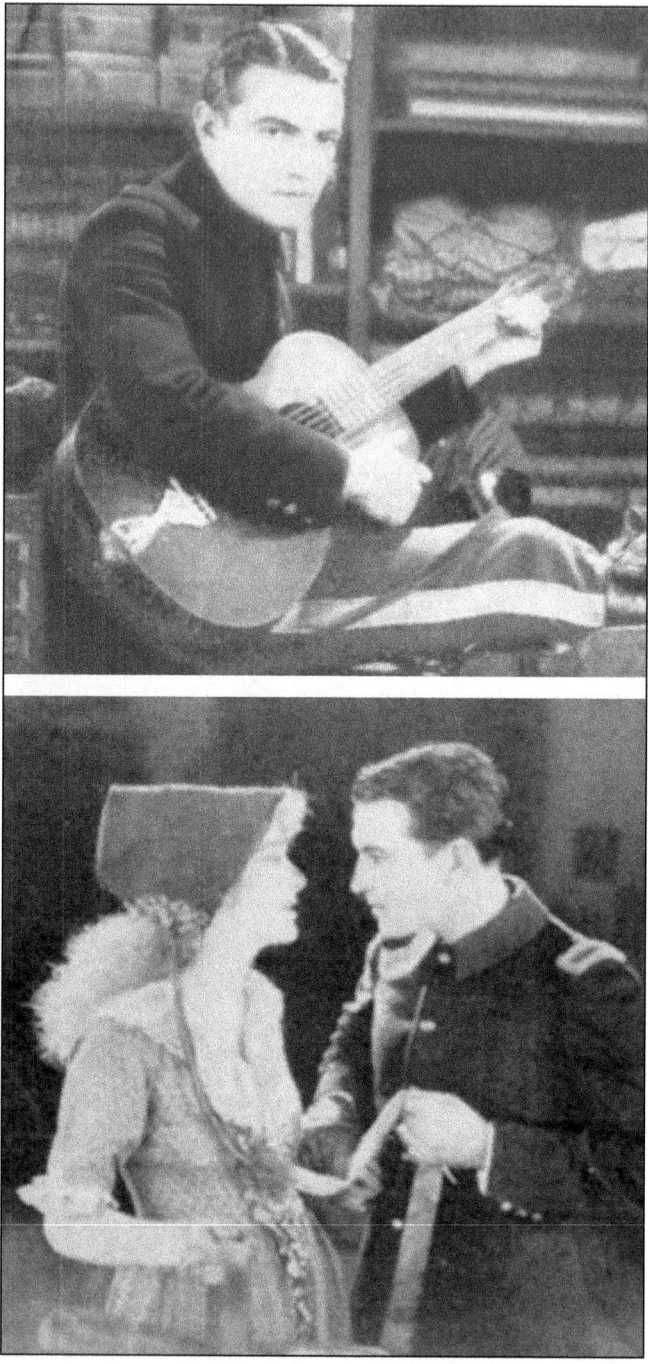

Two scenes from Sidney Olcott's *Ranson's Folly* (1926), starring Richard Barthelmess and Dorothy Mackaill.

THE AMATEUR GENTLEMAN (1926)
INSPIRATION-FIRST NATIONAL
PRODUCER: SIDNEY OLCOTT
DIRECTOR: SIDNEY OLCOTT
SCENARIO: Lillie Hayward, based on a novel by Jeffery Farnol
LENGTH: 8 REELS
CAST: Richard Barthelmess, Dorothy Dunbar, Gardener James, Nigel Barrie, Brandon Hurst, John Miljan, Edwards Davis, Billie Bennett, Herbert Grimwood, Gino Corrado, Sidney De Gray, John Peters

Synopsis: This story of murder among London nobility follows Richard Barthelmess as Barnabas Barthy, the son of a former prizefighter. As the sole surviving son, Barnabas inherits his father's fortune, and moves to London to live a gentleman's life. Along the way, he meets Lady Cleone, falls in love, and faces his rival for her affection.

In London, Sir Mortimer seethes with jealousy for the love of Lady Cleone. Barnabas becomes friendly with Viscount Deveham, buys a horse, and enters the steeplechase. Sir Mortimer enacts treachery, turns Lady Cleone's brother against him, and enters the race to best Barnabas. Unfortunately for him, his efforts fail, and Barnabas wins the race and earns the social standing for which he sought. To spite Lady Cleone, Sir Mortimer buys the outstanding debts from her worthless brother and has creditors threaten him with prison. In desperation, her brother kills the creditors, and then in another fight, kills Sir Mortimer. Barnabas returns to his home discouraged and disillusioned. Lady Cleone follows him, and together, they face a new life united by love.

The *New York Times'* reviewer, Mordaunt Hall, wrote in his review, "Colorful views of old England were depicted in this story of the days when haughty heroines dallied with villainous knights. Although this picture is not alive with suspense, it has its captivating moments, due to the frank and simple manner in which it has been produced and Richard Barthelmess's sympathetic portrayal of Barnabas Barty, the handsome son of an ex-pugilist and innkeeper, who, on inheriting a huge fortune, aspires to be a gentleman."

Variety's reviewer said, "A costume picture crammed with action and a not uninteresting story. Richard Barthelmess does a modified

Beau Brummel, rides to win in an antiquated steeplechase race, rough and tumbles a bit and makes of it satisfactory fare for the bigger and better houses ... Barthelmess does sincerely and well, ably supported by a good sized detachment of male cast members. There are only two women prominent ... nothing to be ashamed of by anyone in this release. The censors can't arbitrarily clip a foot and it gives Barthelmess all kinds of opportunities besides being sufficiently romantic."

The Amateur Gentleman print advertisement as it appeared in many magazines around the country.

Richard Barthelmess as the prizefighter's son who inherits a fortune and becomes a London gentleman, in Sidney Olcott's *The Amateur Gentleman* (1926).

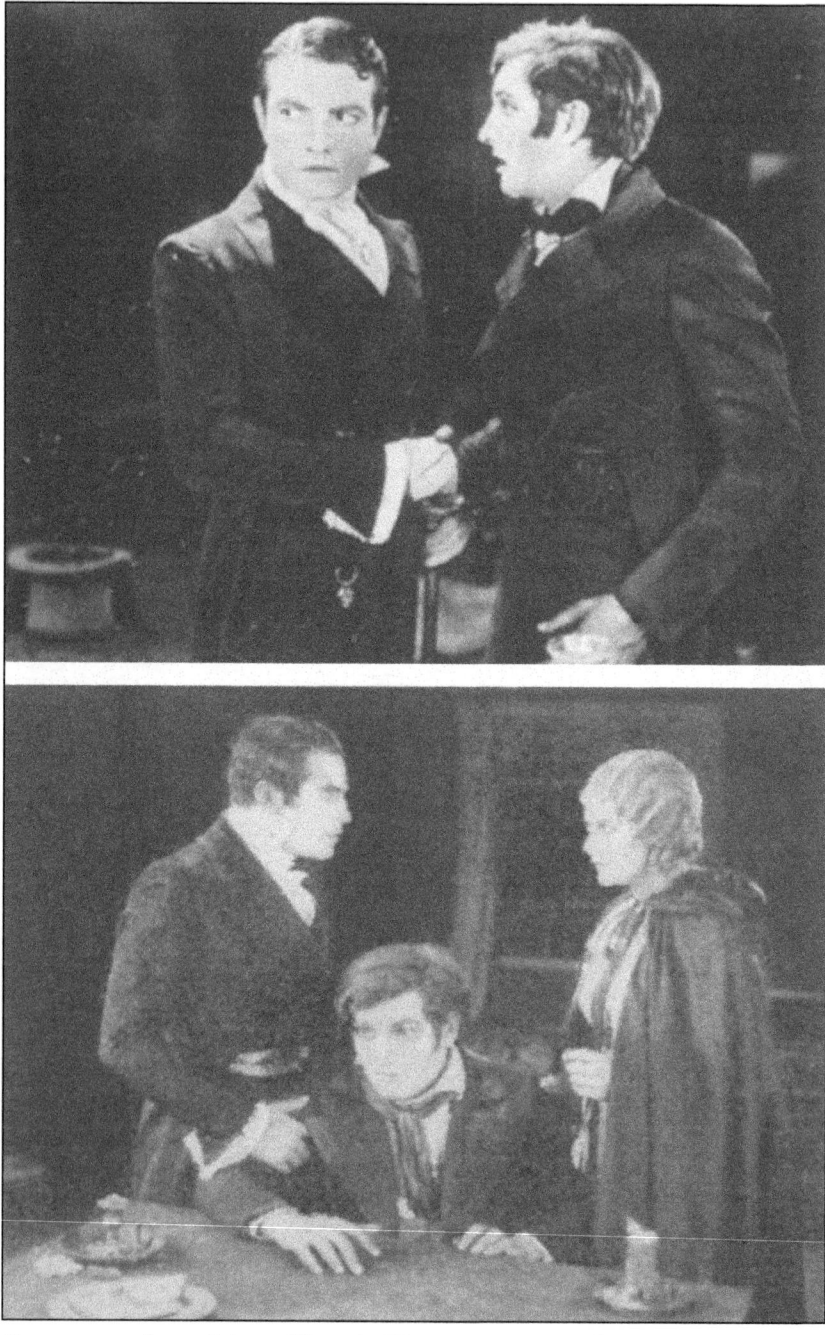

Two scenes from Sidney Olcott's *The Amateur Gentleman* (1926): (TOP) **Richard Barthelmess and Gardner James, and** (BOTTOM) **Barthelmess, James, and Dorothy Dunbar.**

THE WHITE BLACK SHEEP (1926)
INSPIRATION-FIRST NATIONAL
PRODUCER: SYDNEY OLCOTT
DIRECTOR: SYDNEY OLCOTT
SCENARIO: Jerome N. Wilson and Agnes McKenna, based on a story by Violet E. Powell
LENGTH: 7 REELS
CAST: Richard Barthelmess, Patsy Ruth Miller, Constance Howard, Erville Alderson, William H. Tooker, Gino Corrado, Albert Prisco, Sam Appel, Col. G. L. MacDonell, Templar Saxe
SYNOPSIS: As Robert Kincarin, the son of a British Army Colonel, Richard Barthelmess plays a young man assuming the guilt for a theft committed by his fiancée, played by Patsy Ruth Miller. For the alleged crime, his father renounces him. Robert joins the British forces in Palestine, and while engaged, encounters a traitorous desert chieftain, El Rahib, and defends Zelie, a Greek dancer, from him. In turn, Zelie saves Robert and restores him to health.

Robert takes on the disguise of a mute beggar, enters the camp of El Rahib intent on discovering his secret plans to attack the British. He is discovered and tortured, but later escapes and tells his father of El Rahib's treachery. The tribesmen are overtaken, Enid confesses her role in the original theft, Robert is cleared of the charges, and he and Zelie find ultimate happiness.

Mordaunt Hall wrote in his *New York Times* review, "This is the film in which Richard wore a full beard for the first time. Sidney Olcott directed the story's absurd situations involving Arabs and their antics with white men in the Sahara desert. There is plenty of sand in Richard Barthelmess's new production, *The White Black Sheep*. There are also enough mounted Arabs who ride over the nice-looking desert. As a matter of fact the scenic effects in this production would pass muster on any screen, but the story is quite another matter. There must be a frightful scarcity of motion picture material if a producer can enthuse over the incidents in *The White Black Sheep* . . . the acting in this affair is just about what is required by the yarn."

A reviewer for *Variety* wrote, "There are more than a couple of raps coming to this picture. The first might be one of those 'What the well-dressed picture actor should not wear,' and the answer would be for Richard Barthelmess to lay off of the dress clothes he wore in this picture. It made him look like a fellow without any neck and a hunch on his back. Then, Sidney Olcott has turned out a picture that doesn't get anywhere outside of a couple of suspense scenes toward the end of it. The third rap will to a great extent exonerate Olcott, and that is the story is one of those things the screen has had time and again, and a great many times a whole lot better. Total all three of these and the chances are that you'll find the answer: a cluck."

Advertisement for the Sidney Olcott film, *The White Black Sheep* (1926).

Patsy Ruth Miller, Richard Barthelmess, and William H. Tooker, in Sidney Olcott's *The White Black Sheep* (1926).

Richard Barthelmess as the disowned son who redeems himself in the Orient, in Sidney Olcott's *The White Black Sheep* (1926).

THE PATENT LEATHER KID (1927)
FIRST NATIONAL
PRODUCER: ALFRED SANTELL
DIRECTOR: ALFRED SANTELL
SCENARIO: Winifred Dunn, based on an adaptation by Adela Rogers St. Johns and a story by Rupert Hughes
LENGTH: 12 REELS
CAST: Richard Barthelmess, Molly O'Day, Arthur Stone, Matthew Betz, Lawford Davidson, Raymond Turner, Hank Mann, Walter James, Lucien Prival, Nigel de Brulier, Fred O'Beck, Cliff Salam, Henry Murdock, Charles Sullivan, John Kolb, Al Alleborn
SYNOPSIS: While World War One rages in Europe, a boxer in the lower East side of New York shows little affection for his country. Curly Boyl is pictured with natural traits, a man who can stand up against the best of fighters and bring them down for the count. Yet, his weaknesses are brought out when his girl leaves him to entertain troops in France, and Curly is drafted along with his trainer, Puffy.

One entrenched in the war, Curly is shown as a shaking spectacle, while his stuttering trainer, Puffy, who would never have dared to put on gloves in the boxing ring, proves to be a man of steel under fire. When Puffy is shot and killed, Curly is spurred on to take battlefield chances, and reveals his true, brave nature in a shell hole when he plunges ahead to bomb a church belfry. His trainer's death inspires his hatred for the enemy. Curly is badly injured and becomes partially paralyzed. Later, while watching a military parade and seeing the American flag unfurled, his previously paralyzed hand slowly rises in salute.

Mordaunt Hall, writing his review in the *New York Times*, praised Richard's work in this film more highly than any other, saying "Under the direction of Alfred A. Santell, who has already made his mark in the motion picture world, Richard Barthelmess, in a film called *The Patent Leather Kid*, excels any performance he has hitherto given. There is not a single flaw in his acting throughout this long feature . . . it is an interesting character study, for the hero in this case is pictured with natural traits, a man who can stand up against the best of fighters and bring them down for the count. Yet his weaknesses are brought out, and when he becomes a doughboy, he is seen as a shaking spectacle, while his stuttering trainer, Puffy, who would have never dared to put the gloves on against any of the Kid's ring opponents, proves under fire to be a man of steel." The reviewer also noted some telling effects accomplished with sound in the presentation of the picture while at the Globe Theater in New York, including the use of phonograph voices synchronized during the prize fight scenes and piped through the loud speakers into the auditorium.

Variety agreed in its review: "For Barthelmess, perfect, even if Barthelmess is made to play what at times is a repulsive role, that of a slacker during wartime, and admittedly so . . . Barthelmess is such a big portion of this long film, in action and work, that he must come before the picture itself . . . probably the reddest red-fire finish any picture ever has had. The Patent Leather one, in battle and performing a valiant act of or which he was decorated, after all of his professed cowardice, is under the care of his sweetie." The review went on to note the use of amplifiers in broadcasting synchronized sound from disc recordings to supplant ringside noises during the big fight scenes.

The Patent Leather Kid print advertisement as it appeared in many magazines around the country.

Richard Barthelmess and Molly O'Day in Alfred Santell's *The Patent Leather Kid* (1927).

(TOP) "The Kid" in the ring, and (BOTTOM) his girlfriend argues with the manager in Alfred Santell's *The Patent Leather Kid* (1927).

(TOP) **Curly "the Kid"** admired by a throng of hangers-on, and (BOTTOM) unwillingly conscripted in the draft, in Alfred Santell's *The Patent Leather Kid* (1927).

(TOP) **Knee deep in the flooded trenches at zero hour, and** (BOTTOM) **caught in crossfire at a shell hole in Alfred Santell's** *The Patent Leather Kid* **(1927).**

(TOP) **In trying to save his pal, Curly realizes his first desire to fight, and** (BOTTOM) **a tank rolls over Curly, in Alfred Santell's** The Patent Leather Kid **(1927).**

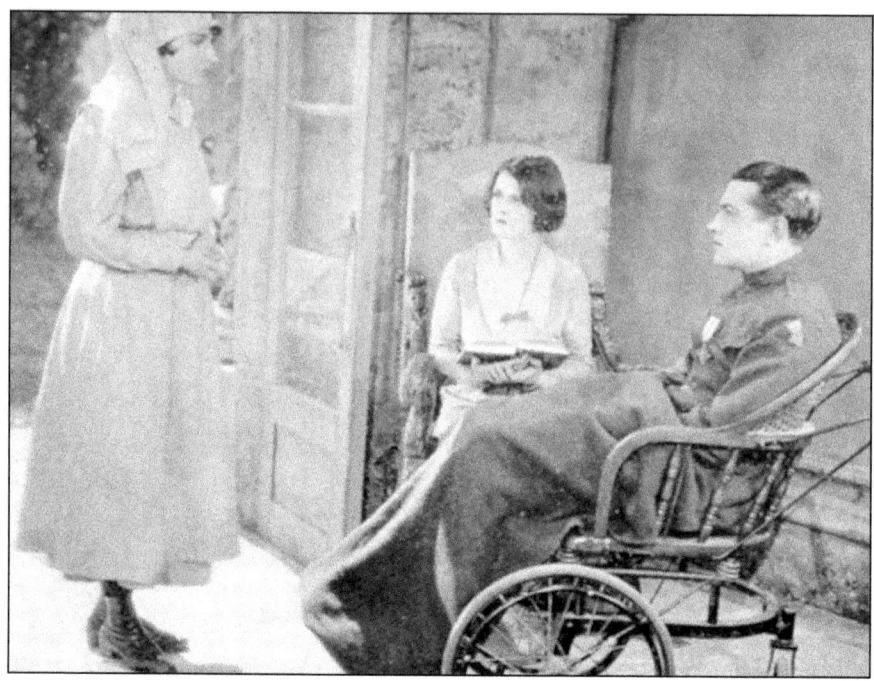

A nurse announces the decoration ceremony for the next day, in Alfred Santell's *The Patent Leather Kid* (1927).

THE DROP KICK (1927)
FIRST NATIONAL
PRODUCER: MILLARD WEBB
DIRECTOR: ALFRED SANTELL
SCENARIO: WINIFRED DUNN
LENGTH: 7 REELS
CAST: Richard Barthelmess, Barbara Kent, Dorothy Revier, Hedda Hopper, Alberta Vaughn, Eugene Strong, James Bradbury, Jr., Brooks Benedict, Mayme Kelso, George Pearce
SYNOPSIS: This story of college football and suicide follows Richard Barthelmess as Jock Hamill, a star of his college football team. The coach's wife, Eunice, flirts shamelessly with him, and spends money above and beyond her husband's income. To finance her extravagances, the coach embezzles money from the university, and when he is caught, he commits suicide rather than face up to his mistake. Eunice creates a trap and seduces Jock into promising marriage. In the moment of her seduction, Jock is discovered with her and suspected of murdering the coach.

The big game follows, and Jock nearly loses the game by failing to perform as usual. But in a final surprise, he returns to his old prowess and drop kicks the winning play. His mother exposes the truth of the coach's suicide, and Jock is saved from the disgrace.

Mordaunt Hall commented in the *New York Times*, "The story of *The Drop Kick*, Richard Barthelmess's latest screen adventure, is one wherein the producers and others have successfully dodged anything in the form of human psychology. It is the type of picture that may appeal to those who have a sneaking suspicion that the hero won't win the girl or even the football game . . . Considering the picture and the fact that he is not to blame for some of the hero's queer acts, Mr. Barthelmess gives a good performance."

Variety's reviewer wrote, "This picture has several weaknesses, but should be a moderate money-maker with the Barthelmess name . . . Barthelmess remains young-looking enough for college and handles his part well . . . photography was off in spots, possible due to a bad print. Most of it was of the better class. The football game is a weakness in production, failing to impress as much as most of its predecessors in college pictures."

The Drop Kick newspaper advertisement as it appeared in the *Lima News*.

Four scenes from Alfred Santell's *The Drop Kick* (1927), featuring (TOP RIGHT AND LOWER LEFT) **Alberta Vaughn, and** (LOWER RIGHT) **Dorothy Revier.**

THE NOOSE (1928)
FIRST NATIONAL
PRODUCER: HENRY HOBART
DIRECTOR: JOHN FRANCIS DILLON
SCENARIO: H. H. Van Loan and Willard Mack, based on adaptation by James T. O'Donohoe
LENGTH: 8 REELS
CAST: Richard Barthelmess, Alice Joyce, Lina Basquette, Montagu Love, Robert E. O'Connor, Jay Eaton, Thelma Todd, Ed Brady, Fred Warren, Charles Giblyn, Alice Joyce, William Walling, Robert T. Haines, Ernest Hilliard, Emile Chautard, Romaine Fielding, Yola d'Avril, Corliss Palmer, Kay English, Cecil Brunner, Janice Peters, Ruth Lord, May Atwood

SYNOPSIS: As Nickie Elkins, a hijacker, Richard Barthelmess meets a gangster he believes is his father. From him, he learns that his mother is the governor's wife. Nickie kills the gangster, is arrested, tried, and sentenced to die at the gallows. When the governor's wife takes an interest in his case, she intervenes and tries to save his life by begging her husband, the governor, to pardon him on the day of the execution. Capital punishment is explored in graphic detail in this powerful tale.

Mordaunt Hall wrote in the *New York Times*, "The piece is amply loaded with tragic irony and sentiment, so loaded that it occasionally splits and the pieces must be forced back by devices somewhat shopworn. As, for example, when the Governor's wife goes into a trance before calling the warden of the prison to put off the execution. A better method could be found, although the obvious supposition is that mother love will triumph over everything from

Lina Basquette with Richard Barthelmess in John Francis Dillon's *The Noose* (1928).

mistaken identity upwards . . . Mr. Barthelmess is not always at his best in the picture, being designed by nature less for a bootlegger and more for a football hero."

Variety wrote in its review, "It is an extremely well directed and played drama, with meller tendencies, a touch of the underworld with a real cabaret scene one of the standouts, but underneath the rest, a virile story of suspensive qualities that are all taken advantage of. Barthelmess' Nickie is a natural for him, although Barthelmess is more likable in action. That's where he sins. Nevertheless, Barthelmess has a distinctive individuality on the screen, and it's very valuable, for few own it. He always suggests impulsiveness, and that's suspense in itself, continually."

(TOP) **Alice Joyce and Richard Barthelmess, and** (BOTTOM) **Lina Basquette, in John Francis Dillon's *The Noose* (1928).**

THE LITTLE SHEPHERD OF KINGDOM COME (1928)
AKA KENTUCKY COURAGE (1928)
FIRST NATIONAL
PRODUCER: ALFRED SANTELL
DIRECTOR: ALFRED SANTELL WITH RICHARD A. ROWLAND AND HENRY HOBART
SCENARIO: Bess Meredyth, based on a novel by John Fox Jr.
LENGTH: 8 REELS
CAST: Richard Barthelmess, Molly O'Day, Nelson McDowell, Martha Mattox, Victor Potel, Mark Hamilton, William Bertram, Walter Lewis, Gardner James, Ralph Yearsley, Gustav von Seyffertitz, Robert Milasch, Claude Gillingwater, David Torrence, Eulalie Jensen, Doris Dawson, Walter Rogers
SYNOPSIS: The story follows Richard Barthelmess as Chad, a Kentucky-born orphan growing up during the American Civil War. After being adopted by Major Buford, Chad attends a school in Lexington. When he hears of the outbreak of war, he joins the Union Army and loses the affection of his foster father and his sweetheart, Margaret Dean.

As a Captain, Chad is sent to his hometown on war duties, and rediscovers his childhood sweetheart, Melissa Turner. Their old romance is rekindled and Chad soon forgets Margaret. His foster father dies, and it is revealed that he had been a blood relative of the Buford family all along. He is offered the Major's estate if he will return to Kentucky, but chooses instead to remain with Melissa.

Mordaunt Hall wrote in the *New York Times*, "The best that may be said of this picture is that it is only fair. Mr. Barthelmess does not make a good rugged type of youthful hero and many of the good parts have been cut from John Fox Jr.'s *The Little Shepherd of Kingdom Come* on which the plot is based . . . as a book went smoothly and logically along with a natural swing; the picture does not. There are gory fights, rainstorms, and horseback riding, making a turbulence of what was once a particularly fine story. Mr. Barthelmess, in the title role, is all right as soon as he gets to the college stage of his career. In earlier life, however, when he is homeless and alone, he is absurd."

According to a reviewer writing in the *Lima News*, "An outstanding performance, in addition to that of the star, is given by Molly

O'Day, the clever seventeen-year old girl who plays opposite Barthelmess. It was this same Molly, who in her first important part in *The Patent Leather Kid*, became a screen sensation overnight . . . a worthy picturization of this novel of the last decade, and again illustrates the adaptability of this screen star."

A reviewer for the *Appleton Post Crescent* wrote, "*Tol'able David* has been re-incarnated — reborn under the magic touch of Richard Barthelmess, who once again has created a barefoot boy . . . as Chad Buford, the Kentucky mountain lad, who dreamed of the settlement's books and grand persons, Dick Barthelmess has added another lovable and unforgettable portrait to his already brilliant gallery. Throughout the last few years, Barthelmess has grown to be more than a name or even a personality, merely incidental designations. He has become symbols: Romance to Everygirl, Son to Everymother, or the Man-boy. He is a very real Peter Pan refusing to grow up, a mirror reflecting the boyhood days of Everyman. If these United States ever decided to erect a monument to American youth, then this selfsame *Tol'able David* and *Little Shepherd* will be its model — idealistic — composite — the culmination of the great American crucible. Dick, they call him — all of them! And that's significant. It's boyish and yet manly. Only chums and buddies call a man named Richard by the more intimate and friendly "Dick." Girls, too. It's irresistible. Dick Barthelmess as Chad Buford is a revelation, startling and breathtaking.

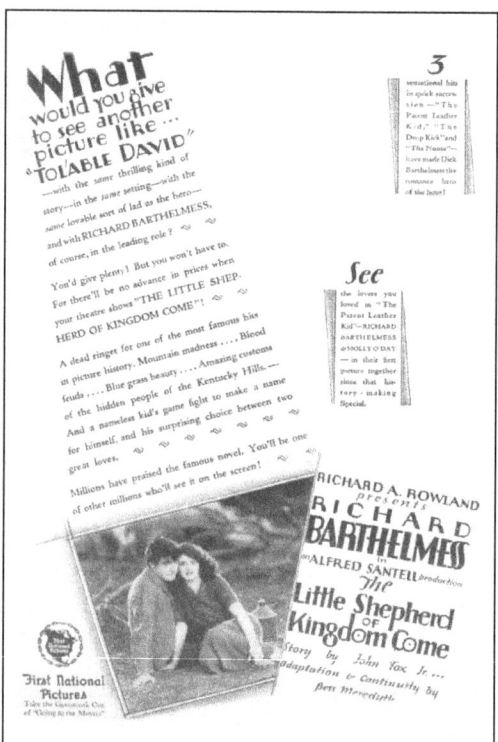

The Little Shepherd of Kingdom Come print advertisement as it appeared in many magazines around the country.

It is uncanny that a man should be able to etch a delicate character such as Chad after the six-year interval since David. *The Little Shepherd of Kingdom Come* will long occupy the deepest recesses of the American heart because Dick Barthelmess has given it flesh and blood and soul; because only the screen's man-boy could have imbued it with feeling and understanding."

Richard Barthelmess as Chad Buford, a barefoot boy of the Kentucky hills, in Alfred Santell's *The Little Shepherd of Kingdom Come* (1928).

Two scenes from Alfred Santell's *The Little Shepherd of Kingdom Come* (1928).

WHEEL OF CHANCE (1928)
FIRST NATIONAL
PRODUCER: ALFRED SANTELL WITH RICHARD A. ROWLAND
DIRECTOR: ALFRED SANTELL
SCENARIO: Gerald C. Duffy, based on a story, *Roulette*, by Fannie Hurst
LENGTH: 7 REELS
CAST: Richard Barthelmess, Lina Basquette, Warner Oland, Margaret Livingston, Bodil Rosing, Ann Schaefer, Sidney Franklin, Martha Franklin
SYNOPSIS: Richard Barthelmess plays Russian twins, Nickolai and Schmulka Turkeltaub. After the apparent death of Schmulka, the Turkeltaub family immigrates to America. Years pass, and Nickolai becomes a prominent district attorney engaged to marry.

Unknown to him, his twin brother, Schmulka, survived, and has grown to manhood under the name, Jacob Talinef. A midwife, Janscha Talinef, brought him to America as a youth, and Jacob lived a life very different than his brother. A gangster and a drunkard, Jacob accidentally kills a promiscuous girlfriend and goes on trial for murder. As fate would have it, his long-lost brother is assigned to the bizarre case and reunited with his twin. His mother pleads for leniency, and after the trial, Jacob serves a brief prison term and is finally reunited with his family.

In his *New York Times* review, Mordaunt Hall wrote, "It is all about two brothers who don't know one another at the more or less crucial time. It is not a masterpiece of any art save that of stretching the long arm of coincidence way beyond its breaking point. There is plenty of Mr. Barthelmess in the picture, for he occupies every scene at least once; very often twice. One part he takes is that of a young assistant district attorney trying his first murder case; the other is that of being the defendant in that same case. In this latter position he adopts a disguise, to be sure, but it is thin enough so that the audience, used to this sort of thing, never doubts that Mr. Barthelmess 'A' is really the brother of Mr. Barthelmess 'B.'"

Variety's reviewer wrote, "Two angles give this picture good value. First is the excellent handling of a dual role by Richard Barthelmess, and second is a certain O. Henry quality in the story of twin brothers, separated by chance in Russia during childhood and coming together years later in New York, each the product of the mystic chances of life . . . picture has many bits of fine suggestion and Barthelmess plays the dual role of the brothers well, achieving striking effects in contrasts while making both portraits convincing with acting at once authentic and legitimate . . . dramatic passages are skillfully managed in a vein of quiet emphasis, and the cast never over-emphasizes. Technical production is first rate."

Advertisement for the Alfred Santell film, *Wheel of Chance* (1928).

Richard Barthelmess as Jason, the bad twin brother, in Alfred Santell's *Wheel of Chance* (1928).

Richard Barthelmess as Nickolai, the good twin, with his fiancé, played by Lina Basquette, and his mother, played by Bodil Rosing, in Alfred Santell's *Wheel of Chance* (1928).

Nickolai, a prosecuting attorney, finds himself involved in the trial of Jason without knowing the man is his long-lost brother, dual roles played by Richard Barthelmess in Alfred Santell's *Wheel of Chance* (1928).

OUT OF THE RUINS (1928)
FIRST NATIONAL
PRODUCER: JOHN FRANCIS DILLON
DIRECTOR: ALFRED SANTELL
SCENARIO: Gerald C. Duffy, based on a story by Sir Philip Gibbs
LENGTH: 7 REELS
CAST: Richard Barthelmess, Marian Nixon, Eugene Pallette, Robert Frazer, Emile Chautard, Bodil Rosing, Rose Dione
SYNOPSIS: As Lieutenant Pierre Dumont, Richard Barthelmess pals with another soldier, Paul Gilbert, during World War One. The two take a leave and visit Paris, where Pierre meets his Paul's sister, Yvonne, and falls in love. The two lovers are torn apart when Pierre must return to the front lines. During a brief lull in the fighting, Pierre leaves his regiment without leave and returns to Paris to marry Yvonne. When his conscience strikes him with guilt for the desertion, Pierre returns to the troops, is court-martialed, and sentenced to die by firing squad. At the last moment, his comrades refuse to kill him, and Pierre is allowed to live out the war.

Thinking Pierre is dead, Yvonne gives in to her parents who force her into an arranged marriage. Suddenly, Pierre appears in Paris to reunite with Yvonne, and her father reports him to the Army authorities. His friend, Paul, tells the commandant of the profound love between Pierre and Yvonne, and he solves the problem by declaring Pierre officially dead. The couple is then free to start live anew under a different name and find true happiness.

In the *New York Times*, Mordaunt Hall wrote, "The outstanding features of this production are Richard Barthelmess's restrained acting and the intelligent performance of the beautiful Miss Nixon . . . quite a number of the incidents are expertly filmed and the romance between Pierre and Yvonne is admirably acted."

In *Variety*, another reviewer wrote, "Not much of a feature for Richard Barthelmess. It lacks the guts of the stories he has had of late . . . even as a part war picture, not much action. Played languidly. In fact, the tempo is irritating. All of the principals seemed trained for the same pace . . . picture won't do Barthelmess any good but one miss in a row of hits can't hurt him now."

In the town of Appleton, *Out of the Ruins*, Richard's 1928 silent film, was exhibiting at the same time as Al Jolson's *The Jazz Singer*. Page from *The Appleton Post Crescent*, August 28, 1928, page 14.

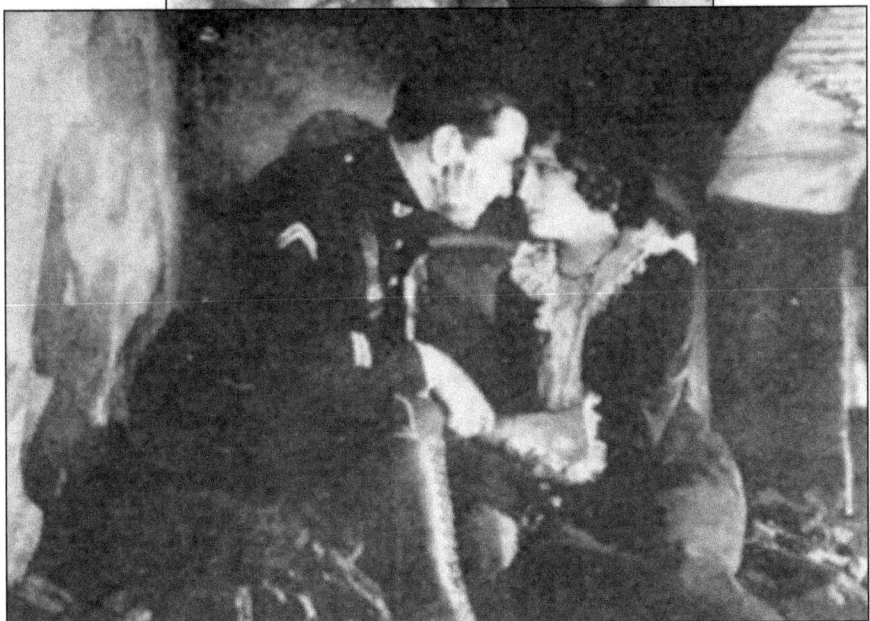

Richard Barthelmess with Marian Nixon in Alfred Santell's *Out of the Ruins* (1928). It was the last silent movie Richard made.

Scarlet Seas (1928)
First National
Producer: John Francis Dillon and Richard A. Rowland
Director: John Francis Dillon
Scenario: Bradley King, based on a story by W. Scott Darling
Length: 7 reels
Cast: Richard Barthelmess, Betty Compson, Loretta Young, James Bradbury, Jr., Jack Curtin, Knute Erickson
Synopsis: This story of mutinous sailors and shipwrecks follows Richard Barthelmess as Steve Donkin, a world-weary sailor who puts his schooner to port off the shore of Apia. He ventures into the town and meets a prostitute, Rose, and witnesses the local authorities ordering her to leave her waterfront dive and move away from the island. Rose asks Steve to take her to Shanghai, and he consents. On the way, his schooner sinks in the middle of the Pacific Ocean. Rose, Steve, and another sailor are cast adrift in a small lifeboat. Tension mounts and tempers clash and as food and water supplied deplete. The sailor attacks Steve, and is knocked overboard in the fight. Rose and Steve continue on their perilous journey close to death, but are soon rescued by a passing ship. Once on board, they find themselves in the middle of a mutiny. Donkin brings the violent eruption under control and rescues the ship's Captain. He and Rose are free to continue their love, as the boat heads to a safe harbor.

"Life on the ocean wave, with flaming ships, mutineers, a cabaret girl and a sympathetic Captain with his pale-faced daughter," wrote Mordaunt Hall in the *New York Times*, "quite a number of queer incidents crop up in the course of this nautical yarn, which may make a good diversion for those youngsters who are interested in gullet-slitting pirate yarns in which it is quite obvious that, although the hero really hasn't an earthly chance, he's going to win out in the end, odds or no odds. Mr. Barthelmess does very well in the circumstances. He is, however, to blame for the story, as it is presumed that he selected it."

Variety wrote in its review, "One of those pictures which keeps promising more than it ever attains. It also has been over-sounded. Outside of these two faults, with the aid of the Barthelmess name, it shouldn't do much box-office harm and will likely gross moderately. Strand audience gave full evidence of this feature's failure to meet its obligation at that point where Barthelmess rushes into the stateroom to save the girl, the next flash showing the men half-way through a half-hearted struggle. Dillon built up this sequence well enough to make balconies applaud just prior to the anticipated battle, but the obvious bad cutting and unconvincing action let the house down with a bump from which neither the film nor customers quite recovered."

The reviewer went on to describe the awkward use of the primitive foray into sound production: "Synchronization has gone out after everything, the score being superior to the effects. Latter parallel each other during the brawl in the joint and the abandoning of ship, one nullifying the other, and especially in this case, because they come close together. It'll make many a patron wish for the silent version, where a little headwork would have made the sound fit and consistent instead of overemphasizing. Door knocks are particularly ridiculous, listening as sledgehammer blows as Barthelmess starts searching what seem to be deserted cabins. A crude interruption of suspense for which there is no excuse."

Richard Barthelmess as Steve, the seafarer who has no faith in God, man, or woman, until a shipwreck, a mutiny, and an innocent girl regenerate him in John Francis Dillon's *Scarlet Seas* (1928).

Betty Compson and Richard Barthelmess in John Francis Dillon's *Scarlet Seas* (1928).

WEARY RIVER (1929)
FIRST NATIONAL
PRODUCER: RICHARD A. ROWLAND
DIRECTOR: FRANK LLOYD
SCENARIO: Bradley King, based on a story by Courtney Ryley Cooper, with dialogue by Thomas J. Geraghty
LENGTH: 8 REELS
CAST: Richard Barthelmess, Betty Compson, George Stone, Louis Natheaux, Raymond Turner, Gladden James, William Holden
SYNOPSIS: Richard plays Jerry, a gangster framed by an enemy, convicted, and sent to prison. While there, he leads the prison orchestra, and writes a song, inspired by a metaphorical utterance of the chaplain to the effect that, "The weariest river finds its way to the sea." In prison, he becomes a model prisoner, and the warden takes a fatherly interest in him. On his release, he makes a

vaudeville debut singing the film's title song, "Weary River," and later, while broadcasting, his erstwhile sweetheart, Alice, hears him and resolves to stay away from him so that he will go straight. But Jerry's interest in vaudeville is only half-hearted, and moves from job to job. When his criminal past is recalled, he drifts back into his old criminal life. Then, Alice reappears and, with the help of the warden, accomplishes what is taken for granted as his everlasting redemption. In time, he becomes a singing star on radio and marries Alice.

Mordaunt Hall wrote in the *New York Times*, "Richard Barthelmess was heard as well as seen last night from the screen of the Central Theater in a First National Vitaphone picture called *Weary River*. The chief attribute of this banal jailbird tale is that it has some interesting prison sequences, and perhaps there are those who may enthuse over Mr. Barthelmess's rendition of a song, also known as "Weary River." He does sing it quite well, but it would take a far better singer and a much better song to atone for the lack of imagination and suspense in this photoplay, which is one of those that slip from silence to sound every now and again."

Mordaunt Hall commented about the dialogue lines in the script, and observed the numerous times a character said, "Hello." Hall wrote, "If three crooks meet each one says 'Hello' adding the name of the man he is greeting. It is to be supposed, that this is the technique of the talking films. You even hear a kiss in this effusion. It is a pity that Mr. Barthelmess should waste his talent on such a hopeless hodge-podge as this. His acting, even in the would-be lachrymose scenes is not without merit."

"Measured from any angle, *Weary River* is a money picture for First National and a credit to Richard Barthelmess, Frank Lloyd, Betty Compson, and almost every artist associated in bringing it to the screen," wrote the reviewer for *Variety*. "A catalog of its merits includes the revelation by Richard Barthelmess of a melodious, vibrant tenor with which he sings the song, "Weary River," if he sings it, and which, take odds, will cause heavy chattering among the femme fans. Barthelmess emerges as possibly the first of the veteran film stars to register a clean-cut wow in the articulate cinema. His voice has human warmth, and he uses it with an unexpected range of effect. Always he is natural, sincere, nicely repressed, conveying by deft suggestion the shades of meaning, which speak to the sympathies. His singing is not only a climax to his performance but a new and interesting phase in his career."

Norbert Lusk wrote in *Picture Play*, "Richard Barthelmess' most effective picture since *The Patent Leather Kid* is his latest, *Weary River*. In spite of the so-called poetic title, the film is lively and entertaining, though the story is not the most remarkable ever filmed, and Mr. Barthelmess breaks his long silence to speak and sing. He does both very well, indeed, but he hasn't denied the report that a double sings in his stead . . . It is true this is not nearly as inspired as Jerry's song, but it has been directed with inspiration and acted uncommonly well, not only by Mr. Barthelmess, but by Betty Compson, of course, and Louis Natheaux, George Stone, and the once-familiar Gladden James. As in *The Barker*, Miss Compson shines as an audible actress."

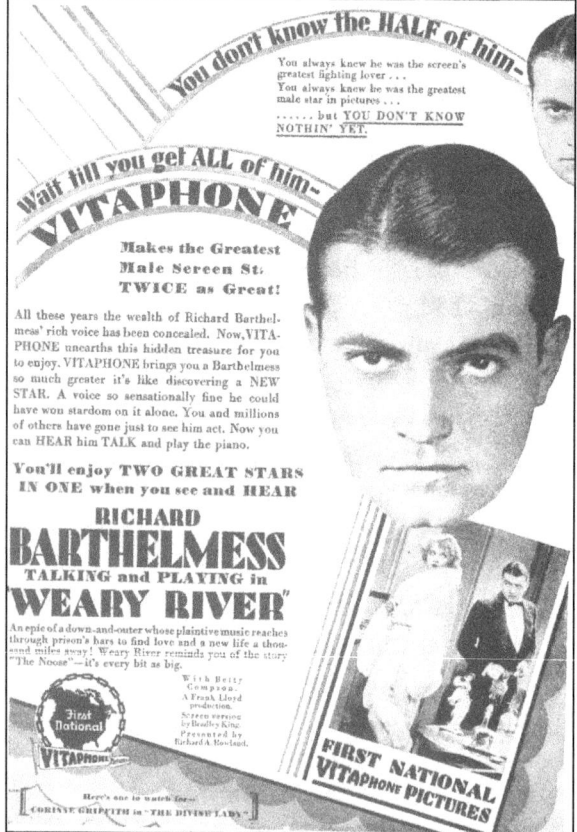

Weary River print advertisement as it appeared in many magazines around the country.

Richard Barthelmess as Jerry, the singing convict, in FrankLloyd's *Weary River* (1928).

Four scenes featuring Richard Barthelmess in Frank Lloyd's *Weary River* (1928).

Drag (1929)

First National
Producer: Richard A. Rowland
Director: Frank Lloyd
Scenario: Bradley King, based on a novel by William Dudley Pelley
Length: 9 reels
Cast: Richard Barthelmess, Lila Lee, Lucien Littlefield, Alice Day, Katherine Ward, Tom Dugan, Margaret Fielding.
Synopsis: The story follows Richard Barthelmess as David Carroll, a newly positioned editor of a small, Vermont newspaper. Along with his publishing work, David has written a musical play, and dreams of seeing it produced. Two young women are the center of his attention: Allie Parker, the daughter of a kindly couple running the boardinghouse where he lives, and Dot, the most sophisticated girl in town. David marries Allie, although he is more attracted to Dot. When David goes to New York to attempt to interest producers in his musical he meets up with Dot, now successful as a costume designer. She introduces him to some show business professionals,

Advertisement for the Frank Lloyd film, *Drag* (1928).

hoping to help him sell his play. While there together, David and Dot fall in love. He makes his fidelity to Allie clear to Dot, and she leaves for Paris disappointed. David sends for Allie to join him in New York, but when she arrives, her whole family is in tow. David follows Dot to Paris.

In the *New York Times*, Mordaunt Hall wrote in his review, "A talking picture in which the greeting 'Hello' is spoken so often that it becomes laughable was presented last night at Warner's Theater. In this feature, known as *Drag*, Richard Barthelmess figures as a young man who is imposed upon in an utterly absurd fashion by his wife's parents and her brother . . . Mr. Barthelmess acquits himself favorably . . . this is all told through spoken lines that are frequently awkward, halting, and amateurish."

Two scenes with Alice Day and Richard Barthelmess in Frank Lloyd's *Drag* (1929).

A reviewer in *Variety* disagreed, writing to exhibitors, "Another wow Richard Barthelmess picture following on the heels of *Weary River*, and making more secure than ever the screen position of this long-reigning young star. *Drag* is human, real, and persistently delightful. It possesses that seldom-encountered, intangible thing: an intelligent approach."

YOUNG NOWHERES (1929)
FIRST NATIONAL
PRODUCER: FRANK LLOYD
DIRECTOR: FRANK LLOYD
SCENARIO: Bradley King Wray, based on a story by Ida A. R. Wylie
LENGTH: 7 REELS
CAST: Richard Barthelmess, Marion Nixon, Bert Roach, Anders Randolph, Raymond Turner, Jocelyn Lee
SYNOPSIS: This story of courtship during Christmas in New York follows Richard Barthelmess as Albert "Binky" Whalen, a lonely elevator operator in an apartment house. When his employer leaves to visit family in California for the holidays, Binky's girlfriend, Annie Jackson, visits him. The couple goes to Coney Island for day of fun. Exhausted at the end of the day in the amusement parks, Binky and Annie fall asleep on the beach and don't wake until dawn. They return home wet, cold, and with a touch of pneumonia. Annie takes ill and is rushed to the hospital. Binky spends his last dollar to buy her a coat, and takes her to the luxurious apartment owned by his employer to rest. When the owner returns unexpectedly on Christmas Eve, he has them arrested. A kindly night court judge dismisses the case and lectures Binky's employer for spoiling their happiness.

"A charmingly simple talking picture . . . this new film makes no pretensions concerning action or length, but it moves along with an appealing naturalness, just like a breath of life," wrote Mordaunt Hall in the *New York Times*. "It carried with it a tear or two and an occasional smile. It is almost Barriesque in its idea and the mere fact that the producers have not sought to encumber it with glittering cabaret scenes, bright-eyed blondes or artificial villains enhances its value as a rational and pleasant entertainment. It is without a doubt a yarn that is better suited to Mr. Barthelmess than anything in which he has appeared since *Tol'able David*. And he is ably supported by the winsome Miss Nixon who delivers her lines with careful thought."

A *Variety* reviewer wrote, "Artistic successes have a way of being less than tumultuous at the pay box and this picture is a definite attempt at something a little finer and more imaginative than the usual Hollywood hokum. But for $2 it's commercially silly, and far from adding gloss the Broadway engagement probably netted the picture injury through inevitably prejudicing its chances by false pretensions. Running sixty-five minutes, *Young Nowheres* is the cinemas equivalent to a short story as distinguished from a full-length, many-episode novel. It deals with a situation rather than a plot and bases appeal entirely on humanity. Dickens and O. Henry, in collaboration, would have turned out something of the sort . . . Barthelmess, since *The Patent Leather Kid*, has been identified with a series of interesting and for the most part successful pictures. Probably through his own knowledge of values he manages to get good stories . . . *Young Nowheres* should do okay as a Barthelmess programmer, winning friends even if others view it with impatience."

Advertisement for the Frank Lloyd film, *Young Nowheres* (1929).

(TOP RIGHT AND BOTTOM) **Director Frank Lloyd gives instructions to Marian Nixon and Richard Barthelmess while filming his human drama, Young Nowheres (1929).** (TOP LEFT) **Maria Nixon and Richard Barthelmess in the film.**

THE SHOW OF SHOWS (1929)
WARNER BROS.
PRODUCER: DARRYL ZANUCK
DIRECTOR: JOHN ADOLFI
SCENARIO: J. Keirn Brennan and Frank Fay
LENGTH: 15 REELS
CAST: All star production, including Richard Barthelmess, John Barrymore, Beatrice Lillie, Louise Fazenda, Lloyd Hamilton, Frank Fay, Myrna Loy, Noah Beery, Winnie Lightner, Alice White, Dolores Costello, Grant Withers, Loretta Young, Ann Sothern, Ben Turpin, Lupino Lane, Jack Mulhall, Chester Morris, Chester Conklin, Betty Compson.

SYNOPSIS: This huge, 124-minute film was a showcase for nearly every star on the Warner Brothers lot, and included many who were not under contract to that studio. The revue was said to cost nearly $1 million, and the film boasts full-color on all but twenty-one minutes. There is no story or plot. It is a vaudeville show, filmed on a grand scale, with a finale running for nearly an entire reel. John Barrymore is the standout among the hundreds of people on the screen. His soliloquy from *Henry VI* was startling and dramatic, a tantalizing preview of what could be done with the works of Shakespeare in the new talking picture technology.

Mordaunt Hall wrote in his review in the *New York Times*, "One has the opportunity of seeing something like seventy-seven performers like Ben Turpin and Chester Conklin and younger ones . . . the various sketches in which they are seen are frequently amusing and Frank Fay does an excellent job as master of ceremonies. He is now and again aided by Mr. Barthelmess and others, including that film dog star, Rin-Tin-Tin, who barks his message . . . But after leaving the plethora of scenes, there is one that stands out above all the others, and that is John Barrymore's Shakespearian impersonation."

A reviewer in *Variety* wrote, "Film could have stood two or three masters of ceremonies. It was noticeable that both Barrymore and Barthelmess evidently declined to kid with or be kidded by Fay. Barthelmess rigidly introduces one number and Barrymore serves as his own trail blazer, though with something of a gag tag line."

"John Barrymore was undeniably the outstanding hit of this film, wrote another reviewer in *Photoplay*. "His performance in a classic interlude from the *Henry VI* soliloquy, plunged in the midst of the film chaos of jazz music, satire, adagio performers, and chorus girls, seemed out of place. Yet it supplies the one striking and genuinely significant note, but also the most popular episode in this latest and most lavish of the film extravaganzas."

The Show of Shows print advertisement as it appeared in many magazines around the country.

SON OF THE GODS (1930)
FIRST NATIONAL
PRODUCER: FRANK LLOYD
DIRECTOR: FRANK LLOYD
SCENARIO: BRADLEY KING
LENGTH: 93 MINUTES
CAST: Richard Barthelmess, Constance Bennett, Dorothy Matthews, Frank Albertson, Barbara Leonard, James Eagle, Mildred Van Dorn, King Ho Chang, Geneva Mitchell, E. Alyn Warren, Ivan Christie, Anders Randolf, George Irving, Claude King, Dickey Moore, Robert Homans

SYNOPSIS: The story of racism and courtship among Chinese students follows Richard Barthelmess as Sam Lee, seemingly the wealthy son of one of the richest Chinese merchants in San Francisco. In college, Sam faces the stilted, barely tolerant attitude of the white students by working hard to prove himself. He knows he is accepted only because of his money, so he takes work that leads him to the French Riviera. There, he meets a novelist who introduces him to Allana, played by Constance Bennett, a classy American girl with whom he falls in love. Allana dismisses all talk of his background, but when she learns he is genetically Chinese, she denounces him. After stunning Sam with the stinging blows of her riding whip, Sam retreats with a broken heart to his home. After his father dies, Sam learns that he was adopted, and that his natural parents were white. In the end, Allana sees the error of her racism and returns repentant to him for a happy reunion.

"After a none too hopeful beginning, Richard Barthelmess's latest talking film, *Son of the Gods* plods its weary way through banal episodes until the final happy fade-out — that is, happy for the two leading characters involved in the romance," wrote Mordaunt Hall in the *New York Times*. "In the program, it is set forth that Mr. Barthelmess gives to this production a 'whimsical something rarely achieved even by the greatest of actors.' This quality is conspicuous by its absence, for Mr. Barthelmess is not the genius who can turn to good account the character allotted to him in this uninspired narrative of a young man who believes himself to be Chinese. When considered as seriously as it is possible, this yarn is violently inconsistent in most of its action ... Mr. Barthelmess occasionally speaks a few words of Chinese, and after having started in that language in a conversation with his supposed father, the two finally decide to talk English. Mr. Barthelmess is calm, a stoic, in fact, through most of the scenes. He does not excel in speaking his lines, both Constance Bennett, who figures as Allana, and Claude King, who has a minor role doing far better with the dialogue than Mr. Barthelmess."

Variety's reviewer wrote, "Excepting for treatment the delicate subject of a Chinaman in love with a white girl, and vice versa, realism is sacrificed to an obvious narrative device in order to convert the Chinaman into a while man for the final clinch ... fine performances by everyone from Barthelmess down, and the restrained direction of the always-shrewd Frank Lloyd maintains interest despite the things which the mind fastens on critically en route . . . some such similar makeshift was used years ago to convert the late Valentino's sleep Arab into undiluted Caucasian. Regardless of Anglo-Saxon conventions probably rendering this race metamorphosis necessary, the effect is to riddle the illusion and expose the machinery of Hollywood."

Son of the Gods print advertisement as it appeared in many magazines around the country.

Richard Barthelmess as a young Oriental who collides with prejudice in Frank Lloyd's *Son of the Gods* (1930).

Constance Bennett (TOP RIGHT) and Richard Barthelmess in three scenes from Frank Lloyd's *Son of the Gods* (1930).

THE DAWN PATROL (1930)
FIRST NATIONAL
PRODUCER: ROBERT NORTH
DIRECTOR: HOWARD HAWK
SCENARIO: Howard Hawks, Dan Totheroh, Seton Miller, based on a story, *The Flight Commander*, by John Monk Saunders
LENGTH: 12 REELS
CAST: Richard Barthelmess, Douglas Fairbanks, Jr., Neil Hamilton, Frank McHugh, Clyde Cook, James Finlayson, Gardner James, William Janney, Edmund Breon, Jack Ackroyd, Harry Allen, Dave O'Brien
SYNOPSIS: As Dick Courtney, Richard Barthelmess plays an ace pilot integral to a team of flyers in World War One. Major Brand, the head of their flying unit, is disillusioned and embittered through the horrors of war, and transfers away from their unit before he has a nervous breakdown. Dick is promoted to the position, and in

turn, becomes equally disillusioned when he sees the barely trained youths sent to his unit to replace flyers downed in battle. The deaths of these novices weigh heavily on Dick, and in a moment of patriotism, he takes to the skies to battle the Germans. Dick is killed, and his buddy, Douglas Scott, is promoted to fill the Major's role. Like his predecessors, he becomes disillusioned and bitter after a short time and is given raw recruits to replace the latest dead flyers. The futility of war drags on with stark and wearying repetition.

A reviewer in the *New York Times* wrote, "*The Dawn Patrol* met with approval ... the picture has as an underlying motive that same theory first presented by Laurence Stallings and Maxwell Anderson in the raucous whimsicalities, the deep purposes of *What Price Glory?* It is the futility of war. In *The Dawn Patrol* the motive forms a background, one dressed with the roar of airplane motors, sky raids, and lonely rides through the clouds, battle, and destruction. There are no bands; there is no heroine dressed in a manner to faintly suggest the crinoline days ... When planes are flying there are whole fleets in the sky at once; when guns are fired there are entire batteries. Finally, toward the end, Richard Barthelmess takes it upon himself to bomb a city. The explosion would have practically won the war. First National has spent its powder and shot lavishly, and *The Dawn Patrol* holds the interest. Both Mr. Barthelmess and Douglas Fairbanks, Jr. do well as Courtney and Scott, respectively. And neither is an easy part."

The *Variety* reviewer penned, "Another air picture, and a good one. *Dawn Patrol* should do business for it holds the attention throughout, provides several tense sequences, and compares favorably with the handful of worthy sequels to *Wings*. It is not much of a picture for starring, although Richard Barthelmess contributes another of his dependable performances."

Andrew Sarris wrote in *You Ain't Heard Nothin' Yet*, "*The Dawn Patrol* (1930) was Hawk's first all-talking film, and its history is typical of Hawks' luck in the matter of reputation and name recognition. The film was released at a time when the screen was saturated with imitations of Lewis Milestone and Erich Maria Remarque's *All Quiet on the Western Front* and James Whale and Robert Sheriff's *Journey's End*, not to mention such fondly remembered twenties classics as King Vidor's *The Big Parade* and

William Wellman's Oscar-winning *Wings*. Consequently, the critics, though favorably disposed toward *The Dawn Patrol*, tended to dismiss it in the hope that they genre would sooner or later peter out. Nevertheless, the movie was well liked by the public and fondly remembered for years despite a glossier 1938 re-make starring Errol Flynn, David Niven, and Basil Rathbone, and directed by Edmund Goulding."

The Dawn Patrol print ad as it appeared in magazines around the country.

Richard Barthelmess and Neil Hamilton in Howard Hawks' *The Dawn Patrol* (1930).

Two scenes of Richard Barthelmess as the gallant ace flyer turned commander in Howard Hawks' *The Dawn Patrol* (1930).

Two scenes from Howard Hawks' *The Dawn Patrol* (1930): (TOP) with Neil Hamilton, and (BOTTOM) with Douglas Fairbanks, Jr., watching a flyer downed by the enemy.

Douglas Fairbanks, Jr., and Richard Barthelmess in Howard Hawks' *The Dawn Patrol* (1930).

THE LASH (1930)
FIRST NATIONAL
PRODUCER: FRANK LLOYD
DIRECTOR: FRANK LLOYD
SCENARIO: Bradley King, based on a story, *Adios*, by Lanier Bartlett and Virginia Stivers Bartlett
LENGTH: 79 MINUTES
CAST: Richard Barthelmess, Mary Astor, David Howard, James Rennie, Marian Nixon, Fred Kohler, Barbara Bedford, Robert Edeson, Arthur Stone, Mathilde Comont, Erville Alderson.
SYNOPSIS: The story follows Don Francisco Delfina, a Southern California nobleman in 1848, during the days of California's admission to the Union. After suffering injustices at the hands of the Americans, Don retaliates and disguises himself as El Puma, a dashing, Robin Hood-like bandit and outlaw. He hates as he loved, which is with all of his body and soul. In his alternate role, Don Francisco risks love to accomplish revenge. He rides through the sweeping panorama of the glorious California countryside at the

head of his bandits, righting wrongs in the manner of Robin Hood and risking everything for love's reward. In a desperate errand of hate, he leads a revolt against tyrannical land agents and politicians. His activities are finally halted when his sister falls in love with a "Gringo," and he seeks exile in Mexico. There, he discovers romance with Rosita Garcia, played by Mary Astor.

Mordaunt Hall wrote in the *New York Times*, "Beautiful panoramic views and a great herd of stampeding cattle are to be seen in *The Lash*, the current talking picture at the Winter Garden, in which Richard Barthelmess plays the leading role. It is not an especially perturbing tale, but its scenes in the open are always interesting . . . Mary Astor plays Rosita. Marian Nixon is Delfina's sister. James Rennie plays Howard. None of the performances is particularly impressive."

"A good action talker in the western romantic strain," wrote a reviewer in *Variety*. "It suits Barthelmess all the way. While the picture is first released in New Orleans and right before Christmas, it probably will not be generally turned loose until after that day to preserve its full draw. It should be another Barthelmess money film . . . this story doesn't place the Americans in a very favorable light after the conquest of California, but it does give Barthelmess opportunities to be unusually heroic."

The film was widely released in normal 35mm format, but it was filmed on the large 65mm Vitascope guage.

The Lash print ad as it appeared in magazines around the country.

Richard Barthelmess as Don Francisco, the bandit-hero, in Frank Lloyd's *The Lash* (1930).

The Stolen Jools (1931)
Also known as The Slippery Pearls

NATIONAL VARIETY ARTISTS-
PARAMOUNT-NATIONAL SCREEN
SERVICE
DIRECTOR: WILLIAM McGANN
LENGTH: 20 MINUTES
CAST: All-star, including Richard Barthelmess, Warner Baxter, El Brendel, Wallace Beery, Charles Butterworth, Joe E. Brown, Gary Cooper, Maurice Chevalier, Fifi D'Orsay, Claudia Dell, Bebe Daniels, Stuart Erwin, Frank Fay, Douglas Fairbanks, Jr., Richard "Skeets" Gallagher, Wynne Gibson, Mitzi Green, Garry Hayes, Hedda Hopper, Allen Jenkins, Eddie Kane, Buster Keaton, Laurel & Hardy, Dorothy Lee, Edmund Lowe, J. Farrell MacDonald, Polly Moran, Charles Murray, Our Gang, Eugene Pallette, Jack Oakie, Edward G. Robinson, Charles "Buddy" Rogers, Norma Shearer, Lowell Sherman, Barbara Stanwyck, Bert Wheeler, Robert Woolsey.
SYNOPSIS: A madcap, two-reel satire in which Norma Shearer is the victim of a robbery. A galaxy of Hollywood stars is under investigation by Detective Eddie Kane. Wallace Beery appears as the police station sergeant.

In a review appearing in the *Appleton Post Crescent*, the talking-picture comedy was praised as a winner. "Never before has such a

Three scenes from Frank Lloyd's *The Lash* (1930): (TOP) **Marian Nixon, Robert Edeson, and Richard Barthelmess;** (MIDDLE) **James Rennie and Richard Barthelmess;** and (BOTTOM) **Mary Astor and Richard Barthelmess.**

galaxy of stars been assembled for one picture," the reviewer stated. "They come from all the producing companies; they represent every type of actor from dramatic to slapstick; every barrier has been let down to make this the funniest, the most hilarious production ever projected on a screen. The list of players alone is enough to make motion picture history. Any one of them, as the star of a film, is enough to send the crowds to the theater. Put them together and there is a picture of untold possibilities.

"The entire motion picture industry, from scenarists to house managers, is devoting a portion of the coming week to gaining funds to be used in support of the national home for retired and disabled actors," read an article appearing in the *Decatur Herald*. "With thousands of actors out of work, due to the national financial depression and to changes in theater entertainment, the national home's income has been greatly reduced in recent months. Making and presentation of *The Stolen Jools* is the result of the moving picture industry's contribution to the cause. Theater patrons will be asked for donations . . . ."

THE FINGER POINTS (1931)
FIRST NATIONAL
PRODUCER: JOHN FRANCIS DILLON
DIRECTOR: JOHN FRANCIS DILLON
SCENARIO: Robert Lord and John Monk Saunders, from a story by W. R. Burnett
LENGTH: 9 REELS
CAST: Richard Barthelmess, Fay Wray, Regis Toomey, Robert Elliot, Clark Gable, Oscar Apfel, Robert Gleckler, Noel Madison
SYNOPSIS: In a story based on the murder of Jake Lingle murder case, Richard Barthelmess plays Breckenridge Lee, a fresh young kid from the South, who gets a job with a major newspaper. His first assignment on gangsters gets his name in the paper and earns some notoriety among the underworld. He tries to play straight, and barely makes a living on the meager weekly salary of a reporter. In a short time, men from the local gangsters approach him about slanting the news to influence public opinion. Lee regularly takes money from the underworld for keeping their machinations out of the newspaper. Once in their clutches, he betrays his trust to his

newspaper and learns to shake down the gangsters by shielding them. With the power of the press behind him, they initially leave Lee alone. Fay Wray plays Marcia Collins, a girl reporter on the paper. She is aware of his activities, pleads with him to free himself from the underworld, and refuses to give him attention or take his rang until he goes straight. Unfortunately, when one story breaks that the gangsters wanted hushed, they put him on the spot, and then make him pay for his double-cross. In a suspenseful climax, Lee is gunned down in a blaze of bullets.

"Richard Barthelmess plays the young reporter, who charges as high as $100,000 for keeping gang secrets out of his paper, heads a splendid cast, and the film offers some vivid and authentic melodrama, comparable sometimes in its savage honest with the best films of its kind seen this season," wrote Mordaunt Hall in the *New York Times*.

". . . it doesn't hold much," wrote a reviewer in *Variety*. "Where Barthelmess stands well and where gangster fever is in high, plus the phase of the reporter who runs the underworld of the town, this picture should do well. In other spots it calls for support . . . ."

The Finger Points print advertisement as it appeared in many publications around the country.

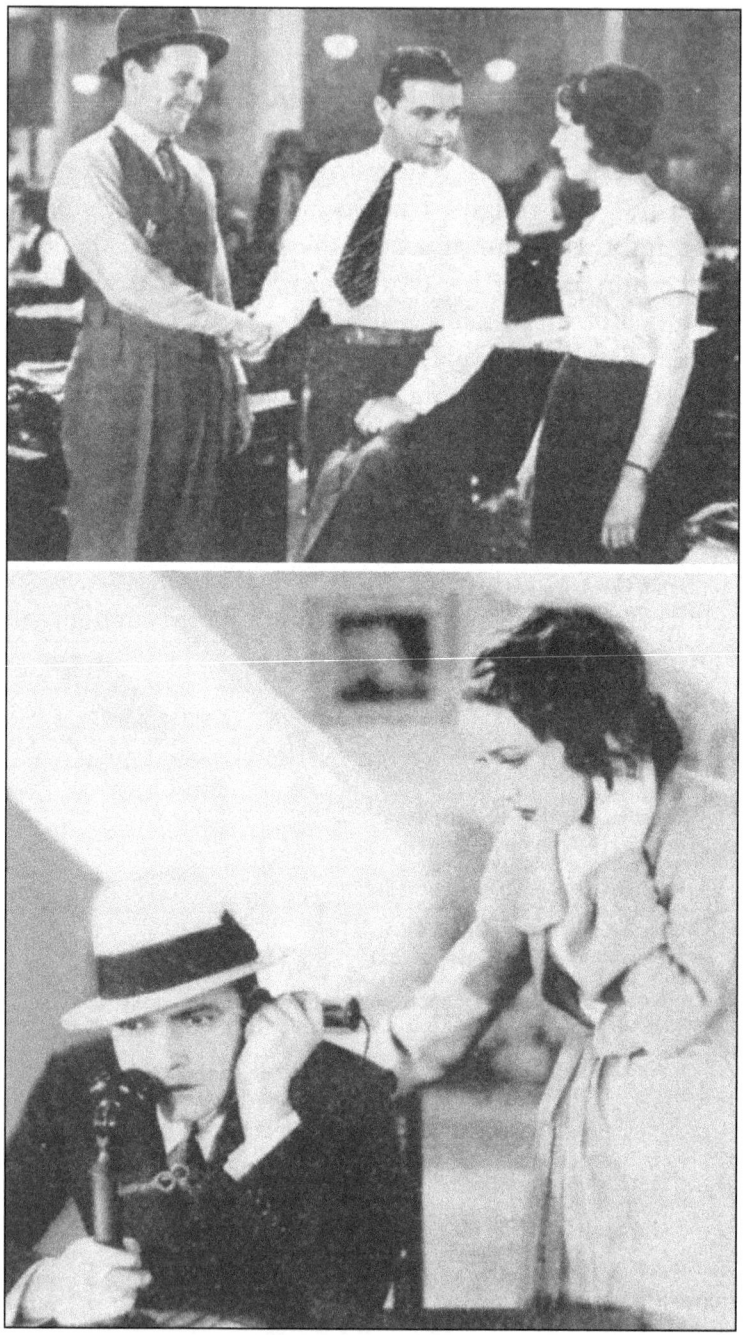

Two scenes from Frank Lloyd's *The Finger Points* (1931):
(TOP) **Regis Toomey, Richard Barthelmess, and Fay Wray,** and
(BOTTOM) **Richard Barthelmess and Fay Wray.**

THE LAST FLIGHT (1931)
FIRST NATIONAL
PRODUCER: WILLIAM DIETERLE
DIRECTOR: WILLIAM DIETERLE
SCENARIO: John Monk Saunders, based on a novel, *Single Lady*, by John Monk Saunders
LENGTH: 8 REELS
CAST: Richard Barthelmess, Helen Chandler, David Manners, Johnny Mack Brown, Elliot Nugent, Walter Byron, Luis Alberni, Yola d'Avril, George Irving, Wallace MacDonald
SYNOPSIS: Nikki, a drifting screwball, takes up with war-wracked former aces endeavoring to kill boredom in Paris after the War. These young aviators, trained to kill and downed by the Armistice, are trying to fine release for their torn nerves, and discharge mental energy before the bar at the Claridge, tossing off human sparks while civilization picks up the loose ends of greed, beauty, and sordidness. With the help of the peculiar young woman, nearly all of them make a wreck of their lives. The wandering story explores the mental states of these people, and along the way, Richard, as Cary Lockwood, falls in love with Nikki. At one point they stand before the grave of history's greatest lovers, Abelard and Heloise, and pledge their love, while trying to find themselves in a new world of peace.

A reviewer for *Variety* wrote, "Barthelmess is the consistent performer here, and with the usual wisdom of surrounding himself with a good looking and able group of young male actors. That's the usual Barthelmess background with the usual single woman decoy. It's been Barthelmess's successful system and no reason why it shouldn't work here . . . if the crowd can understand that girl character in this picture, the film is an undoubted grosser. The vagueness of the femme role and her reason for being, which at no time is made altogether clear except to those who might have read the story in magazine form or book, is a deterrent."

Mordaunt Hall wrote in the *New York Times*, ". . . a curious but often brilliant study of the post-war psychology of four injured American aviators. Their mad waggery and reckless drinking ends darkly for three of them, but the fourth, Cary Lockwood, played by Richard Barthelmess, finds happiness with a girl named Nikki, whose humor and outlook on life has a great deal in common with that of the fliers . . . Helen Chandler's performance as Nikki is exceptionally fine. Mr. Barthelmess is efficient in his role."

The Last Flight newspaper advertisement as it appeared in the Burlington Daily Times News.

The Last Flight was also released under the title, Nikki and her War Birds. This newspaper advertisement appeared in many cities across America.

Richard Barthelmess as a war-wracked pilot unwinding in Paris in William Dieterle's *The Last Flight* (1931).

Two scenes with Helen Chandler as Nikki, a drifting screwball, who takes up with former flying aces, played by Richard, Johnny Mack Brown, Elliott Nugent, Walter Byron, and David Manners, in William Dieterle's *The Last Flight* (1931).

ALIAS THE DOCTOR (1932)
FIRST NATIONAL
PRODUCER: JACK WARNER
DIRECTOR: MICHAEL CURTIZ
SCENARIO: Houston Branch and Charles Kenyon, based on a play by Emric Foeldes
LENGTH: 69 MINUTES
CAST: Richard Barthelmess, Marian Marsh, Lucille La Verne, Norman Foster, Oscar Apfel, John St. Polis, George Rosener, Boris Karloff, Adrienne Doer, Wallis Clark, Nigel De Brulier, Arnold Lucy, Reginald Barlow
SYNOPSIS: Richard played Karl Muller, an orphan living on a farm in Bavaria as an adopted son. He grows up to be a zealous student at a medical fraternity along with his lazy brother, Stephan. Both go to Munich to study medicine. Karl is at the top of the class while Stephan is barely passing. When Stephan attempts an illegal operation, which proves fatal for a young woman, Karl is the one who sacrifices his career as a doctor and takes the wrap with the three-year prison term. When he gets out, he finds Stephan is dead and a sick child needs an operation. He conceals his identity, assumes the name of his stepbrother, and he performs brilliant surgery on the child, although he is practicing without a license. With this act, he becomes world-renowned. His deception is revealed, and the shock affects his foster mother's brain. He is the only man who can perform the operation, so he pleads before the medical hospital council, who finally allow him to operate. Unfortunately, being that he is now Stephan, he can no longer marry Lottie, as she is now his sister.

Originally titled, *Environment*, the film's title was changed along with a change of directors. Howard Hawks was set to handle the directing job, but prolonged work on *Scarface* with Paul Muni forced him to relinquish the job to Michael Curtiz. The Hays office had objected to the ending of *Scarface*, and the original twenty-eight-day shooting schedule stretched to sixty-days. Hawks was forced to abort the Barthelmess film, and Michael Curtiz, who had proven to be difficult for Richard while making *Cabin in the Cotton*, was hastily recruited to fill the director's role.

Mordaunt Hall, in his review in the *New York Times*, said the film was "produced with praise-worthy earnestness and painstaking attention to surgical details, it is not precisely an entertaining subject. The scenes in a hospital operating room are undoubtedly set forth with authentic atmosphere, but they are no more dramatic than they are cheering." Hall also said, "Mr. Barthelmess does as well as is possible in the circumstances with his role." Boris Karloff appeared as an autopsy surgeon who seemed disappointed when an operation was successful. His presence was harnessed as an obvious symbol of the shadow of death."

In *Variety*, a reviewer wrote, "Strictly a Barthelmess picture, he sustains whatever tempo *Alias the Doctor* possesses. Calling for impressive dramatic moments, even the star's histrionic skill skates on thin ice to lend it realism. There are a couple of tense moments, but at best the picture is just a fair programmer, and would not merit the grind run booking as at the Winter "Garden were it not for other contributing factors."

Alias the Doctor print advertisement as it appeared in magazines around the country.

Richard Barthelmess as Karl Muller, assuming the identity of his dead brother, and taking his job as a practicing surgeon, in Michael Curtiz' *Alias the Doctor* (1932).

Marian Marsh with Richard Barthelmess in Michael Curtiz' *Alias the Doctor* (1932).

Richard Barthelmess in Michael Curtiz' *Alias the Doctor* (1932).

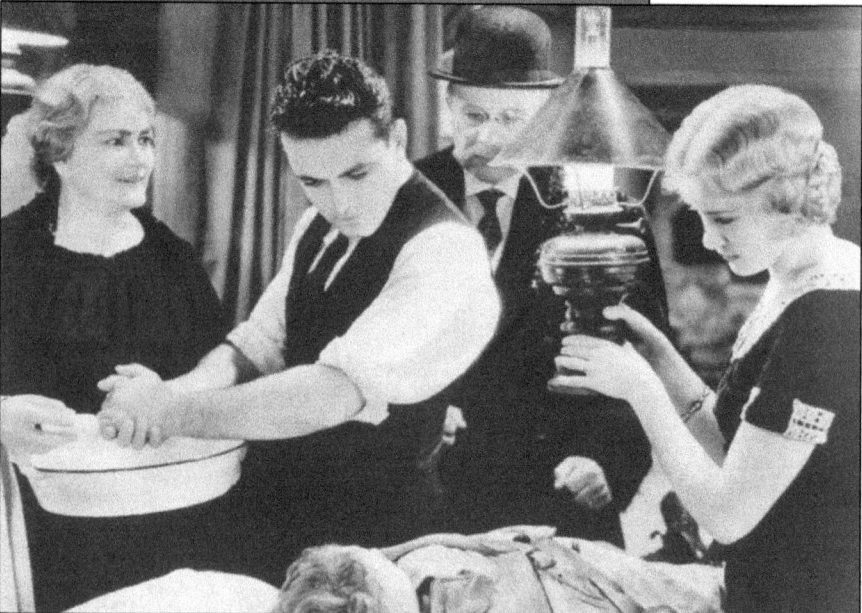

With assistance from Lucille LaVerne and Marian Marsh, Richard Barthelmess saves the life of a boy in a gruesome operating scene in Michael Curtiz' *Alias the Doctor* (1932).

Cabin in the Cotton (1932)

First National
Producer: Jack Warner, Hal B. Wallis, Darryl F. Zanuck
Director: Michael Curtiz
Scenario: Paul Green, based on a novel by Harry Harrison Kroll
Length: 78 minutes
Cast: Richard Barthelmess, Bette Davis, Dorothy Jordan, Hardie Albright, David Landau, Berton Churchill, Dorothy Peterson, Russell Simpson, Tully Marshall, Henry B. Walthall, Edmund Breese, John Marston, Erville Alderson, William Le Maire, Clarence Muse
Synopsis: Marvin Blake, a sharecropper's son, feels the need to help those in his community overcome poverty and ignorance. Madge, the plantation owner's daughter, encourages Blake to get an education. After his graduation, Marvin works as a clerk in a local general store, and while there, Marvin learns the proprietor is cheating. Now in love with Madge, Marvin stands up for the rights of the plantation tenants and exposes the cheating planters.

Cabin in the Cotton, a popular feature on American television in late evening showings, was not enjoyed by Mordaunt Hall of the *New York Times* in 1932. He said in his review, "There is undoubtedly a certain sincerity about most of the episodes of the pictorial conception of Henry Harrison Kroll's novel, *The Cabin in the Cotton* ... it is a film which seldom awakens any keen interest and Richard Barthelmess, who appears as Marvin Blake, gives a careful but hardly an inspired performance. His general demeanor lacks the desired spontaneity and often he speaks his lines in a monotone."

Variety's reviewer wrote, "Picture proves again that a book that attracts a good deal of attention isn't necessarily screen material. Subject matter here doubtless has dramatic power in its essence, but it doesn't come through to the audience from the screen. Less than a moderate grosser all around, probably with its weakest reaction in the big cities ... picture is not well done and it presents Barthelmess in another luke-warm role, a role which he plays without vigor."

Variety also noted: "Best this hero can do in the embarrassing situation is to gasp, 'Madge!' This was much too much for the Strand audience that witnessed the opening. They broke down in merriment. Bad cutting may have had something to do with the untoward reaction. Or maybe the censor wrecked it. Picture has all the flaws of an adapted book. Incident is blurred and character is foggy."

Richard Barthelmess as the poor country boy torn between loyalty to his people and the debut he owes to the slave-driving overlord of the cotton country, in Michael Curtiz' *Cabin in the Cotton* (1932).

Bette Davis as Madge, the fascinating daughter of the rich plantation lord, with Richard Barthelmess in Michael Curtiz' *Cabin in the Cotton* (1932).

Betty Davis and Richard Barthelmess at the grand ball in Michael Curtiz' *Cabin in the Cotton* (1932).

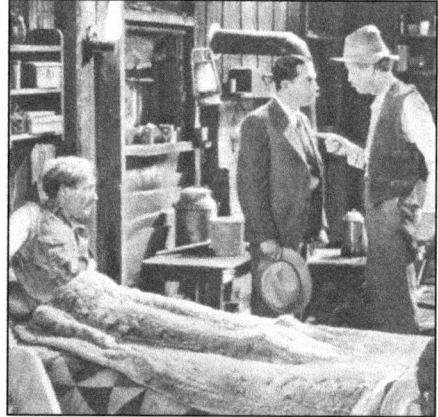

Henry B. Walthall (LEFT) was a pioneering actor in the early days of filmmaking at Biograph with D. W. Griffith. Here he is with Richard Barthelmess in Michael Curtiz' *Cabin in the Cotton* (1932).

CENTRAL AIRPORT (1933)
FIRST NATIONAL
PRODUCER: HAL B. WALLIS
DIRECTOR: WILLIAM A. WELLMAN
SCENARIO: Rian James and James Seymour, based on a story, *Hawk's Mate*, by Jack Moffitt
LENGTH: 74 MINUTES
CAST: Richard Barthelmess, Sally Eilers, Tom Brown, Glenda Farrell, Grant Mitchell, Harold Huber, James Murray, Claire McDowell, Willard Robertson, Arthur Vinton, Charles Sellon, Robert W. Craig, Harold Huber, Milton Kibbee, Toby Wing, Irving Bacon, Louise Beavers, Harry Bradley, James Bush, James Donlan, Lester Dorr, Dick Elliott, James Ellison, Glenda Farrell, Betty Jane Graham, Harrison Greene, Charles Lane, Sam McDaniel, John Miller, J. Carroll Nash, Theodore Newton, Bradley Page, Russ Powell, Jed Prouty, George Regas, Harry Semels, Phil Tead, Fred Toones, John Vosper, Lucille Ward, John Wayne, Charles Williams, Jack Wise
SYNOPSIS: A courageous aviator, Jim Blaine and his brother Neil are rivals not only as daredevil flyers, but also for the love of parachutist Jill Collins. When Jim's airplane crashes in a storm, he is stripped of his license. Forced to take a bank job, Jim watches as his brother, Neil, takes a job as a test pilot. When Jill's brother crashes in an air show, Jim takes his place. When he is injured in a freak accident, his brother, Neil, takes his place in the air show. Later, Jim discovers his brother in bed with Jill, and punches him before learning they were married the night before. Neil's plane disappears during a storm, and Jim takes to the air in search of him. He finds the downed plane, but cannot land due to heavy fog. In a stirring climax, all the cars in the city line up in an airfield with headlights burning and light the path for him to find earth and safely land. Jim finally realizes the depth of love his brother has for Jill, and leaves town to allow the couple to live happily.

On the night of May 3, 1933, Mordaunt Hall of the *New York Times* saw *Central Airport*. The next day, the newspaper published his review in which he said, "Just when last night's thunderstorm was at its height the Warner Bros. presented their picture *Central Airport*, which, be it known, starts with an electric storm. Thus some of the spectators had the opportunity of comparing the real storm with the one turned out in Hollywood, and it must be admitted that in sound effects and lightning the producers had done very well. The only pity is that the story of this film, which is now at the Warner's Strand, is a most obvious affair with possibly a last idea in its favor. Richard Barthelmess is the stellar performer in *Central Airport* and most of his acting causes one to think that he wished the picture to go into foreign countries without dialogue. He shrugs his shoulders, grimaces and gives one the impression that none of the other characters with whom he converses would possibly appreciate what he was saying if he did not outdo the average Continental in gesticulating . . . the closing sequence, which takes place in Havana waters, is moderately effective, with scores of automobiles all tooting their horns to direct the aviator lost in the supposedly thick fog."

A reviewer in *Variety* wrote, "There's a thrill in *Central Airport's* moments, and just enough of those moments to cover up deficiencies in practically every other department, from story to cast . . . story is the worst offender, although one extremely harmful bit of casting is almost as big a reason for the general shortcomings . . . Barthelmess is what the scenarist ordered as the daredevil flyer who takes more chances than he should after his brother cops his girl. The dialog has him in accidents all over the world, although only two of the crack-ups are shown. At the finish, Barthelmess is minus and eye and gimps in one leg.'"

In an interview appearing in the *Times Recorder*, one writer expressed that the preview audience went home feeling that they had about the most thrilling evening of their lives. "If more thrills could have been put in a picture, *Central Airport* would have had them!" said the reviewer. ". . . the almost unbelievable thrills which abound in this spectacular drama of daring and self-sacrifice are at times completely overshadowed by the tense and gripping love story that truly classify *Central Airport* as one of the best screen romances of the year. Parachute jumps, wrecks in passenger and stunt planes, at sea and on land, sensational and awe-inspiring as they are, serve as ingredients which build up an enthralling love interest to greater and greater degrees until the powerful denouement in the final fadeout . . . Barthelmess is superb in a role that reveals his histrionic genius as never before He lives and breathes in a characterization that few screen idols dare attempt." Sally Eiler's beauty and performance were also highly praised.

Central Airport newspaper advertisement as it appeared in publications around the country.

Richard Barthelmess as a stunt pilot in William Wellman's *Central Airport* (1933).

Richard Barthelmess, Tom Brown, and Sally Eilers in William Wellman's *Central Airport* (1933).

Sally Eilers as a feminine jumper with Richard Barthelmess in William Wellman's *Central Airport* (1933).

Heroes for Sale (1933)
First National
Producer: Hal B. Wallis
Director: William A. Wellman
Scenario: Robert Lord and Wilson Mizner
Length: 73 minutes
Cast: Richard Barthelmess, Loretta Young, Aline MacMahon, Gordon Westcott, Robert Barrat, Grant Mitchell, Burton Churchill, Charley Grapewin, Robert McWade, G. Pat Collins, James Murray, Edwin Maxwell, Margaret Seddon, Arthur Vinton, Robert Elliott, John Marston, Willard Robertson, Arthur Hoyt, Ward Bond, Eddy Chandler, Frank Darien, Douglass Dumbrille, Hans Fuerberg, Eddie Graham, George Irving, Milton Kibbee, John Miller, Henry Otho, Inez Palange, Bob Perry, Lee Phelps, Dewey Robinson, Guy Usher, Charles C. Wilson, Tammany Young
Synopsis: The social drama follows Richard Barthelmess as Tom Holmes, a soldier in World War One. When his comrade, Lieutenant Roger Winston, fails to carry out a mission to capture a German prisoner, Tom assumes the task and bravely captures the German. Before he can return, a burst of shellfire fells Tom, and Roger, believing him dead, escorts the prisoner to the superior officers. He ungratefully takes full credit for the daring capture, is decorated for bravery, and returns to America posing as a victorious soldier, belying the cowardly fact of his actions.

Unknown to Tom, Germans capture Tom wounded and dying, and after taking morphine for his pain, he returns home after the war addicted to the drug. He confounds Roger with his reappearance, and feeling guilty for his cowardly actions, Roger finds work for Tom in his father's bank. Tom struggles with the banking job because of his morphine cravings, and must quietly search out the illicit drug on the streets. When discovered borrowing money from the bank vault to fund his habit, he is fired, and Roger does nothing to save him or his job.

As time passes, Tom is sent to a sanitarium to break his addiction, and emerges penniless but determined to start his life over. He meets Ruth, a young woman working in a laundry, and they fall in love. Tom invents a machine to revolutionize commercial laundry, and earns a fortune. Fate again turns against him in a riot in where workers are killed. His friend, Max, collects the royalties while Tom takes a prison term for allegedly causing the riot. When he emerges five years later from prison, his son is grown, and he finds that Max has saved all his royalties, faithfully depositing them in a bank account. Tom turns the money over to his friend, Mary Dennis, who runs a small boarding house and shares her meager earnings feeding the many homeless people who come by for a free meal. Local police wrongly believe Tom is a Communist, and drive him away from town. On the road as a homeless wanderer, he encounters Roger, now destitute from the failure of his father's bank, and Tom forgives him for the wrong done during the war. Tom's son never sees his father again, but Mary erects a memorial to him and his benevolence, while using his donated savings to feed the thousands of lost souls who turn up for meals.

The *New York Times* critic, Mordaunt Hall, wrote, "A bewildering plot burdened Richard's next film, *Heroes for Sale*. Halfway into the picture about a character called Roger Winston and his prisoner-seeking foray into No Man's Land, his capture by Tom Holmes, played by Barthelmess, Roger's wounding and subsequent addiction to morphine, the story took a ninety degree turn to a second plot. The new story showed Tom starting a new life in Chicago where his wife is killed in a labor strike. If there be any connection between the stories, it is only that of Tom's unbroken misfortune. Mr. Barthelmess carries on bravely under the afflictions which befall to the lot of Tom."

A reviewer for the *Newark Advocate* wrote, "Occasionally, there is a story coming out of Hollywood broad enough in scope to demand the serious attention of all. Such is the story contained in *Heroes for Sale* . . . to Richard Barthelmess is given the lead role, which he carries in typical Barthelmess style to give a performance equal to some of his best parts and far superior to his recent pictures . . . The picture takes a straight-from-the-shoulder punch at the ruthless use of machines to replace workmen. It shows how Barthelmess as an employee of a laundry was instrumental in helping an inventor friend sell the firm on a laborsaving device. The intent is harmless enough, but when the firm changes ownership, more improvements are made to the extent that practically all workers lose their jobs. One of the high points of the picture shows a mob, incited over the loss of their jobs, marching to destroy the machines which robbed them of a living. Barthelmess makes a vain effort to divert this mob, but is unsuccessful. The climax is reached when his wife follows, only to meet death in the clash between mob and police. *Heroes for Sale* is a picture that may be recommended without reservation. If you have the admission price, the picture will give you something to reflect upon; if you don't have, never mind, because you probably know the story too well."

Heroes for Sale newspaper advertisement as it appeared in the *Newark Advocate*.

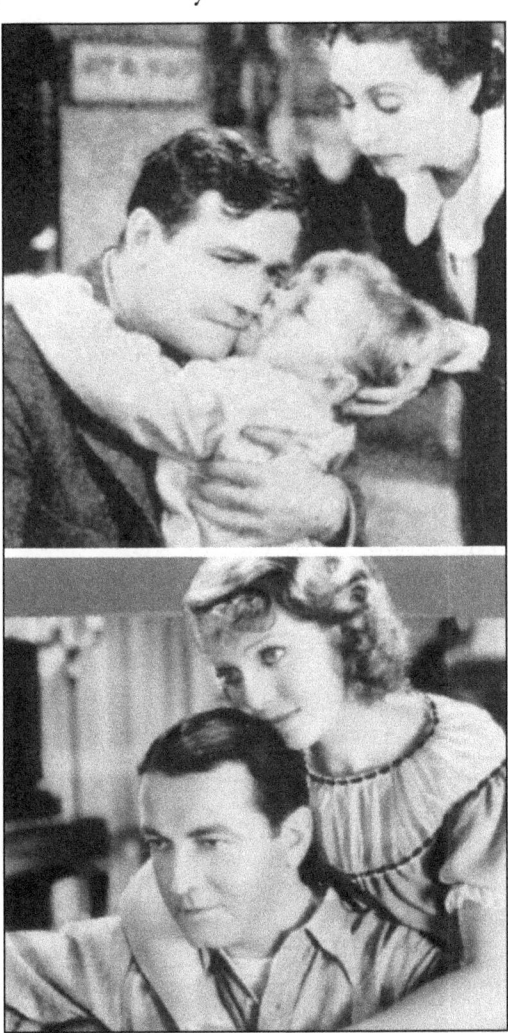

Two scenes from William Wellman's *Heroes for Sale* (1933): (TOP) with Aline MacMahon, and (BOTTOM) with Loretta Young.

Richard Barthelmess as the forgotten war hero in William Wellman's *Heroes for Sale* (1933).

MASSACRE (1934)
FIRST NATIONAL
PRODUCER: ROBERT PRESNELL, SR.
DIRECTOR: ALAN CROSLAND
SCENARIO: Ralph Block and Sheridan Gibney, based on a story by Robert Gessner
LENGTH: 70 MINUTES
CAST: Richard Barthelmess, Ann Dvorak, Dudley Digges, Henry O'Neil, Claire Dodd, Robert Barrat, Arthur Hohl, Sidney Toler, Clarence Muse, Charles Middleton, Tully Marshall, Wallis Clark, William V. Mong, DeWitt Jennings, Juliet Ware, James Eagles, Frank McGlynn, Sr., Agnes Narcha, Douglass Dumbrille, William B. Davidson, Henry Kolker, George Blackwood, Samuel S. Hinds, Philip Faversham
SYNOPSIS: The story follows Richard Barthelmess as Chief Joe Thunder Horse of the Sioux tribe. The Indian, after an absence of several years, returns to his studies at the Haskell Institute. After graduating, he finds employment as a stunt rider in a Western show at the Chicago World's Fair. His success performing before eager

audiences earns him top dollar, and he enjoys making a public spectacle of his position. People see him driving an expensive car with the name of the show painted along the side with his own name, and when requested, Joe gives crack shot demonstrations. His true heritage becomes uppermost on his mind when his girlfriend, Norma, shares decorative accessories of Indian lore, and Joe realizes he knows nothing about his background.

When he learns his father is near death, Joe returns to the reservation, and is faced with the corrupt white leadership and poor medical conditions surrounding his father. When his father dies, Joe holds a funeral in traditional Indian style. In the middle of the occasion, the undertaker assaults Joe's sister, Jenny. Joe beats the offending man behind his car and is the arrested for attempted murder. A court-appointed attorney pleads for a guilty verdict, and before sentence can be passed, Joe escapes with the aid of his girlfriend.

After fleeing to Washington, D.C., Joe reports his troubles to the head of the Bureau of Indian Affairs. J. R. Dickinson, the head of the office, stands up for Joe's rights, but before meaningful action can follow, the beaten undertaker dies and Joe is arrested for murder. After a second jail escape, the corrupt land agents are brought to justice, and Joe asks his girlfriend for her hand in marriage.

Mordaunt Hall wrote in his review in the *New York Times*: "Mr. Barthelmess's make-up is excellent. When in the show ring, he wears a black wig, which he doffs in his dressing tent and appears without artificial hair, but nevertheless still reminds one of a Sioux. Mr. Barthelmess gives a vigorous and effective performance."

A reviewer in *Variety* wrote, "Persecution of the redskin under the white administrators of Indian affairs in the southwest is the not-so-timely subject of Massacre. Film attempts to modernize a tepid subject by setting the action at the time of the last Chicago World's Fair. Richard Barthelmess stars as an Indian with Broadway playboy ideas, and upon his shoulders rests the assignment of drawing about all *Massacre* will get. Not likely to be much despite the all-around technical excellence of the production and the sincerity behind the theme. Barthelmess is yes and no in the role . . . ."

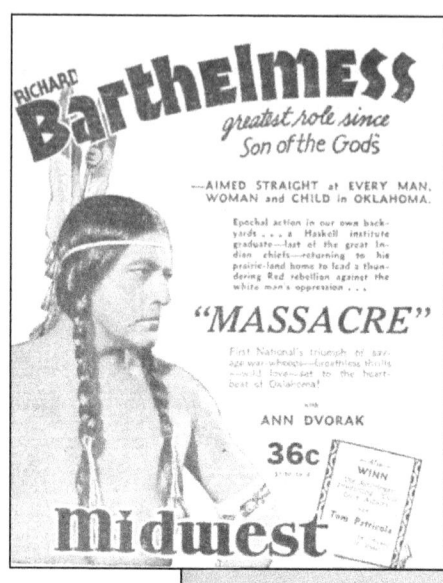

Massacre newspaper advertisement as it appeared in many publications around the country.

Richard Barthelmess as Joe Thunderhorse in Alan Crosland's *Massacre* (1934).

Two scenes from Alan Crosland's *Massacre* (1934): (TOP) Richard Barthelmess in the trial scene with Dudley Digges as the prosecutor and Ann Dvorak watching the proceedings. (BOTTOM) Richard with Sioux Indians angered by the government agents.

A Modern Hero (1934)
Warner Bros.
Producer: Jack Warner
Director: George W. Pabst
Scenario: Gene Markey and Kathryn Scola, based on a novel by Louis Bromfield
Length: 71 minutes
Cast: Richard Barthelmess, Jean Muir, Dorothy Burgess, Marjorie Rambeau, Florence Eldridge, Verree Teasdale, Dorothy Burgess, Hobart Cavanaugh, William Janney, Arthur Hohl, Theodore Newton, J. M. Kerrigan, Maidel Turner, Mickey Rentschler, Richard Tucker, Judith Vosselli, Theodore Lorch, Louise Beavers, Mary Baker, Lester Dorr, Ralph Brocks, David Thursby, Betty Boyd, Gordon Elliott, Eric Wilton, George Reed, Howard Hickman, Theresa Harris, Madame Sul-Te-Wan.
Synopsis: Richard Barthelmess plays Pierre Radier, a bareback rider in a circus, who is weary of life on the road. While traveling from town to town, Pierre meets Joanna Ryan, played by Jean Muir, and their brief affair results in an unplanned pregnancy. Pierre offers to leave the circus and marry Jean, despite advice from his alcoholic mother against it.

Jean tells Pierre she would rather marry a more stable man in town, so when Henry Mueller, a worker in the circus, asks Pierre to join him in a new business, he asks his mother for money. She refuses, and Pierre then takes up with a wealthy widow. She lends him money to start the business, a bicycle shop, which becomes a great local success. Pierre starts down the road to financial freedom, soon branching out into owning an auto factory and munitions manufacturing. His illegitimate son grows up, and Pierre finances his education, while taking up with an endless succession of attractive women.

Pierre's life takes a downward spiral beginning with the accidental death of his son in an auto accident. Then, he loses his fortune in the stock market crash, and his marriage dissolves. While penniless, he returns to his mother, now working as a fortuneteller, and they plan to move to Europe to begin life again.

In the *New York Times*, Mordaunt Hall wrote, "It is an earnest, sketchy and spiritless account of Pierre Radier's rise and fall that they offer at the Strand in the film version of Mr. Bromfield's novel. This is the story of a man who failed because he succeeded . . . although Richard Barthelmess' faultless coiffure is streaked with gray at the end, whatever of sadness and defeat there is in him as he confesses to his mother that he has failed in the tricky business of living scarcely touches the audience."

A reviewer in *Variety* wrote, "With an ace director at the helm, a box office star in the top spot, a strong cast of supporting players, and a novel by a name writer, studio has turned out a picture that won't make the grade . . . of the cast, Barthelmess stands out, although he doesn't ever quite convince."

Advertisement for the G. W. Pabst film, *A Modern Hero* (1934).

Richard Barthelmess as a circus acrobat in G. W. Pabst's *A Modern Hero* (1934).

Two scenes from G. W. Pabst's *A Modern Hero* (1934): (TOP) **with William Janney, and** (BOTTOM) **with Mickey Rentschler and Jean Muir.**

Midnight Alibi (1934)
Warner Bros.
Producer: Jack Warner
Director: Alan Crosland
Scenario: Warren Duff, based on a story, *The Old Doll's House*, by Damon Runyon
Length: 59 minutes
Cast: Richard Barthelmess, Ann Dvorak, Helen Chandler, Helen Lowell, Henry O'Neil, Robert Barrat, Robert McWade, Purnell Pratt, Harry Tyler, Paul Hurst, Arthur Aylesworth, Vincent Sherman, Eric Wilton, Boothe Howard, Water Law, Edward Keane, Allan Wood, Heinie Conklin, David Callis, Ethel Wales, Gus Reed, Tom Costello, Buck Russell, William B. Davidson, Ben Hendricks, Frank La Rue, Philip Morris, James Donlan, Charles Hickman, Carl McBride, Renee Whitney, Walter Walker, Milton Kibbee, Stanley Mack, Lee Phelps, Robert Warwick, Harry Seymour.
Synopsis: Richard was cast as a tough, young gambler, Lance McGowan, first followed as he meets Joan Morley, the sister of his rival, Angie the Ox. He finds Angie has taken over control of several of his gambling clubs, and when the man discovers Lance with Joan, she warns him to stay away and instructs her henchmen to kill him. Shots are fired, and while fleeing, Lance drops over a fence into the garden of an old woman, Abigail Ardsley, now living in seclusion.

Lance returns to pour out his love to Joan, and is again discovered by her brother, Angie. A shot is fired by one of Lance's men, killing Angie. Lance is arrested for the murder, and when he is put on trial, Abigail makes a stunning entrance into the courtroom with an alibi for her young, gambler friend. He is acquitted, and returns to thank Abigail, finding Joan waiting for him to renew their relationship.

A reviewer for the *New York Times* wrote, "All things considered, First National has made a little plot go a long way. And the credit, of course, is due largely to the cast. Mr. Barthelmess, Miss Lowell and Miss Chandler, with the emphasis upon Miss Lowell, have turned in good performances."

A reviewer in *Variety* wrote, "Pretty much of an all-around miss. Barthelmess' name may help the picture somewhat in the grinds and duals, but picture won't help him anywhere. Gangster yarn that's badly miscast. Barthelmess in the central role just adds one more to the series of improbabilities about the film; he's never for a moment believable as a touch guy and the slang never seems to fit his lips . . . trimmed down to essentials, the story's pretty sappy and unconvincing, and that's what was done in the filming. It was pulled down, rather than built up. All the obvious story faults remain plus the use of amazingly bad dialog throughout, and the mentioned miscasting."

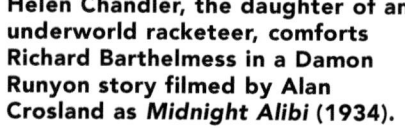

Helen Chandler with Richard Barthelmess in Alan Crosland's *Midnight Alibi* (1934).

Helen Chandler, the daughter of an underworld racketeer, comforts Richard Barthelmess in a Damon Runyon story filmed by Alan Crosland as *Midnight Alibi* (1934).

Four Hours to Kill! (1935)

PARAMOUNT
PRODUCER: ARTHUR HORNBLOW, JR.
DIRECTOR: MITCHELL LEISEN
SCENARIO: Norman Krasna, based on a play, *Small Miracles*, by Norman Krasna
LENGTH: 70 MINUTES
CAST: Richard Barthelmess, Helen Mack, Ray Milland, Gertrude Michael, Roscoe Kearns, Ray Milland, Charles C. Wilson, Henry Travers, Noel Madison, Paul Harvey, Olive Tell, Lee Kohlmer, Bodil Rosing, Lois Kent, Bruce Mitchell, John Buettner, Alfred Delcambre, Sam Ash, Frank Losee, Jr., Robert Kent, Craig Reynolds, Paul Gerrits, Gertrude Astor, Sheila Darcy, John Howard
SYNOPSIS: This thrilling murder mystery follows Richard Barthelmess as Tony Mako, a murderer doomed to hang. While handcuffed to a detective, the two have four hours to kill before the train departs to take him to his hanging. They attend a theater show where he sees the wife of Noel Madison, the man who testified against him. He brushes closely to the manager in the lobby of the theater and deftly takes the manager's gun. He calls Madison to tell him his wife needs him at the theater, and quietly waits in a phone booth to shoot Madison on arrival at the theater. Madison arrives, Barthelmess is discovered, and shot.

The *New York Times* reviewer wrote, "Norman Krasna's play *Small Miracles*, which ran for fourteen weeks at the Golden Theater this season, has been transferred intact, except for its title, to the screen of the Paramount Theatre. Known in its film form as *Four Hours to Kill*, the picture is a gripping, although extremely theatrical, melodrama with a neatly dovetailed plot, a uniformly excellent cast and well-paced direction . . . Richard Barthelmess as the convict, Tony Mako contributes what is probably one of his finest performances."

Four Hours to Kill newspaper advertisement as it appeared in the *Zanesville Signal*.

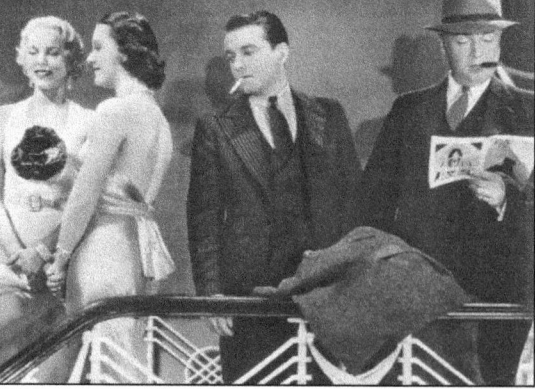

Richard Barthelmess as a hunted criminal handcuffed to a detective, played by Charles C. Wilson, in Mitchell Leisen's *Four Hours to Kill* (1935).

Two scenes from Mitchell Leisen's *Four Hours to Kill* (1935): (TOP) Richard Barthelmess with detective Charles C. Wilson, as they kill four hours in a theater while waiting for the train to take Barthelmess to his hanging. (BOTTOM) Dorothy Tree, wife of the theater manager, brushes by the condemned killer unknowing he has stolen a gun and plans to kill her husband, the man who gave testimony that convicted him for murder.

The Spy of Napoleon (1936)
Also known as The Invader, The Man who Changed His Mind, and The Man Who Lived Again
Twickenham-Unity Productions
Producer: Julius Hagen
Director: Maurice Elvey
Scenario: Frederick V. Merrick, based on a novel by Baroness Emmuska Orczy
Length: 98 minutes
Cast: Dolly Haas, Richard Barthelmess, Francis L. Sullivan, Frank Vosper, Lynn Harding, Henry Oscar, Marjorie Mars, Brian Buschell, Wilfrid Caithness, James Carew, Stafford Hilliard, George Merritt, C. Denier Warren

Frank Nugent, reviewing the film for the *New York Times*, said the cast appeared to "wander unguided through large sets and small scenes like a party of befuddled tourists." He said the British Unity Film troupe could "scarcely avoid resembling a jig saw puzzle which has not merely been badly assembled, but misses several key pieces . . . at least, that is our impression of the story, although it is so muddled we cannot guarantee it. The cast deserved better treatment, for there are a number of competent players in it: Dolly Haas, Richard Barthelmess, Francis Sullivan and the late Frank Vosper among them."

"Julius Hagen has made a praise-worthy production of this historical spy story, but it still has little to give it appeal outside of the domestic market," wrote a reviewer in *Variety*. "If the casting of Richard Barthelmess was intended to strengthen the film, it was a gamble that has not succeeded, for his performance is colorless in a picture that has many good acting studies . . . sets are spacious, but mostly studio-ish with the exception of lakeside exteriors and paddle steamer scenes. Photography and lighting are adequate. Sound is probably the weakest element in the film's construction."

The Postman Always Rings Twice (1936)
Opened February 25, 1936
Director: Robert Sinclair
Written by James M. Cain with Mary Philips
Cast: Joseph Greenwald, Mary Philips, Richard Barthelmess, John

Dolly Haas and Richard Barthelmess in Maurice Elvey's *The Spy of Napoleon* (1936).

Kearney, Joseph Cotton, Dudley Clements, Charles Halton, May Holsman, Queena Belotti, Walter Vonnegut, Al Cunningham, Philip Ryder

In 1936, Richard returned to the New York stage in *The Postman Always Rings Twice*. He made a striking, professional stage debut as a California vagrant who takes a job in a gas station because he took a fancy to the peculiar beauty of the wife of the station owner.

In the cast was Mary Philips, one of the most popular leading women in the theater. She had appeared in several successful stage plays in New York prior to *The Postman Always Rings Twice*, and with this new play, essayed the role of Cora Papadakis.

Joseph Cotton, later to achieve fame in *Citizen Kane* and many other motion pictures, appeared in a small role as a policeman. His work in this play followed a great deal of radio and stock work, and a few New York appearances in *Tonight or Never, Absent Father,* and *Accent on Youth.*

Brooks Atkinson of the *New York Times* thought the play version of the novel by James M. Cain translated well as a drama. "It turned up callously at the Lyceum last evening with Richard Barthelmess as the snide killer and Mary Philips as the killeress" he wrote. "Nearly everything that the stage can do for such an impetuous exercise in crime, Mr. Cain and his theater associates have done with considerable technical skill, and many of the twelve scenes sputter with garish excitement."

Atkinson also wrote about Richard's performance: "As the reckless lover of a gas station strumpet, Mr. Barthelmess does a blameless job in his first starring appearance on Broadway. He is pleasantly forthright, although he lacks the rasp and bite that are needed to make Frank Chambers a credible adventurer. He is up against some excellent actors in his stage debut . . . ."

Richard Barthelmess and cast on the Broadway stage of the Lyceum Theater in the second auto crash scene from the play, *The Postman Always Rings Twice* (1936).

ONLY ANGELS HAVE WINGS (1939)
COLUMBIA
PRODUCER: HOWARD HAWKS
DIRECTOR: HOWARD HAWKS
SCENARIO: Jules Furthman, based on a story by Howard Hawks
LENGTH: 121 MINUTES
CAST: Cary Grant, Jean Arthur, Richard Barthelmess, Thomas Mitchell, Rita Hayworth, Allyn Joslyn, Sig Ruman, John Carroll, Noah Beery, Jr., Melissa Sierra, Lucio Villegas, Forbes Murray, Cecilia Callejo, Pat Flaherty, Pedro Regas, Pat West, Manuel Maciste, Harry A. Bailey, Ky Robinson, Jack Lowe, Victor Travers, Al Rhein, Ed Randolph, Francisco Maran, Lou Davis
SYNOPSIS: The story follows Cary Grant as Geoff Carter, the head of a second-rate airline service in the Peruvian Andes. Geoff and the other pilots are forced to fly in treacherous weather each day, and their devil-may-care attitude toward the perils they face shocks Bonnie Lee, a showgirl played by Jean Arthur, stranded in the high mountains. At first, she cannot tolerate their casual attitude toward imminent mortality, but as days pass, she accepts their show of bravado as part of their job.

Richard Barthelmess, as Bat MacPherson, is another pilot who moves through the story with an air of guilt hanging over his head. In an earlier accident, Bat carelessly cost the life of one of their comrades. Because of his neglect, those at the airport view him with disdain. To make his life worse, he is saddled with a faithless wife, Judith, played by Rita Hayworth. When Judith makes a play for Geoff, he rebuffs her misguided show of affection, and shows attention only for Bonnie Lee. She stands by helplessly during an exciting turn of events, leading up to Geoff's death-defying flight through terror-filled skies.

According to Frank Nugent in the *New York Times*, "Mr. Hawks, whose aviation melodramas must, we suspect, drive airline stock down from two to three points per showing, has produced another fatality littered thriller in *Only Angels Have Wings* (even the title is ominous) . . . not content with the fell set-up, Mr. Hawks, as author, has chosen to add a few dramatic and romantic complications. Miss Arthur enters the scene as a stranded showgirl, and a less convincing showgirl than Miss Arthur would be hard to find. Enter, too,

Richard Barthelmess as a pilot with a black blot on his record and a wife who, by some strange coincidence, used to be Mr. Grant's fiancé."

"Mr. Hawks has staged his flying sequences brilliantly," Nugent went on to assess. "He has caught the drama in the meeting of a flier and the brother of the man he killed. He has made proper use of the amiable performing talents of Mr. Grant, Miss Arthur, Thomas Mitchell, Mr. Barthelmess, Sig Ruman and the rest. But when you add it all up, *Only Angels Have Wings* comes to an overly familiar total. It's a fairly good melodrama, nothing more."

A reviewer in the *Hollywood Reporter* wrote, "Barthelmess gives an unusually impressive delineation of an outcast flyer in a deadpan effort to re-establish himself among the flying clan. The part has mounting sympathy, with Barthelmess making the most of it."

Variety's reviewer related, "Columbia has a winner . . . with a good name cast it's certain for big returns . . . subplot has Barthelmess coming on the scene with Rita Hayworth (one of the

Only Angels Have Wings print advertisement as it appeared in many publications around the country.

Richard Barthelmess as Bat MacPherson in Howard Hawks' *Only Angels Have Wings* (1939).

dancing Cansinos family) as his wife. Latter is the girl who made Grant dour. Barthelmess is another disgraced aviator, but he more than vindicates himself with some very dangerous flying to a rescue job, and in another sequence, when he's transporting nitroglycerine . . . every facet of *Only Angels Have Wings* is big league. The Grant-Arthur cynicism and unyielding romantics are kept at a high standard. Thomas Mitchell's devoted aide is never permitted to become banal, and there are opportunities in plenty where it might so have been. Rita Hayworth as Barthelmess' wife is likewise impressive. She's a good-looking gal with an ah-voom chassis. Barthelmess is perhaps a bit too deadpan in his performance, but the bitterness is made plausible by his past, due to an unheroic episode when he based out of a crashing plane and permitted his pilot to crack up. Barthelmess' new mechanic physiognomy fits the plot situation well."

Three scenes from Howard Hawks' *Only Angels Have Wings* **(1939)**: (TOP) **with Rita Hayworth;** (CENTER) **with Gary Grant and Thomas Mitchell;** (BOTTOM) **Hayworth, Grant, and Jean Arthur.**

The Man Who Talked Too Much (1940)
Also known as Broadway Lawyer, and The Sentence
Warner Bros.
Producer: Edmund Grainger, Jack Warner
Director: Vincent Sherman
Scenario: Walter DeLeon and Earl Baldwin, based on a play by Frank R. Collins
Length: 75 minutes
Cast: George Brent, Virginia Bruce, Brenda Marshall, Richard Barthelmess, William Lundigan, George Tobias, John Litel, Henry Armetta, Alan Baxter, David Bruce, Clarence Kolb, Louis Jean Heydt, Marc Lawrence, Edwin Stanley, Kay Sutton
Synopsis: The story follows George Brent as Stephen Forbes, a hot young prosecuting lawyer who successfully wins the death sentence for a man. When he learns the truth about the innocence of the convicted man, his remorse over having been responsible for sending him to his death causes him to change career paths. He becomes a defense attorney, and grows rich defending racketeers guilty of various crimes. After a frame-up, he sees the errors of his ways.

Bosley Crowther wrote in the *New York Times*, "For a straight gangster picture, which should be fast and concise, it is ponderously slow and windy and as transparent as a goldfish bowl. There are two identically suspenseful sequences, at the beginning and at the end, when innocent men linger painfully in the shadow of the electric chair while people rush around madly to save them. And that's about all the suspense there is. George Brent plays the title role in a perpetually sullen mood, and Virginia Bruce tags wistfully after him as his doting but apparently unrequited secretary. Richard Barthelmess chips in with a conventionally dour gangster performance...."

A reviewer in *Variety* wrote, "This is a remake of *The Mouthpiece* produced by Warner Bros. back in 1932 when anything in the way of a gangster film was usually big box office. The essence of the story itself has been done and redone to a crisp in pictures. It's about the lawyer who suffers remorse when, as an assistant district attorney, he sends an innocent kid to the chair. He quits as prosecutor, but goes hungry in his own practice until a gang leader, Richard Barthelmess, persuades him to defend the mob for very fancy coin. This enables Brent to pay off his bills...there's nothing distinguished the performances . . . however, the film has some importance in again showing Barthelmess on a screen. The ex-star is miscast as a soft-spoken gang chief, but his speaking ability rates more and better chances."

The Man Who Talked Too Much newspaper advertisement as it appeared in the *Lima News*.

A scene from Vincent Sherman's *The Man Who Talked Too Much* (1940), featuring George Brent, Virginia Bruce, William Lundigan, and Richard Barthelmess.

THE SPOILERS (1942)
UNIVERSAL
PRODUCER: FRANK LLOYD
DIRECTOR: RAY ENRIGHT
SCENARIO: Lawrence Hazard and Tom Reed, based on the novel by Rex Beach
LENGTH: 87 MINUTES
CAST: John Wayne, Randolph Scott, Marlene Dietrich, Richard Barthelmess, Margaret Lindsay, Harry Carey, George Cleveland, Samuel S. Hinds, Russell Simpson, William Farnum, Marietta Canty, Jack Norton, Ray Bennett, Forrest Taylor, Art Miles
SYNOPSIS: In Nome, Alaska, miner Roy Glennister and his partner Dextry, are victimized by a crooked political plot, which involves Alex McNamara and Judge Stillman robbing rightful owners by jumping their claims. With the help of saloon entertainer Cherry Malotte, the men fight to save their gold claim. Along the way, Roy befriends Helen Chester, the niece of Judge Stillman, but believes she is an accomplice in the mine jumping. Despite his feelings and suspicions, Roy saves the Judge from hanging, and in the end, Glennister delivers a rousingly just reward to McNamara by way of an epic fistfight.

This was the fourth version of the famous story by Rex Beach, and made cinema history with the original version in 1915 starring William Farnum and Kathlyn Williams in the roles played by John Wayne and Marlene Dietrich. In an interesting bit of casting, William Farnum played the role of Wheaton in this version made some twenty-seven years later.

The *New York Times* reviewer wrote, "Having pinched the muscles of John Wayne and Randolph Scott and found them solid, Ray Enright has leaped to a safe perch on a camera boom and let them slug it out for Marlene Dietrich's well-manicured hand in *The Spoilers*." Richard played the "Bronco Kid" who, in his youth, used to win the affection of Cherry Malotte, played by Marlene Dietrich, only to later earn a hearty rebuff when he returned. "Perhaps Cherry's complex affections seem a bit amusing at this distance, and thank Mr. Enright and Miss Dietrich's witty playing for keeping them so," continued the *New York Times*. "Sprinkled with double entendres nearly as frankly cut as Miss Dietrich's gowns, the author and producer have kept their tongues firmly in their cheeks, even when stout Mr. Wayne and Mr. Scott begin tearing up the set. It's a lovely brawl."

"Richard Barthelmess gives a creditable performance as the gambler," wrote a reviewer in *Variety*, "while other good characterizations are turned in by Hinds, Harry Carey, George Cleveland, Russel Simpson and William Farnum. Yes, the same William Farnum now in an obscure role, who nearly thirty years ago made cinema history in the part currently being played by John Wayne."

The *Spoilers* newspaper advertisement as it appeared in the *Coshocton Tribune*.

Richard Barthelmess with Marlene Dietrich in Ray Enright's *The Spoilers* (1942).

The Mayor of 44th Street (1942)
RKO
Producer: Cliff Reid
Director: Alfred E. Green
Scenario: Lewis Foster and Frank Ryan, based on a story by Robert Andrews
Length: 86 minutes
Cast: George Murphy, Anne Shirley, William Cargan, Richard Barthelmess, Joan Merrill, Freddy Martin, Rex Downing, Millard Mitchell, Mary Wickes, Eddie Hart, Robert Smith, Marten Lamont, Walter Reid, Lee Bonnell, Ken Lundy, Esther Muir, John Dilson, Wayne McCoy, Lola Jensen, Rosemary Coleman, Jane Woodworth, Gerald Pierce, Jane Patton, Norman Mayes, Mike Lally, Clarence Hennecke, Frank O'Connor, Richard Martin, David Kirkland, Pete Theodore, Linda Rivas, Matt Moore, John McGuire, Donald Kerr, Eddie Hart, Jack Gardner, George Ford, Monte Collins, Jr., Ken Christy, Jack Byron, Reginald Barlow.
Synopsis: The story follows George Murphy as Joe Jonathan, a struggling, ex-vaudevillian, who tries to keep his business straight while dealing with shady characters. He opens an agency for dance bands, and helps out local youths by helping them obtain jobs at dance events. Because of the racketeering tactics of its former proprietor, the cops are watching the agency closely. With the aid of Jessie Lee, played by Anne Shirley, Joe is making a success of the business until he runs afoul of the local gang leader, Blitz McKarg, played by Rex Downing, and helps another gangster, Ed Kirby, played by Richard Barthelmess, earn a parole by offering him a chance at employment. He comes to regret the action, as the ex-con uses his influence with the agency to resume a blackmailing operation and commit extortion.

This RKO release was prepared as a vehicle for musical comedy star, George Murphy. The film featured the musical numbers, "Your Face Looks Familiar," "Heavenly, Isn't He?" "Let's Forget It," "You're Bad For Me," "A Million Miles From Manhattan," and the Oscar-nominated, "When There's a Breeze on Lake Louise." In one number, Murphy is seen dancing with exuberant style. In his final film role, Richard played a character called Ed Kirby.

In a review in the *New York Times*, Bosley Crowther hated the film, and made no mention of Richard. It was just as well, because he felt the film was dismal. "Unless your toleration of the genius jitterbug is complete and unassailable you would do well to maintain restraint toward RKO's The Mayor of 44th Street, for the type of wacky youngster which goes around howling and hooting at bands, making himself a nuisance as well as an unholy sight, is here-in presented not only as an abomination to the human race but also as a heavy contributor to the delinquency of adults. It takes a lot of patience to bear with the little rascals in this case. And, for that matter, it takes patience to bear with *The Mayor of 44th Street*."

A reviewer for *Variety* wrote, ". . . is a lightly textured drama providing top B-grade of entertainment through meritorious work by the cast and director. Lacking sufficient marquee voltage for key spots, picture nevertheless will provide strong support in the regular runs.

The Mayor of 44th Street newspaper advertisement as it appeared in the *Newark Advocate*.

Two scenes from Alfred E. Green's *The Mayor of 44th Street* (1942): (TOP) **Richard Barthelmess with George Murphy and Anne Shirley, and** (BOTTOM) **with Rex Downing.**

Part 3: Portrait Gallery

Richard Barthelmess in 1917 at the time he first appeared in motion pictures.

Portrait of Richard Barthelmess ca. 1918.

Portrait of Richard Barthelmess ca. 1918.

Portrait of Richard Barthelmess ca. 1919.

Portrait of Richard Barthelmess ca. 1920.

Portrait of Richard Barthelmess ca. 1920.

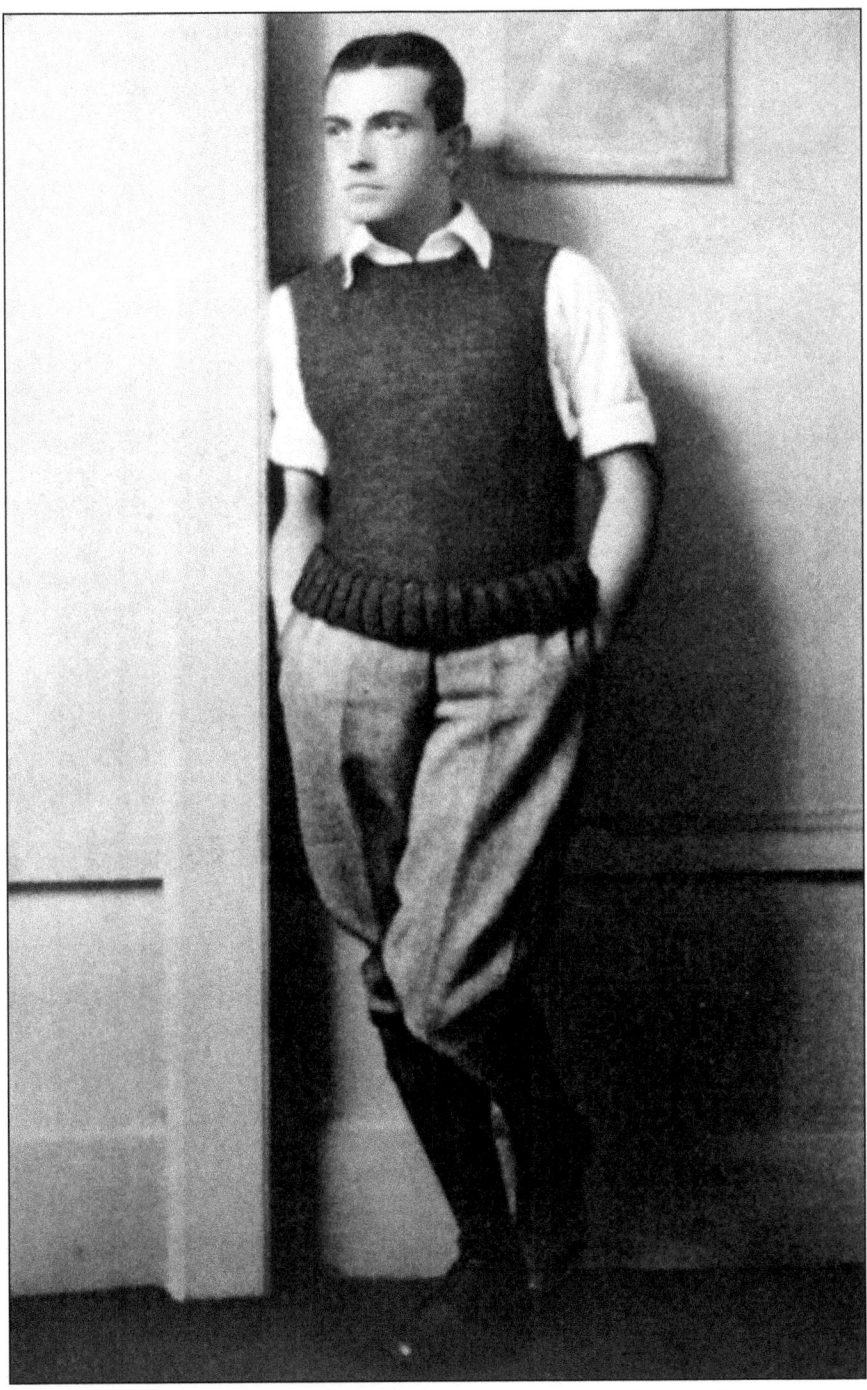

Portrait of Richard Barthelmess ca. 1920.

Portrait of Richard Barthelmess as David Bartlett in *Way Down East* (1920).

Portrait of Richard Barthelmess ca. 1922.

Portrait of Richard Barthelmess ca. 1923.

Portrait of Richard Barthelmess in *The Fighting Blade* ca. 1923.

Portrait of Richard Barthelmess ca. 1924.

Portrait of Richard Barthelmess ca. 1924.

Portrait of Richard Barthelmess ca. 1925.

Portrait of Richard Barthelmess ca. 1926.

Portrait of Richard Barthelmess ca. 1927.

Portrait of Richard Barthelmess ca. late 1920s.

Portrait of Richard Barthelmess ca. late 1920s.

Portrait of Richard Barthelmess ca. late 1920s.

Portrait of Richard Barthelmess ca. late 1920s.

Portrait of Richard Barthelmess ca. late 1920s.

Portrait of Richard Barthelmess ca. late 1920s.

Portrait of Richard Barthelmess ca. early 1930s.

Portrait of Richard Barthelmess ca. early 1930s.

Part 3: Portrait Gallery

Portrait of Richard Barthelmess ca. early 1930s.

Portrait of Richard Barthelmess ca. early 1930s.

Portrait of Richard Barthelmess ca. early 1930s.

Portrait of Richard Barthelmess ca. early 1930s.

Portrait of Richard Barthelmess ca. mid-1930s.

Portrait of Richard Barthelmess ca. mid-1930s.

Portrait of Richard Barthelmess ca. mid-1930s.

Portrait of Richard Barthelmess ca. mid-1930s.

Portrait of Richard Barthelmess ca. mid-1930s.

Portrait of Richard Barthelmess ca. mid-1930s.

Portrait of Richard Barthelmess ca. late 1930s.

Portrait of Richard Barthelmess ca. late 1930s.

Portrait of Richard Barthelmess ca. late 1930s.

Portrait of Richard Barthelmess ca. late 1930s.

Appendix
The Plays and Motion Pictures of Mary Hay

HEARTS OF THE WORLD (FILM) (1918)
D. W. GRIFFITH PRODUCTION COMPANY
DIRECTOR: D. W. GRIFFITH
SCENARIO: D. W. Griffith (as M. Gaston de Tolignac); translated by (D. W. Griffith) as Captain Victor Marier
CAST: Lillian Gish, Robert Harron, Dorothy Gish, Adolph Lestina, Josephine Crowell, Jack Cosgrove, Kate Bruce, Ben Alexander, Marion Emmons, Francis Marion, Robert Anderson, George Fawcett, George A. Siegmann, Fay Holderness, L. Lowry, Eugene Pouyet, Anna Mae Walthall, Yvette Duvoisin, Herbert Sutch, Alphonse Dufort, Jean Dumercier, Jules Lemontier, Gaston Riviere, Georges Loyer, George Nichols, Mrs. Mary Gish, Mary Harron, Jessie Harron, Johnny Harron, Noel Coward
LENGTH: 11 REELS

EASTWARD HO! (FILM) (1919)
FOX FILM CORPORATION
DIRECTOR: EMMETT J. FLYNN
SCENARIO: ROY SOMERVILLE
CAST: William Russell, Lucille Lee Stewart, Johnnie Hines, Charles A. Stevenson, Mary Hay, Robert Cain, Thomas Delmar, Colin Chase, Dorothy Dickson, Carl Hyson
LENGTH: 5 REELS

ZIEGFELD GIRLS OF 1920 (PLAY)
OPENING MARCH 8, 1920
DANSE DE FOLLIES
TOTAL PERFORMANCES: 78
DIRECTOR/PRODUCER: FLORENZ ZIEGFELD, JR.
CAST: Fanny Brice, Cameron Sisters, Sybil Carmen, Peggy Eleanore, W. C. Fields, Thomas Handers, Mary Hay, Vanda Hoff, John Price Jones, Allyn King, Lillian Lorraine, Kathlene Martyn, Arthur Milliss, Prince Royle, Princess Wha-Letka

SALLY (PLAY)
OPENING DECEMBER 21, 1920
NEW AMSTERDAM THEATER
TOTAL PERFORMANCES: 561
DIRECTOR/PRODUCER: FLORENZ ZIEGFELD, JR.
CAST: Walter Catlett, Barbara Dean, Leon Errol, Irving Fisher, Mary Hay, Alfred P. James, Alta King, Frank Kingdom, Mary McDonald, Marilynn Miller, Gladys Montgomery, Jacques Rebiroff, Stanley Ridges, Phil Riley, Vivian Vernon, Betty Williams

WAY DOWN EAST (FILM) (1920)
D. W. GRIFFITH-UNITED ARTIST
PRODUCER: D. W. GRIFFITH
DIRECTOR: D. W. GRIFFITH
SCENARIO: Anthony Paul Kelly, based on the stage play by Lottie Blair Parker
CAST: Lillian Gish, Richard Barthelmess, Lowell Sherman, Burr McIntosh, Mary Hay, Creighton Hale, Kate Bruce, Edgar Nelson, Porter Strong, Mrs. David Landau, Josephine Bernard, Mrs. Morgan Belmont, Patricia Fruen, Florence Short, Vivia Ogden, Porter Strong, George Neville, Edgar Nelson, Emily Fitzroy, Norma Shearer
LENGTH: 13 REELS

Marjoliane (Play) (1922)
Broadhurst Theater
Opening January 24, 1922
Total Performances: 136
Director: Russell Janney
Cast: Albert G. Andrews, Irving Beebe, Daisy Belmore, Colin Campbell, Royal Cutter, E. L. De Brocq, Worthe Faulkner, Irving S. Finn, Mary Hay, Maurice Holland, Lennoxe Paule, Merle Stevens, Nellie Strong, Olga Treskoff, Paul Warren, Addeson Youngs

Mary Jane McKane (Play) 1923
Imperial Theater
Opening December 25, 1923
Total Performances: 151
Director/Producer: Arthur Hammerstein
Cast: Eva Clark, Laura De Cardi, Mary Hay, James Heenan, Keene Twins, Kitty Kelly, Louis Morrell, Stanley Ridges, Hal Skelly, Dallas Welford

New Toys (Film) 1925)
Inspiration-First National
Producer: John S. Robertson
Director: John S. Robertson
Scenario: Josephine Lovett, based on a story by Agnes Smith
Cast: Richard Barthelmess, Mary Hay, Clifton Webb, Katherine Wilson, Francis Conlon, Bijou Fernandez, Tammany Young, Pat O'Connor, Jules Jordan, Jacob Kingsbury
Length: 8 reels

Treasure Girl (Play) (1928)
Alvin Theater
Opening November 8, 1928
Total Performances: 68
Director: Alex A. Aarons

CAST: Charles Barron, Frank G. Bond, Walter Catlett, Norman Curtis, John Dunsmure, Stephen Francis, Virginia Franck, Paul Frawley, Victor Garland, Ferris Hartman, Mary Hay, Dorothy Jordan, Gertrude Lawrence, Peggy O'Neill, Edwin Preble, Clifton Webb

GREATER LOVE (PLAY) (1931)
LIBERTY THEATER
OPENING MARCH 2, 1931
TOTAL PERFORMANCES: 8
DIRECTOR/PRODUCER: MARTIN JONES
WRITTEN BY BRUCE SPAULDING, MARY HAY, ANTHONY BAIRD, AND NELLA STEWARD
CAST: John Breeden, Brenda Dahlen, Douglas Gillmore, Mary Hay, Jack McKee, Edith Meiser, Catherine Proctor, Muriel Stone, Fred Sullivan

Bibliography

"Alias the Doctor." By Mordaunt Hall in the *New York Times*, March 3, 1932, page 22.

"Alias the Doctor." *Variety*, March 8, 1932.

"All Talking Movie Pleasing Big Crowds at the Majestic." *The Sheboygan Press*, August 16, 1928, page 16.

"Alla Nazimova, of Screen Fame, Is Dead." *The Waterloo Daily Courier*, July 13, 1945, page 2.

"Amateur Gentleman." *Variety*, August 18, 1928.

"Amateur Gentleman." By Mordaunt Hall in the *New York Times*, August 17, 1926, page 15.

"A Modern Hero." By Mordaunt Hall in the *New York Times*, April 20, 1934, page 17.

"A Modern Hero." *Variety*, April 24, 1934.

"Another Tol'able David Role for Our Dick in the Kentucky Hills." *The Appleton Post Crescent*, April 13, 1928, page 12.

Astor, Mary. *A Life on Film*. New York: Delacourte Press, 1967.

"A Plea for Privacy." By Helen Louise Walker in *Photoplay*, September 1928, page 65, 121.

"A Terribly Intimate Portrait." By Beatrice Wilson in *Motion Picture Classic*, May 1924, page 38-39.

"A Wealthy Manufacturer's Son." By Delight Evans in *Photoplay*, January 1919, pages 96, 97.

"Bab's Burglar." The *Newark Advocate*, December 10, 1917, page 6.

"Bab's Burglar." *Variety*, November 9, 1917.

"Bab's Diary." The *Iowa Citizen*, November 27, 1917, page 6.

"Bab's Diary." The *Newark Advocate*, October 19, 1917, page 7.

"Bab's Diary." The *Newark Advocate*, October 26, 1917, page 10.

"Bab's Diary." The *Indianapolis Star*, October 8, 1917, page 12.

"Bab's Diary." *Variety*, October 5, 1917.

Balyeat, Peggy. "Barthelmess — the Unwilling Vamp." *Pantomime*, March 18, 1922.

Barry, Iris. *D. W. Griffith American Film Master*. New York: Doubleday & Company, Inc., 1965.

"Barthelmess Between Pictures." By John Carlisle in *Silver Screen*, June 1933, page 21.

"Barthelmess is Back." By Miriam Teichner in *Modern Movies*, December 1939, pages 45, 64.

"Barthelmess Dead at 68." The *Herald Express Examiner*, Saturday, August 17, 1963.

Barthelmess, Richard. "The True Story of My Life" in *Movie Weekly*, April 11, 1925, pp. 14, 15, 33.

"Barthelmess — the Unwilling Vamp." By Peggy Balyeat in *Pantomime*, March 18, 1922.

"Barthelmess To Marry." The *Morning Oregonian*, August 23, 1927.

"Beautiful City, The." By Mordaunt Hall in the *New York Times*, November 23, 1925, page 25.

"Beautiful City, The." *Variety*, November 25, 1925.

"Behind the Headlines of Barthelmess' Comeback." By Roger Carroll in *Motion Picture Magazine*, April 1939, page 28, 75.

"Big Estate for Dorothy Gish." The *Valley Independent*, June 27, 1968, page 2.

Bodeen, De Witt. "Pauline Frederick." *Films in Review*, February 1965, 69-90.

"Bondboy, The." The *Daily Northwestern*, December 13, 1922, page 8.

"Bondboy, The." The *Mexia Evening News*, October 29, 1922, page 6.

"Bondboy, The." The *New York Times*, October 9, 1922, page 10.

"Boots." The *Daily Kennebec Journal*, February 27, 1919, page 3.

"Boots." The *Sandusky Star Journal*, November 14, 1919, page 13.

"Boots." The *New York Times*, March 10, 1919, page 9.

"Bright Shawl, The." The *New York Times*, Mar 13, 1922, page 18.

"Bright Shawl, The." By Frederick James Smith in *Photoplay*, July 1923.

"Bright Shaw, The." *Variety*, April 26, 1923.

"Broken Blossoms." By Julian Johnson in *Photoplay*, August 1919, page 20.

"Broken Blossoms." The *Coshocton Tribune*, May 4, 1920, page 8.

"Broken Blossoms." *Pictures and Picturegoer*. March 27, 1920, page 316, 317.

"Broken Blossoms." The *New York Times*, May 23, 1916, page 15.

Brown, Karl. *Adventures with D. W. Griffith*. Farrar, Straus and Giroux, 1973.

"Call Mr. Ponce de Leon." By Herbert Howe in *Photoplay*, January 1918, page 39, 40.

"Cabin in the Cotton." By Mordaunt Hall in the *New York Times*, September 30, 1932, page 17.

"Cabin in the Cotton." *Variety*, October 4, 1932.

"Camille." The *Fredericksburg News*, January 15, 1918, page 1.

"Camille." The *Indianapolis Star*, October 23, 1917, page 11.

"Camille." The *Sheboygan Press*, January 14, 1918, page 7.

"Cast of Celebrities Assembled by Barthelmess in Filming Bright Shawl. *Screenland*, May 18, 1923, page 11.

"Central Airport." By Mordaunt Hall in The *New York Times*, May 4, 1933, page 20.

"Central Airport Thrills Preview Audience." The *Times Recorder*, May 24, 1933, page 7.

"Central Airport." *Variety*, May 9, 1933.

"Classmates." By Mordaunt Hall in the *New York Times*, December 30, 1924.

"Classmates." *Variety*, December 31, 1924.

"Close Up." By Joseph Henry Steele in *Photoplay*, March 1930, pages 99, 112.

"College Men Needed Says Barthelmess. The *Mansfield News*, July 20, 1925, page 5.

Connell, Brian. *Knight Errant–A Biography of Douglas Fairbanks, Jr.* New York: Doubleday & Company, 1955.

"Cut in Movie Stars' Salaries Starts in a Few Months." The *Reno Evening Gazette*, November 28, 1931, page 9.

"Dawn Patrol–With the Air Force." The *New York Times*, July 11, 1930, page 22.

"Dawn Patrol, The." *Variety*, July 16, 1930.

"Dick An Etching of Richard Barthelmess." By Joseph Henry Steele in the *New Movie Magazine*, February 1932, pages 61, 99.

"Dick Barthelmess and Mary Hay, His Wife, Starring in New Toys." The *Mansfield News*, July 20, 1925, page 5.

"Dick Barthelmess Builds His Ideal Home." The *New Movie Magazine*, March 1932, pages 46, 47.

"Dick's Different." By E. E. Barrett in the *Picturegoer*, December 1926, pages 16, 17.

"Dick's New Film." *Picture Show*, May 21, 1927, page 19.

"Dick's New Leading Woman." By Agnes Smith in *Photoplay*, January 1925, page 73, 74.

"Dorothy Gish, Actress, Is Dead." The *New York Times*, June 6, 1968.

"Drag." By Mordaunt Hall in The *New York Times*, June 21, 1929, page 17.

"Drag." *Variety*, June 26, 1929.

"Drop Kick, The." By Mordaunt Hall in the *New York Times*, September 20, 1927, page 32.

"Drop Kick, The." The *Lima News*, September 19, 1927, page 7.

"Drop Kick, The." *Variety*, September 21, 1927.

"D. W. Griffith Rites Tuesday." The *Dallas Morning News*, July 25, 1948.

"Early Days in the Movies." By Rupert Hughes in *Saturday Evening Post*, April 13, 1935, page 31.

"Early Days in the Movies – Part 2." By Rupert Hughes in *Saturday Evening Post*, April 13, 1935, page 118.

"Early Days in the Movies – Part 3." By Rupert Hughes in *Saturday Evening Post*, April 6, 1935, page 18.

Elwood, Muriel. *Pauline Frederick on and off the Stage*. Chicago: A. Kroch, 1940.

"Enchanted Cottage, The." By Mordaunt Hall in the *New York Times*, January 18, 1926.

"Enchanted Cottage, The." *Variety*, April 16, 1924.

"Eternal Sin, The." The *Mansfield News*, July 19, 1917, page 7.

"Eternal Sin, The." The *Washington Post*, June 3, 1917, page 44.

Everson, William K. *American Silent Film*. New York: Oxford University Press, 1978, pages 164-167.

"Experience." The *New York Times*, August 8, 1921, page 12.

"Experience." *Variety*, August 12, 1921.

Eyman, Scott. *The Speed of Sound*. New York: Simon & Schuster, 1997.

Fairbanks, Douglas Jr. *The Salad Days*. New York: Doubleday, 1988.

"Famous Danseuse to Appear at the American." The *Evening Telegram*, August 19, 1918, page 7.

"Famous Juliets." By Jerome Hart in *Motion Picture Classic*, March, 1923.

"Fighting Blade, The." The *Lima News*, November 18, 1923, page 19.

"Fighting Blade, The." The *Coshocton Tribune*, September 21, 1924, page 10.

"Fifteen Years of Film Fame." By Richard Barthelmess in *Picturegoer Weekly*, June 10, 1933.

"Finger Points, The." By Mordaunt Hall in the *New York Times*, March 28, 1931, page 15.

"Finger Points, The." *Variety*, April 8, 1931.

"First Marriage is Frenzy But Second Marriage" By Gladys Hall in *Movie Mirror*. New York: Movie Mirror Publishing Company, March 1934, pages 59, 88.

"For Valour." The *Middletown Press*, April 16, 1918, page 6.

"For Valour." *Variety*, November 23, 1917.

"Four Hours to Kill!" The *New York Times*, April 11, 1934, page 27.

"Four Hours to Kill." The *Zanesville Signal*, May 9, 1935, page 7.

Fox, Charles Donald. *Famous Film Folk*. New York: George H. Doran Company, 1925, page 32.

"Frenzy Says Dick." By Gladys Hall in *Movie Mirror*. New York: Movie Mirror Publishing Company, February 1934.

"Fury." The *Lima News*, March 25, 1925, page 18.

"Fury." *Variety*, February 15, 1923.

"Girl Who Stayed at Home, The." The *Coshocton Tribune*, November 17, 1920, page 10.

"Girl Who Stayed at Home, The." The *Elvira Chronicle*, June 7, 1920, page 6.

"Girl Who Stayed at Home, The." The *New York Times*, March 24, 1919, page 11.

Gish, Lillian. *The Movies Mr. Griffith and Me*. New Jersey: Prentice-Hall, Inc., 1969.

"Gloria's Romance." The *Daily Kennebec Journal*, July 18, 1916, page 3.

"Gloria's Romance." The *Frederick Maryland News*, July 31, 1916, page 14.

"Gloria's Romance." The *Indianapolis Star*, May 22, 1916, page 8.

"Gloria's Romance Shown." The *New York Times*, May 23, 1916.

"Great Change in Motion Pictures For This Season." The *Decatur Daily Review*, August 19, 1928, page 21.

Griffith, Linda Arvidson. *When the Movies Were Young.* New York: Dover Publications, 1969.

Griffith, Richard. *The Film Til Now.* Great Britain: Fletcher & sons, Ltd., 1967.

"Golden Youth–Review." *Picture Show*, April 2, 1927, page 14.

"He Might Be the Richest Man in the World – D. W. Griffith." By Frederick James Smith in *Photoplay*, December 1926, page 30-31, 106.

Henderson, Robert M. *D. W. Griffith His Life and Work.* New York: Oxford University Press, 1972.

"Heroes for Sale." The *Newark Advocate*, July 21, 1933, page 6.

"Heroes for Sale-Jobless Drifter Well Portrayed by Barthelmess." The *Newark Advocate*, July 22, 1933, page 4.

"Heroes for Sale." The *New York Times*, July 22, 1933, page 14.

"He Took College Seriously." By Charleson Gray in *Motion Picture*, February 1930.

"High Salaried Actors Aim to Protect Free Lance Groups." By Elizabeth Yeaman in the *Hollywood Citizen-News*, March 11, 1933.

"Hit the Trail Holiday." The *Lincoln Daily Star*, March 18, 1917, page 20.

"Hit the Trail Holiday." The *Marion Star*, February 8, 1919, page 26.

"Hit the Trail Holiday." *Variety*, June 14, 1918.

"Hollywood's Hall of Fame." By Herbert Howe in the *New Movie Magazine*, July 1931, pages 40, 41, 120.

"Hope Chest, The." The *Mansfield News*, March 28, 1919, page 20.

"Hope Chest, The." The *Sandusky Star Journal*, November 14, 1919, page 13.

"Hope Chest, The." The *New York Times*, January 6, 1919, page 11.

"Hope Chest, The." *Variety*, January 10, 1919.

Hopper, Hedda. *From Under My Hat*. New York: Doubleday & Company, 1952.

Horseman, Victoria. *Made in Heaven*. Chicago: Bonus Books, 1991, page 21.

"Idol Dancer, The." By Burns Mantle in *Photoplay*. New York: June 1920, page 20.

"Idol Dancer, The." The *New York Times*, March 29, 1920, page 12.

"I Have Said Good-bye to Youth." By Gladys Hall in *Modern Screen*, January 1935.

"I'll Get Him Yet." The *Lima News*, August 12, 1919, page 17.

"I'll Get Him Yet." The *New York Times*, May 19, 1919.

"In Cromwellian Days-Fighting Blade Review." The *New York Times*, Mar 13, 1922.

"Intimate Portrait of a Man with Black Hair." *Photoplay*, January 1929, pages 39, 144.

"Just a Song at Twilight." *Variety*, December 29, 1916.

"Just Suppose." The *Decatur Review*, June 12, 1926, page 9.

"Just Suppose." *Variety*, January 20, 1926.

Katchmer, George A. *Eighty Silent Film Stars*. Jefferson: McFarland and Company, 1991, page 15-24.

"Kentucky Courage (The Little Shepherd of Kingdom Come) Review." By Mordaunt Hall in the *New York Times*, May 14, 1928, page 25.

Lambert, Gavin. *Nazimova*. New York: Alfred A. Knopf, 1997.

"Lash, The." By Mordaunt Hall in the *New York Times*, January 1, 1931, page 31.

"Lash, The." *Variety*, December 17, 1930.

"Last Flight, The." The *Burlington Daily Times* News, January 16, 1932, page 11.

"Last Flight, The." By Mordaunt Hall in the *New York Times*, August 20, 1931.

"Last Flight, The." *Variety*, August 25, 1931, page 17.

Leaming, Barbara. *Bette Davis*. New York: Simon & Schuster, 1992.

"Lillian Gish, Acting Great from Silent Film Era, Dies." The *Dallas Morning News*, March 1, 1993, page 18.

"Little Shepherd of Kingdom Come." The *Daily Northwestern*, August 8, 1928, page 4.

"Love Flower, The." By James Frederick Smith in *Motion Picture Classic*, November 1920, page 20.

"Love Flower, The." The *New York Times*, August 23, 1920, page 9.

"Lucretia Borgia." *Variety*, March 23, 1917.

"Man Who Talked Too Much, The." By Bosley Crowther in the *New York Times*, June 29, 1940, page 12.

"Man Who Talked Too Much." The *Lima News*, July 2, 1940, page 9.

"Man Who Talked Too Much, The." *Variety*, July 03, 1940.

Marion, Frances. *Off with Their Heads!* New York: The Macmillan Company, 1972.

"Massacre, The." By Mordaunt Hall in the *New York Times*, January 18, 1934, page 19.

"Massacre, The." *Variety*, January 23, 1934.

Maturi, Richard, and Mary Buckingham Maturi. *Francis X. Bushman A Biography and Filmography.* Jefferson, NC: McFarland & Company, Inc., 1998.

Maturi, Richard, and Mary Buckingham Maturi. *Beverly Bayne, Queen of the Movies.* Jefferson, NC: McFarland & Company, Inc., 2001.

"Mayor of 44th Street, The." By Mordaunt Hall in the *New York Times*, June 11, 1942, page 27.

"Mayor of 44th Street, The." The *Newark Advocate*, October 26, 1942, page 5.

"Mayor of 44th St, The." *Variety*, March 18, 1942.

McCarthy, Todd. *Howard Hawks The Grey Fox of Hollywood*. New York: Grove Press, 1997.

"Midnight Alibi, The." The *New York Times*, July 4, 1934, page 18.

"Midnight Alibi, The." *Variety*, July 10, 1934.

Mook, Samuel Richard. "The Stars Hit Back." *Picture Play*, January 1930.

"Moral Code at Lyric Today Only." The *Fort Wayne News*, March 15, 1917, page 9.

"My Early Life." By David Wark Griffith in *Focus on D. W. Griffith* by Harry M. Geduld, New Jersey: Prentice-Hall, 1971.

"My Leading Women." By Richard Barthelmess in *Motion Picture Magazine*, February 1925, page 109.

"Nazimova Dies of Heart Attack in Hollywood." *United Press International*, July 13, 1948.

"Nazimova in Film of War Brides Play." New York: *New York Times*, November 13, 1916.

"Nearly Married." The *Coshocton Tribune*, April 30, 1918, page 2.

"Nearly Married." The *Mansfield News*, January 28, 1918, page 5.

"Nearly Married." *Variety*, December 7, 1917.

"New Toys." The *Iowa City Press Citizen*, April 18, 1925, page 6.

"New Toys." The *Mansfield News*, July 21, 1925, page 10.

"New Toys." The *New York Times*, February 17, 1925, page 18.

"Noose, The." *Variety*, March 21, 1928.

"On Location with Richard Barthelmess." By Helen Ludlam in *Screenland*, November 1930, pages 58, 59, 114.

"Only Angels Have Wings." By Frank Nugent in the *New York Times*. May 12, 1939, page 25.

"Only Angels Have Wings." The *Hollywood Reporter*. May 11, 1939.

"Only Angels Have Wings." *Variety*, May 17, 1939.

"Out of the Ruins." The *Appleton Post Crescent*, August 28, 1928, page 14.

"Out of the Ruins." By Mordaunt Hall in the *New York Times*, August 20, 1928, page 21.

"Out of the Ruins." *Variety*, August 22, 1928.

"Patent Leather Kid, The." By Mordaunt Hall in the *New York Times*, August 16, 1927, page 31.

"Patent Leather Kid, The." *Variety*, August 17, 1927.

"Pauline Frederick, Empress of Stormy Emotion." By Eve Golden in *Classic Images*, October 2001.

"Peppy Polly." The *Clearfield Progress*, December 10, 1920, page 5.

"Peppy Polly." The *Decatur Review*, July 25, 1919, page 6.

"Peppy Polly." The *Fort Wayne Journal Gazette*, May 4, 1919, page 11.

"Peppy Polly." The *New York Times*, April 7, 1919, page 11.

Playbill. New York: The New York Theatre Program Corporation, February 1936.

Quirk, Lawrence J. *Fasten Your Seat Belts*. New York: William Morrow and Company, 1990.

Ralston, Esther. *Some Day We'll Laugh*. New Jersey: The Scarecrow Press, 1985.

Ramsaye, Terry. *A Million and One Nights*. New York: Simon and Schuster, 1926.

"Ranson's Folly." By Mordaunt Hall in the *New York Times*, May 31, 1926, page 10.

"Ranson's Folly." *Motion Picture Classic*, August 1926, page 51.

"Ranson's Folly." *Variety*, June 9, 1926.

"Raving Versus Reason." By Emma-Lindsay Squier in *Picture-Play Magazine*, 1921, page 30.

"Rich Man, Poor Man." *Variety*, April 19, 1918.

"Rich Man, Poor Man." The *Trenton Evening Times*, July 16, 1918, page 2.

"Richard Barthelmess." By Aleen Keylin and Suri Fleischer in *Hollywood Album*. New York: Arno Press, 1977, page 25.

"Richard Barthelmess." By Ann Lloyd and Graham Fuller in *The Illustrated Who's Who of the Cinema*. New York: MacMillan Publishing Company, 1983, page 30.

"Richard Barthelmess." By Jake Jacobs in *Films in Review*, January 1953.

"Richard Barthelmess–A Seeker After Romance In Real Life." *Picture Show*, December 31, 1927, pages 16, 17.

"Richard Barthelmess, 68, Dies; Boyish Idol of Silent-Film Era." The *New York Times*, Sunday, August 18, 1963.

"Richard the Tenth." *Motion Picture Magazine*, January 1921, page 22.

"Romances of Famous Film Folk." By Harriette Underhill in *Picture-Play Magazine*, August 1921, pages 69, 99.

"Romantic Mountain Story Features Barthelmess–The Little Shepherd of Kingdom Come." The *Lima News*, September 23, 1928, page 22.

"Romeo and Juliet." By George Blaisdell in *Moving Picture World*, November 4, 1916.

"Romeo and Juliet." *Photoplay*, January 1917.

"Sampascoopies." By Charles G. Sampas in the *Lowell Sun*, March 15, 1945, page 2.

"Sampascoopies." By Charles G. Sampas in the *Lowell Sun*, October 29, 1945, page 2.

Sarris, Andrew. "Howard Hawks." *You Ain't Heard Nothin' Yet*, New York: Oxford University Press, 1998.

"Scarlet Days." By James Frederick Smith in *Motion Picture Classic*, January 1920, page 20.

"Scarlet Days." The *New York Times*, November 10, 1919, page 18.

"Scarlet Seas." By Mordaunt Hall in the *New York Times*, December 31, 1928, page 9.

"Scarlet Seas." *Variety*, January 9, 1929.

"Second Love." By Evelyn Dane in *Screenland*, March 1927.

"Seven Swans." The *Washington Post*, February 10, 1918, page 41.

"Seven Swans." The *Washington Post*, February 11, 1918, page 6.

"Seven Swans." *Variety*, January 4, 1918.

"Seventh Day." The *New York Times*, Mar 13, 1922, page 18.

"Seventh Day." *Photoplay*. April 1922.

"Seventh Day." *Variety*. March 17, 1922.

Shipman, David. *The Great Movie Stars The Golden Years*. New York: Hill and Wang, 1979, pages 45-48.

"Shore Leave." By Mordaunt Hall in the *New York Times*, September 14, 1925, page 16.

"Shore Leave." *Variety*, September 16, 1925.

"Show of Shows." By Mordaunt Hall in the *New York Times*, November 21, 1929, page 24.

"Show of Shows." *Photoplay*, August 1928, page 20.

"Show of Shows." *Variety*, November 27, 1929.

"Silence is Still Golden." By Edward Harrison in the *New York Times*, July 10, 1938.

Slide, Anthony and Edward Wagenknecht. "Snow White." *Fifty Great American Silent Films 1912-1920*. New York: Dover Publications, Inc., 1980.

Smith, Frederick James. "Those Nazimova Eyes!" *Picture Play*, September 1918.

"Snow White." By George N. Shorey in *Motion Picture News*, January 6, 1917.

"Snow White." The *Chillicothe Constitution*, July 23, 1917, page 8.

"Snow White." The *Iowa City Citation*, February 14, 1917, page 5.

"Some Things That Only Dick Barthelmess Knew Til Now." By Joseph Henry Steele in *Motion Picture Magazine*, January 1932, page 51, 103.

"Son of the Gods, The." *Variety*, February 5, 1930.

"Son of the Gods, The." By Mordaunt Hall in the *New York Times*, January 31, 1930, page 24.

"Sonny." The *New York Times*, Mar 13, 1922, page 14.

"Sonny." *Variety*, June 2, 1922.

"Soul of a Magdalene, The." The *Mansfield News*, May 21, 1917, page 7.

"Soul of a Magdalene, The." The *Mansfield News*, July 3, 1917, page 6.

"Soul Fire." By Mordaunt Hall in the *New York Times*, May 6, 1925.

"Soul-Fire." *Variety*, May 6, 1925.

"Soul of a Magdalen, The." *Variety*, May 25, 1917.

Spears, Jack. *Hollywood The Golden Era*. New York: Castle Books, 1971, page 14, 59.

"Spoilers, The." *The Coshocton Tribune*, May 17, 1942, page 9.

"Spoilers, The." The *New York Times*, May 22, 1942, page 27.

"Spoilers, The." *Variety*, April 15, 1942.

"Spy of Napoleon, The." By Frank Nugent in the *New York Times*, June 29, 1940, page 18.

"Spy of Napoleon, The." *Variety*, September 30, 1936.

"Stolen Jools." The *Appleton Post Crescent*, April 4, 1931, page 14.

"Stolen Jools." The *Decatur Herald*, April 5, 1931, page 22.

"Stage Tradition Hit By Pictures." The *Reno Evening Gazette*, November 28, 1931, page 9.

"Streets of Illusion, The." The *Fort Wayne News*, September 13, 1917, page 6.

"Sunshine Nan." The *Bridgeport Telegram*, May 8, 1918, page 8.

"Sunshine Nan." The *Capital Times*, Marcy 19, 1918, page 3.

"Sunshine Nan." The *Evening Telegram*, August 19, 1918, page 7.

"Sunshine Nan." The *Lima Daily News*, June 12, 1918, page 5.

"Sunshine Nan." The *Mansfield News*, August 30, 1918, page 7.

"Timing For Laughs Problem in Talkies." The *Decatur Herald*, September 7, 1930, page 6.

"The Actor on the Cover." *Moving Picture Stories*, May 13, 1921, Vol. XVII, No. 437, page 29.

"The Bulletin Board." *Motion Picture Magazine*, November 1925, page 9.

"The Greatest Star in Hollywood." By Joseph Henry Steele in *Silver Screen*, January 1931, pages 32, 59.

"The Idealistic Builder." By Adele Whitely Fletcher in *Motion Picture Magazine*, October 1922.

"The Luck of Richard Barthelmess." *Pictures and Picturegoer*, April 1923.

"The Noose a Curious Blend of The Sublime and the Ridiculous." By Mordaunt Hall in the *New York Times*, March 19, 1928, page 26.

"The Real Richard Barthelmess. *Screenland*, October 3, 1922, page 7.

"The Story of David Wark Griffith." By Henry Stephen Gordon in *Photoplay*, June 1916, pages 35, 37, 162-165.

"The Story of David Wark Griffith." By Henry Stephen Gordon in *Photoplay*, July 1916, pages 124–129, 131-132.

"The Story of My Life." By Pauline Frederick in *Motion Picture Magazine*, December 1918.

"Three Men and a Girl." The *Humeston New Era*, August 20, 1919, page 6.

"Three Men and a Girl." The *New York Times*, March 31, 1919, page 11.

"Tol'able David." By Edward Weitzel in *Moving Picture World*, December 5, 1921, page 20.

"Tol'able David Shown at Liberty." *Screenland*, January 7, 1922, page 5.

"Tol'able David." The *New York Times*, August 23 1920, page 20.

"Tol'able David." *Variety*, January 16, 1922.

Trotta, Vincent and Cliff Lewis. *Screen Personalities*. New York: Grosset and Dunlap, 1933, page 17.

"Twenty One." The *New York Times*, Mar 13, 1922, page 13.

"Twenty-One." *Variety*, February 21, 1924.

"Valentine Girl, The." The *Fort Wayne News*, April 30, 1917, page 7.

"Valentine Girl, The." *Variety*, May 4, 1914.

Vantol, Jan. "A Lot of Bunk about Stardom." *Hollywood Magazine*, July 1931.

"Voices of Gloria Swanson, John Barrymore." The *Decatur Daily Review*, August 19, 1928, page 21.

Walker, Alexander. *The Shattered Silents*. New York: William Morrow and Company, 1979, pages 133-134, 204.

"War Brides." By Edward Weitzel in *Moving Picture World*, December 2, 1916.

"War Brides." The *Sheboygan Press*, April 20, 1917, page 2.

"War Brides." The *Washington Post*, May 4, 1915, page 6.

"Way Down East." By Alexander Woolcott in the *New York Times*, September 4, 1920, page 7.

"Way Down East." By Burns Mantle in *Photoplay*, December 1920, page 18.

"Way Down East." *Film Daily*, September 12, 1920, page 6.

"Weary River." By Mordaunt Hall in the *New York Times*, January 25, 1929, page 20.

"Weary River." By Norbert Lusk in *Picture Play*, May 1929, page 71.

"Weary River." *Variety*, January 30, 1929.

"What Happened to Pauline Frederick?" By Adela Rogers St. Johns in *Photoplay*, June 1926, 38.

"White Black Sheep, The." By Mordaunt Hall in the *New York Times*, December 21, 1926, page 20.

"White Black Sheep, The." *Variety*, December 22, 1926.

"Wild Primrose." The *Sandusky Star Journal*, December 17, 1919, page 3.

"Wild Primrose." *Variety*, August 16, 1918.

Wing, Ruth. *The Blue Book of the Screen.* Hollywood: The Blue Book of the Screen, Inc., 1923, page 16.

"Weary River." By Norbert Lusk in *Picture Play*, May 1929, page 71.

"What Mrs. Barthelmess Thinks of Richard." By Burt Knight in *Screenland*, April 1926, page 45.

"What'll You Do, Mary?" By Gladys Hall in *Pictures and Picturegoer*, February 1925, pages 54, 55.

"Wheel of Chance, The." By Mordaunt Hall in the *New York Times*, July 2, 1928, page 11.

"Wheel of Chance, The." *Variety*, July 4, 1928.

"Wild Primrose." The *Oxnard Courier*, August 20, 1918, page 3.

Wray, Fay. *On The Other Hand–A Life Story*. New York: St. Martin's Press, 1989.

"High Salaried Actors Aim to Protect Free Lance Groups." By Elizabeth Yeaman in the *Hollywood Citizen-News*, March 11, 1933.

"Young Nowheres." By Mordaunt Hall in the *New York Times*, October 2, 1929, page 28.

"Young Nowheres." *Variety*, October 9, 1929.

"Zukor Tells the Story of Twenty-Five Years." By Adolph Zukor in the *New York Times*, February 28, 1937.

Bibliography

21 (see *Twenty-One*)
Abbott, Charles, 63
Abraham Lincoln 90
Adios (see *The Lash*)
Alias the Doctor 349, advertisement 350, photos 351, 351.
All at Sea 61
Allen, Viola, 7
Allen, Winifred, 28, 142, photo 185.
Amateur Gentleman 289, *The*, advertisement 290, photos 291, 292.
American Tragedy 82
Arthur, Jean, 136, photo 379
Arvidson, Linda, 25, 26.
Astor, Mary, 63, 65, 104, 106, photos 341.
Atkinson, Brooks, 132
Bab's Burglar 20, 178, photo 181.
Bab's Diary 20, 176, advertisement and photo 179.
Bailey, William, photo 18,
Baird, Anthony, 77
Ballin, Mabel, photo 185
Banky, Vilma, 90
Bara, Theda, 13, 20, 28, 148, photo 177.
Barlow, Reginald, 120
Barrymore, John, 65, 90, 102, 100, 140.
Barrymore, Lionel, 135
Bartelemys, Alfred, 7

Bartelemys, Richard Semler (see *Richard Barthelmess*)
Barthelmess, Mary Hay, birth 51, 52, 77, 113, 140, 142, 149, photos 9, 52, 81, 96, 122, 123, 127, 141.
Barthelmess, Richard, in school 8-9, first film 10, college 11-12, making *War Brides* 18, meeting D. W. Griffith 29, making *Broken Blossoms* 36, making *Way Down East* 42, marriage to Mary Hay 46, birth of daughter 51, forming Inspiration Pictures 55, divorce 77, making *The Patent Leather Kid* 78, Academy Award 79, 84, second marriage 82, first sound film 88, 92, on radio 130, in WWII 142, D. W. Griffith's funeral 147, death 149, photos 17, 24, 35, 42, 43, 49, 50-52, 56, 58, 59, 62, 64, 65, 67-69, 72, 73, 81, 82, 86, 89, 92, 94, 96, 98, 107, 109, 112, 113, 115, 117, 118, 121-124, 126, 127, 129, 130, 132-134, 137-139, 141, 143, 147, 149, 173, 175, 179, 181, 183, 185, 187, 191, 192, 196, 199, 202, 207, 210, 211, 213, 214, 217, 218, 220, 221, 223-225, 228, 229, 230, 232-235, 237, 238, 242, 243, 245, 246, 248-252, 254-256, 258-259,

261, 262, 264-266, 268, 269, 272, 273, 275, 276, 278, 279, 281, 282, 284, 287, 288, 291, 292, 294, 295, 298-302, 304-306, 309, 310, 313, 314, 317, 319, 320, 323, 325, 328, 332, 333, 335-338, 340, 341, 344, 347, 348, 351, 352, 354, 357, 358, 361, 362, 364, 365, 367, 368, 370, 372, 373, 375, 376, 378, 379, 381, 383, 386, 387-424.
Barthelmess, Stewart, 113, 149, photos 143, 145.
Bartlett, Lanier, 104
Bartlett, Virginia Stivers, 104
Basquette, Lina, photos 305, 306, 314.
Bassett, Russell, photo 192
Bath, Vivian, 77
Baxter, Warner, photo 132
Bayne, Beverly, 13, 14, 50, 51, photo 160.
Beach, Rex, 140
Beautiful City, The, 280, advertisement 281, photos 281, 282.
Beery, Wallace, 118
Bennett, Constance, photo 333
Berkeley, Gertrude, photo 18
Bickford, Charles, 118
Big Tree, Chief, 84
Billy 7
Biograph 10, 25, 26, 27, 32, 45, 75, 136.
Birth of a Nation, The, 22, 27, 40, 146.
Bitzer, Billy, 41, 42.
Black Beach, The 39
Blackwell, Carlyle, 148
Bogart, Humphrey, 123
Bond Boy, The 48, 246, advertisement 248, photos 248, 249.
Boots 30, 197, advertisement 199, photos 199.
Borzage, Frank, photo 149.

Bow, Clara, 148
Boyer, Charles, 123
Boys Town 139
Brackett, Charles, 146
Brenon, Herbert, 17, 19, 20.
Brent, George, 140, photo 381.
Brewster, Eugene, photo 173
Bridge of San Luis Rey, The 146
Bright Shawl, The, 62, 63, 65, 97, 136, 252, advertisement 254, photos 254-256.
Brinistool, Rev. Emil, 146
Broadway Lawyer (see The Man Who Talked Too Much)
Broken Blossoms 33, 34, 36, 37, 91, 116, 125, 139, 151, 206, sheet music 209, photos 210, 211.
Broun, Heywood, 53
Brown, Johnny Mack, 108, photos 348.
Brown, Karl, 31, 35.
Brown, Tom, photo 358
Bruce, Kate 38, photos 221, 228.
Bruce, Virginia, photo 381
Bryant, Charles, photo 18
Burke, Billie, 15, 151, 155, photo 157.
Burke, Thomas, 33
Bushman, Francis X., 13, 14, 50, 51, photo 160.
Byron, Arthur, photo 134
Byron, Walter, 108, photos 348.
Cabin in the Cotton 110, 111, 353, photos 354.
Cadman, Rev. S. Parkes, 77
Cagney, James, 118, 123, 142.
Cain, James M., 132
Caldwell, Colonel Frank, 37
Caldwell, Dorothy, 46
Caldwell, Jane, 46
Caldwell, Mary Hay (*see Mary Hay*)
Caldwell, Mrs. Frank, 37

Camille 20, 148, 175, advertisement and photo 177.
Camp, Walter, 128
Capra, Frank, photo 138
Captains Courageous 139
Carroll, Roger, 139
Central Airport 120, 355, advertisement 357, photos 357, 358.
Chandler, Helen, 108, photos 348, 370.
Chaplin, Charlie, 36, 88, 90, 95, 136, 148.
Chatterton, Ruth, 88
Chevalier, Maurice, photo 149
Clark, Marguerite, 20, 21, 28, 32, 61, 140, photos 179, 181, 187, 171, 191, 204.
Classmates 267, advertisement 268, photos 269.
Clayton, Marguerite, photo 192, 193.
Cohan, George M., 142
Cohan, George, 28, photos 192, 193.
Cohn, Harry, 137
Coincidence 45
Colbert, Claudette, photo 139
Colby, Anita, photo 145
Coleman, Ronald, 80, 90, 99, 115, 117, 122, photos 129, 132.
Columbia Pictures 133, 136, 137, 139, 140.
Compson, Betty, photo 320
Connell, Brian, 100
Cooper, Gary, 123
Cornwall, Anne, photo 242
Costello, Helene, 85
Crabbe, Buster, 123
Crisp, Donald, 146
Cromwell, Oliver, 68
Crosby, Bing, 123
Crosland, Alan, photo 134
Curtiz, Michael, 110
Daniels, William, photo 149

Darling, Ida, photo 204
Davidson, Max, 25
Davis, Bette 110, photos 134, 354.
Davis, Mildred, 53
Daw, Marjorie, photos 237, 238.
Dawley, J. Searle, 21
Dawn Patrol, The, 99-102, 333, advertisement 335, photos 335-338.
Day, Alice, photos 325
Day, Juliette, 7
Del Rio, Dolores, 90
Dempster, Carol, 31, 38, 151, photos 217, 218, 220, 221, 223, 224, 229.
Di Valantina, Rudolpho (*see Rudolph Valentino*)
Dietrich, Marlene, 140, photo 383.
Digges, Dudley, photo 365
Dinehart, Alan, 118
Don Juan 74
Dove, Billie, 80
Downing, Rex, photo 386
Drag 324, advertisement 324, photos 325.
Dreiser, Theodore, 88
Dressler, Marie, photo 73
Drew, Sidney, 7
Drop Kick, The, 302, advertisement 303, photos 304.
Dunbar, Dorothy, photos 292
Durante, Jimmy, photo 117
Dvorak, Ann 110, photos 134, 365.
Dyer, Elmer, 101
Eagles, Curley, 106
Eagle Wing, Chief, 84
Eastward Ho! 28, 425
Edeson, Arthur, photo 149.
Edeson, Robert, photo 341
Eilers, Sally, photo 358
Einstein, Albert, 92
Ellis, Edward, 7
Emerson, John, 90

Enchanted Cottage, The 69, 263, photos 264-266.
England, John, 70
Environment (see Alias the Doctor)
Essanay 50
Eternal Sin, The 20, 149, 167, photo 168.
Evans, Delight, 33
Evans, Madge, 128, photos 268, 269.
Experience 235, photos 59, 237, 238.
Eyman, Scott, 104
Fairbanks, Douglas Sr., 33, 36, 53, 88, 90,102.
Fairbanks, Douglas Jr., 100, photos 337, 338.
Farnum, William 107, 141, 148.
Fasten Your Seat Belts 110
Fawcett, George 34, 35, photos 196, 217, 218.
Faye, Alice, photo 126
Fedora 25
Fenberg, George M., 21
Fighting Blade, The, 48, 68, 256, advertisement 258, photos 258, 259.
Finger Points, The, 108, 109, 342, advertisement 343, photos 109, 344.
First National Film Corporation 71, 77, 78, 101, 102, 105, 131, 147.
Fitzmaurice, George, photo 59.
Fletcher, Adele, 56
Flynn, Emmett J., 28
Folsey, George, photo 149.
For Valour 142, 182, advertisement and photos 184, 185.
Ford, Henry, II 147
Ford, John, 148
Foster, Lewis R., 141
Four Horsemen of the Apocalypse, The, 32
Four Hours to Kill! 129, 131, 133, 371, advertisement 372.
Fox Film Corporation 74

Fox, William, 13, 74.
Francis, Kay 115
Fury 63, 249, photos 249-252, advertisement 250.
Gable, Clark, 109, 111, 123, photo 133.
Gamest Girl, The, 39
Garmes, Lee, photo 149
Gaynor, Janet, photo 149
Gilbert, John, 88, 99, 117.
Gilmore, J. H., photo 175
Girl of the Golden West, The, 12
Girl Who Stayed at Home, The, 30, 33, 198, advertisement 201, photos 202.
Gish, Dorothy, 10, 22, 27, 28, 30, 31, 32, 63, 83, 87, 136, 149, 150, 151, photos 62, 196, 199, 207, 213, 214, 250-252, 254-256, 281, 282.
Gish, Lillian, 10, 22, 27, 28, 32-34, 41, 42, 44, 45, 71, 83, 88, 91, 136, 146, 149, 150, 151.
Gloria's Romance 16, 151, 155, advertisement 158.
Glyn, Elinor, 66
Golden Boy 133
Golden Youth (see Just Suppose)
Goldwyn, Samuel, 133
Good Earth, The, 139
Goudal, Jetta, 63
Goulding, Edmund, 55, 63
Graham, Carroll, 97
Grant, Cary, 123, 136, photos 379.
Grant, Lawrence, 118, 120.
Grapes of Wrath, The, 140
Graves, Ralph, photos 217.
Greater Love 77, 427
Greatest Question, The, 31
Greely, Evelyn, 20,151
Grey Duck, The, 39
Grey Fox of Hollywood, The, 99
Grey, Ralph, 30
Griffith, Albert, 36

Griffith, Corinne 125
Griffith, David Wark (*see D. W. Griffith*)
Griffith, D. W., 22, 23, 24, 25, 26, 27, 28, 30, 31, 32, 33, 34, 36, 37, 38, 39, 40, 41, 42, 44, 45, 55, 61, 66, 75, 90, 91, 116, 125, 128, 136, death 146, 151, photos 24, 126, 147.
Griffith, Lawrence (*see D. W. Griffith*)
Haas, Dolly, photo 375
Hale, Creighton, 38
Hall, Gladys, 77, 125, 128.
Hamilton Stock Company 11
Hamilton, Neil, photos 335, 337.
Hammerstein II, Oscar, 53
Hammerstein, Arthur, 53
Happy End, The, 55
Harding, Ann, 88
Hardy, Sam, 120
Hardy, Oliver, 136.
Harlow, Jean, photo 133.
Harriman, Averell, 55
Harris, Caroline, 10, 38, 46, photos 7, 9.
Harris, Catherine (*see Caroline Harris*)
Harron, Bobbie, 32, 34, 45, photos 202.
Harron, Tessie, 34
Hartford Film Corporation 12
Hawks, Howard, 99, 101, 102, 131, 136, 137.
Hay, Mary, 27, 28, 37, 38, 44, 45, 46, 51, 53, 54, 66, 75, 76, 77, 80, 114, 148, photos 36, 37, 47, 58, 67, 75, 272, 273.
Hayworth, Rita 137, photos 379.
Hearts of the World 27, 28, 425.
Hedda Gabler 10
Heifetz, Jascha, photo 96.
Hell's Angels 100, 101.
Henderson, Skitch, photo 145.
Henie, Sonja, photos 145.
Hergesheimer, Joseph, 55, 63, photo 56.
Heroes for Sale 359, advertisement 361, photos 361, 362.
Hit the Trail Holiday 28, 152, 190, photos 192, advertisement 193.
Holbrook, Hal, 150
Hope Chest, The, 30, 195, photos 196, advertisement 197.
Houston, Walter, 118
Howard Hawks The Grey Fox of Hollywood 101
Howard, Leslie, 102
Howe, James Wong, photo 149.
Huff, Louise, photo 242, 243.
Hughes, Howard, 100, 101, 131.
Hughes, Rupert, 16, 78.
Hulette, Gladys, 28, 57, photo 175, 232, 234.
Hutchinson, Charles, photo 18
I Never Sang For My Father 149, 150.
I'll Get Him Yet 212, advertisement 213, photos 213, 214.
Ibsen, Henrik, 10
Idol Dancer, The, 33, 38, 39, 219.
Ingram, Rex, 53
Inspiration Pictures 55, 61, 68, 69, 71, 147.
Intolerance 14
Invader, The (see *The Spy of Napoleon*)
James, Gardner, photos 292.
Janney, William, photo 368.
Jannings, Emil, 84, 85.
Java Head 60
Jazz Singer, The, 91
Johnson, Arthur, 10
Jolson, Al, 91
Joyce, Alice, photo 306.
Just a Song at Twilight (Love's Old Sweet Song) 20, 151, 166.
Just Suppose 282, advertisement 283, photos 284.
Kelly, Anthony Paul, 40
Kelly, Helen, photos 238.

Kelly, Kitty, 20
Kennedy, Madge, 28, photo 183.
Keystone Cops 136
King Lear 8
King, Henry, 55, 57, 60, photos 56, 62.
Kirkwood, James, 10
Knight Errant – A Biography of Douglas Fairbanks, Jr. 100
Kodascope 136
La Verne, Lucille, photo 352.
Lash, The, 104, 106, 338, advertisement 339, photos 105, 340, 341.
Last Flight, The, 108, 345, advertisements 346, photos 347, 348.
Laurel, Stan, 136.
Lawrence, Florence, 26
Le Guere, George, 7
Leisen, Mitchell, 131
Lena and the Geese 27
Leslie, Gladys, 151
Letters to Lucerne 140
Lewis, Diana, photo 137.
Lichiman, Alexander, 90
Life of Emile Zola, The, 139
Life on Film, A, 65, 104.
Lights of New York, The, 84, 85.
Lillie, Beatrice, photo 96.
Limehouse Nights 33
Lincoln, Elmo, 136
Little Caesar 102
Little Princess 7
Little Shepherd of Kingdom Come, The, 84, 307, advertisement 308, photos 309, 310.
Lloyd, Frank, 105, 106, photo 328.
Lloyd, Harold, 53, 148, photo 149.
Lombard, Carole, 82, 122, photo 107.
London, Jack, 140
Loos, Anita, 90
Losee, Frank, photo 242.
Love 'Em and Leave 'Em 82

Love Flower, The, 33, 38, 39, 222, advertisement and photos 223, 224.
Love Song, The, 90
Love, Bessie 72, photos 72, 275, 276.
Love, Montagu, 84
Lundigan, William, photo 381.
Lynn, William, photo 134.
Mac, Nila, photo 18.
Mackaill, Dorothy, 83, 128, photos 258, 259, 261, 262, 278, 279, 288.
MacMahon, Aline, photo 361.
Man who Changed His Mind, The (see *The Spy of Napoleon*)
Man Who Lived Again, The (see *The Spy of Napoleon*)
Man Who Talked Too Much, The, 380.
Manners, David, 108, photos 348.
Mantell, Robert B., 7
March, Fredric, 118
Marion, Frances, 13, 146.
Marjoliane 427
Marley, Peverell, photo 149.
Marlowe, Julia, 24
Marmont, Percy, photos 204.
Marsh, Mae, 146, 148, photo 147.
Marsh, Marian, photos 351, 352.
Martin, Freddy, 141
Mary Jane McKane 53, 427.
Massacre, The, 362, advertisement 364, photos 364, 365.
May, Mary, 36
Mayer, Louis B., 99
Mayor of 44th Street, The, 141, 142, 384, advertisement 385, photos 386.
McAvoy, May, 69, 70, photos 69, 264-266.
McCarthy, Todd, 101
McCormick, S. Barret, 154
McCoy, Bessie, 37
McIntosh, Burr, photos 228.
McQuarrie, George, photos 220, 221.

Meighan, Thomas, 53, 88.
Melton, James, photo 134.
Mersereau, Clara, 7
Metro-Goldwyn-Mayer 12, 50, 131.
Midnight Alibi 369, photos 370.
Miljan, John, 118
Miller, Arthur C., photo 59.
Miller, Patsy Ruth, photo 294.
Miss 1917 21
Miss Petticoats 25
Mitchell, Thomas, photo 379.
Mizner, Addison, photo 73.
Moby Dick 100
Modern Hero, A, 366, advertisement 367, photos 124, 367, 368.
Montgomery, Robert, 111
Mook, Samuel, 88, 93.
Moore, Victor, 95
Moral Code, The, 151, 167.
Moran, Lois, photos 284.
Movies, Mr. Griffith, and Me, The, 27
Movietone 90, 97.
Mrs. Wiggs of the Cabbage Patch 11, 154.
Muir, Jean, photo 124
Muni, Paul, 139
Murnau, F. W., 74, 75.
Murphy, George, photo 386
Murray, Johnny, 93, 94.
Murray, Mae, 148
My Dear Children 140
Nagel, Conrad, 120
Naldi, Nita, photo 238
Nazimova, Alla, 10, 16, 18, 19, 32, 144, photos 18.
Nearly Married 180, photo 183.
Negri, Pola, 148
New Toys 66-68, 82, 270, 427, advertisement 271, photos 272, 273.
Nilsson, Anna Q., 151
Nine O'Clock Frolic 36
Nixon, Marian, photos 317, 328, 341.

Noose, The, 84, photos 305, 306.
Novarro, Ramon, photo 149.
Nugent, Elliott, 108, photos 348.
O'Connor, Robert Emmett, 118
O'Day, Molly, 78, photo 298.
O'Neill, Nancy, 25
Of Human Bondage 111
Off With Their Heads 13
Olcott, Sydney, 76
Only Angels Have Wings 138, 377, advertisement 378, photos 378, 379.
Only Son, The, 7
Orchard of Girls, The, 36
Osborne, Marie, 148
Osterman, Katherine, 25
Out of Luck 30
Out of the Ruins 87, 315, advertisement 316, photos 317.
Outward Bound 102
Pabst, G. W., photo 124
Page, Anita, photo 117
Panthea 7
Paramount 21, 104, 107, 109, 129.
Parker, Lottie Blaire, 38
Patent Leather Kid, The, 77-80, 79, 99, 296, advertisement 297, photos 298-302.
Patrick, Jerome, photo 204
Patton, John, 62
Peggy 16
Pennington, Ann, 21, 28.
Peppy Polly 205, advertisement and photos 207.
Peter Ibbetson 65
Petit, Dutch, photo 121
Petrova, Mme., 7
Petrova, Olga, 20, 28, 151, photo 173.
Phillips, Mary, 132
Pickford, Jack, 8, 10.
Pickford, Lottie, 10
Pickford, Mary, 10, 26, 27, 28, 33, 36,

53, 88, 90, 91 127, 136, 146, 148, photos 127, 147, 149.
Pinchot, Ann, 34
Pippa Passes 26
Plane No. 4 (see *Only Angels Have Wings*)
Postman Always Rings Twice, The, 132, 374.
Powell, Richard, 72
Powell, William, 71, 80, 82, 97, 63, 115, 116, 122, 127, 128, photos 64, 107, 132, 137, 282.
Prosser, Monty, 136
Quirk, Lawrence J., 111
Ralston, Esther, 116
Ranson's Folly 83, 84, 284, advertisement 286, photos 287, 288.
Reardon, Mildred, photo 238
Redmond, Harry, photo 79.
Reed, Florence, 149
Reid, Cliff, 141
Reid, Wallace, 22
Rennie, James, photo 341.
Rentschler, Mickey, photo 368
Revier, Dorothy, photos 304
Reynolds, Harry, 101
Rhinehart, Mary Robert, 20
Rich Man, Poor Man 189, advertisement and photos 191.
Ring, Frances, 53
Rita Hayworth, The Time, The Place, and The Woman 137
RKO 141, 142.
Robertson, John S., 68, 70, photos 68, 72.
Robinson, Edward G., 63
Rockett, Al, 78
Rogers, Ginger, 148
Romeo and Juliet (film) 13-14, 71, 159, photo 160.
Romola 24, 136.
Rosher, Charles, photo 149

Rosing, Bodil, photo 314
Ross, Thomas, 7
Rotter, Fritz, 140
Rowland, Richard A., 78
Ryan, Frank, 141
Sally 36, 426
Sampas, Charles G., 142
Santell, Alfred 78, photo 79.
Sargent, Jessica Stewart, 135, photos 96, 112, 113, 115, 118, 122, 123, 126.
Sargent, Stewart (see *Stewart Barthelmess*)
Saunders, John Monk, 102, 108, 109.
Scarface 131
Scarlet Days 30, 31, 33, 104, 213, advertisement 216, photos 217, 218.
Scarlet Seas 88, 318, photos 319, 320.
Schenk, Joseph, 53, 128.
Schubert Brothers 10
Scott, Randolph, 140
Scrambled Wives 61, 140.
Selznick, David O., 120
Selznick, Lewis J., 16, 19.
Sennett, Mack, 10
Sentence, The (see *The Man Who Talked Too Much*)
Seven Swans, The, 186.
Seventh Day, The, 61, 239, advertisement 241, photos 242, 253.
Seymour, Clarine, 38, 44, photos 202, 220, 221.
Shakespeare, William 7, 8, 13, 14, 71.
Shanghai Orchids (see *Four Hours to Kill*)
Sheik, The, 135
Shinn, Everett, 64
Shipman, Dr. Herbert, 46
Shirley, Anne, photo 386
Shore Leave 277, photos 278, 279.
Slippery Pearls (see *The Stolen Jools*)
Smith, Agnes, 67
Smith, Gladys (see *Mary Pickford*)
Smith, H. Montgomery, 46

Snow White 20, 164, advertisement and photos 165.
Son of the Gods 139, 330, advertisement 332, photos 332, 333.
Son of the Sheik 135
Sonny 243, photos 245, 246.
Sorrows of Satan, The, 151
Soul of a Magdalen, The, 20, 151, 172, advertisement 17.
Soul-Fire 273, advertisement 275, photos 275, 276.
Spaulding, Bruce, 77
Speed of Sound, The, 104
Spoilers, The, 140, 382, advertisement 383, photos 383.
Spy of Napoleon, The 374, photo 375.
Squier, Emma-Lindsay, 57
St. Denis, Ruth, 36
Stevenson, Charles, photo 238.
Steward, Nella, 77
Stolen Jools, The, 341
Stone, Arthur, 106
Stone, Lewis, 118
Story of Louis Pasteur, The, 139
Streets of Illusion, The, 174, photo 175.
Struggle, The, 90
Sunrise 74
Sunshine Nan 21, 188, advertisement 189.
Sutch, Herbert, photos 220, 221.
Svengali 102
Swan, The, 91
Swanson, Gloria, 90, 148, photo 149.
Taber, Robert, 24
Talmadge, Constance, 87
Talmadge, Norma, 53, 88, 90.
Tarzan of the Apes 136
Tashman, Lilyan, photo 238
Taylor, Jeremy, 113
Taylor, Robert, 123
Terry, Alice, 53

The Show of Shows 328, advertisement 330.
Three Men and a Girl 202, photos 204.
Tiger Shark 131
Tol'able David 56, 57, 60, 61, 125, 231, advertisement 232, photos 232-235,
Tooker, William H., photo 294
Toomey, Regis, photo 348
Torrence, Ernest, 60, 122, 128.
Tracy, Spencer, 139
Treasure Girl 77, 427.
Tree, Dorothy, photo 373
Twentieth Century Fox 140
Twenty-One 69, 259, advertisement 261, photos 261, 262.
Underhill, Hariette, 38
United Artist Corporation 36, 90.
Universal 140
Unseen Enemy, An, 27
Valentine Girl, The, 170, advertisement and photo 171.
Valentino, Rudolph, 31, 32, 135.
Vallee, Rudy, 131
Vantol, Jan, 102
Vaughn, Alberta, photos 304.
Vidor, Florence, photo 96.
Vincent, Allen, 140
Vitaphone 74
Vitaphone 85, 92, 97.
Von Sternberg, Josef, photo 149.
Walker, Helen Louise, 116
Walker, Stuart, 106
Walthall, Henry B., photo 354
War Brides 16, 17, 18, 19, 20, 32, 144, 161, advertisement and photos 18, 162-163.
Warde, Agnes J., 48
Warner Bros. 74, 92, 88, 104, 109, 110, 111, 123, 131, 147.
Warner, Jack, 100
Way Down East 28, 33, 39, 40, 44, 45,

54, 56, 125, 151, 225, advertisement 227, photos 42, 228, 229, 230.
Wayne, John 140
Weary River 91, 92, 94, 320, advertisement 322, photos 323.
Weaver, Henry, photo 185.
Webb, Clifton, 77
Wentworth, Marion Craig, 18
Whales of August, The, 151
Wheaton, Edna, photo 59
Wheel of Chance 85, 311, advertisement 312, photos 313, 314.
White Black Sheep, The, 293, advertisements 76, 294, photos 294, 295.
White, Pearl, 136
Wild Primrose 151, 193, advertisement 194.
Wilson, Charles C., photos 372, 373.
Wilson, Katherine, 67, 82, 89, photos 89.
Withey, Chester, 45
Woods, Al, 31
Wray, Fay, 108, 109, 125, photos 344.
Yankee Doodle Dandy 28, 142.
Yearsley, Ralph, 61
Young Nowheres 326, advertisement 327, photos 328.
Young, Loretta, 128, photos 138, 361.
Zanuck, Darryl, 100, 110, 111.
Ziegfeld Follies 21
Ziegfeld Girls of 1920, The, 36, 426.
Ziegfeld Midnight Frolic 37
Ziegfeld, Florenz, 36
Zukor, Adolph 13, 21, 36, 104.

THE CAPTIVATING LIVES and groundbreaking accomplishments of fourteen men who dared to gamble their reputations by appearing in the first motion pictures are explored in a richly researched new book, The First Male Stars: Men of the Silent Era. At a time when other actors in the "legitimate theater" scorned the industry, these amazing men not only defied the odds of success but also received a place at the heights of a fascinating business that was a new form of art. Each made an enduring and important contribution to early cinema, although some are forgotten today. Exhaustive research in every major archive of the world has created this compilation of information and images. In this engaging and educational volume, author David W. Menefee reaches into the vaults of history to withdraw countless, unusual details that tell how these men, their roles, and their influence were received in their time, and how their powerful impact still lingers today.

The book includes 114 rare scene photos, portraits, reproductions of full-page film advertisements, and lobby cards.

Actors include:

JOHN BARRYMORE, LIONEL BARRYMORE, RICHARD BARTHELMESS,

JOHN BUNNY, FRANCIS X. BUSHMAN, LON CHANEY, JACKIE COOGAN,

WILLIAM S. HART, TOM MIX, ANTONIO MORENO, JACK PICKFORD,

WALLACE REID, RUDOLPH VALENTINO, AND CRANE WILBUR

AVAILABLE IN SOFTCOVER & HARDCOVER

www.BearManorMedia.com

Here's a small sampling of a few more books published by BearManor Media.

Simply go online for details about these and other terrific titles.

www.BearManorMedia.com

www.ingramcontent.com/pod-product-compliance
Ingram Content Group UK Ltd.
Pitfield, Milton Keynes, MK11 3LW, UK
UKHW021315180426
11947UKWH00015B/1240